Inside the C++ Object Model

Inside the C++ Object Model

Stanley B. Lippman

ADDISON–WESLEY

Boston • San Francisco • New York • Toronto • Montreal
London • Munich • Paris • Madrid
Capetown • Sydney • Tokyo • Singapore • Mexico City

The frontispiece art is an engraving *Knight, Death and the Devil* by Albrecht Dürer, 1471–1528. Courtesy, Museum of Fine Arts, Boston, Massachusetts. Gift of Mrs. Horatio Greenough Curtis in Memory of her Husband, Horatio Greenough Curtis.

The photograph on the back cover is by David Remba.

Extracts on pages 100–112 are from the *Journal of C Language Translation*, Vol. 6, No. 2, December 1994. Copyright 1995, I.E.C.C. Editor/publisher John R. Levine, Trumansburg, New York. Reprinted by permission of the publisher.

Senior Editor: *Tom Stone*
Associate Editor: *Debbie Lafferty*
Associate Production Supervisor: *Patricia A. Oduor*
Copyeditor: *Diane Freed*
Proofreader: *Bunny Ames*
Art Editing Supervisor: *Meredith Nightingale*
Senior Manufacturing Coordinator: *Judith Y. Sullivan*

Library of Congress Cataloging-in-Publication Data

Lippman, Stanley B.
    Inside the C++ object model / by Stanley Lippman.
        p. cm
    Includes bibliographical references and index.
    ISBN 0-201-83454-5
    1. C++ (Computer program language) 2. Object-oriented programming
(Computer science)   I. Title.   II. Title: C plus plus object models
ZA76.73.C153L58   1996
005.13'3 – – dc20   96–6024
                                                                      CIP

The programs and applications presented in this book have been included for their instructional value only.

Access the latest information about Addison-Wesley books from our World Wide Web page: http://www.awl.com/cseng/

Text printed on recycled and acid-free paper.

ISBN 0201834545

10 1112131415 HT   09 08 07

10th Printing   September 2007

Preface

For nearly a decade within Bell Laboratories, I labored at implementing C++. First it was on *cfront*, Bjarne Stroustrup's original C++ implementation (from Release 1.1 back in 1986 through Release 3.0, made available in September 1991). Then it was on to what became known internally as the *Simplifier*, the C++ Object Model component of the Foundation project. It was during the Simplifier's design period that I conceived of and began working on this book.

What was the Foundation project? Under Bjarne's leadership, a small group of us within Bell Laboratories was exploring solutions to the problems of large-scale programming using C++. The Foundation was an effort to define a new development model for the construction of large systems (again, using C++ only; we weren't providing a multilingual solution). It was an exciting project, both for the work we were doing and for the people doing the work: Bjarne, Andy Koenig, Rob Murray, Martin Carroll, Judy Ward, Steve Buroff, Peter Juhl, and myself. Barbara Moo was supervising the gang of us other than Bjarne and Andy. Barbara used to say that managing a software group was like herding a pride of cats.

We thought of the Foundation as a kernel upon which others would layer an actual development environment for users, tailoring it to a UNIX or Smalltalk model as desired. Internally, we called it Grail, as in the quest for, etc. (It seems a Bell Laboratories tradition to mock one's most serious intentions.)

Grail provided for a persistent, semantic-based representation of the program using an object-oriented hierarchy Rob Murray developed and named ALF. Within Grail, the traditional compiler was factored into separate executables. The parser built up the ALF representation. Each of the other components (type checking, simplification, and code generation) and any tools, such as a browser, operated on (and possibly augmented) a centrally stored ALF representation of the program. The Simplifier is the part of the compiler between type checking and code generation. (Bjarne came up with the name *Simplifier*; it is a phase of the original cfront implementation.)

What does a Simplifier do between type checking and code generation? It transforms the internal program representation. There are three general flavors of transformations required by any object model component:

1. *Implementation-dependent transformations.* These are implementation-specific aspects and vary across compilers. Under ALF, they involved the transformations of what we called "tentative" nodes. For example, when the parser sees the expression

   ```
   fct();
   ```

   it doesn't know if this is (a) an invocation of a function represented or pointed to by `fct` or (b) the application of an overloaded call operator on a class object `fct`. By default, the expression is represented as a function call. The Simplifier rewrites and replaces the call subtree when case (b) applies.

2. *Language semantics transformations.* These include constructor/destructor synthesis and augmentation, memberwise initialization and memberwise copy support, and the insertion within program code of conversion operators, temporaries, and constructor/destructor calls.

3. *Code and object model transformations.* These include support for virtual functions, virtual base classes and inheritance in general, operators **new** and **delete**, arrays of class objects, local static class instances, and the static initialization of global objects with nonconstant expressions. An implementation goal I aimed for in the Simplifier was to provide an Object Model hierarchy in which the object implementation was a virtual interface supporting multiple object models.

These last two categories of transformations form the basis of this book. Does this mean this book is written for compiler writers? No, absolutely not. It is written by a (former) compiler writer (that's me) for intermediate to advanced C++ programmers (ideally, that's you). The assumption behind this book is that the programmer, by understanding the underlying C++ Object Model, can write programs that are both less error prone and more efficient.

What Is the C++ Object Model?

There are two aspects to the C++ Object Model:

1. The direct support for object-oriented programming provided within the language

2. The underlying mechanisms by which this support is implemented

The language level support is pretty well covered in my C++ *Primer* and in other books on C++. The second aspect is barely touched on in any current text, with the exception of brief discussions within [ELLIS90] and [STROUP94]. It is this second aspect of the C++ Object Model that is the primary focus of this book. (In that sense, I consider this text to form a bookend to my C++ *Primer*, much as my MFA and MS degrees provide a "fearful symmetry" to my education.) The language covered within the text is the draft Standard C++ as of the winter 1995 meeting of the committee. (Except for some minor details, this should reflect the final form of the language.)

The first aspect of the C++ Object Model is invariant. For example, under C++ the complete set of virtual functions available to a class is fixed at compile time; the programmer cannot add to or replace a member of that set dynamically at runtime. This allows for extremely fast dispatch of a virtual invocation, although at the cost of runtime flexibility.

The underlying mechanisms by which to implement the Object Model are not prescribed by the language, although the semantics of the Object Model itself make some implementations more natural than others. Virtual function calls, for example, are generally resolved through an indexing into a table holding the address of the virtual functions. Must such a virtual table be used? No. An implementation is free to introduce an alternative mechanism. Moreover, if a virtual table is used, its layout, method of access, time of creation, and the other hundred details that must be decided, are all decisions left to each implementation. Having said that, however, I must also say that the general pattern of virtual function implementation across all current compilation systems is to use a class-specific virtual table of a fixed size that is constructed prior to program execution.

If the underlying mechanisms by which the C++ Object Model is implemented are not standardized, then one might ask, why bother to discuss them at all? The primary reason is because my experience has shown that if a programmer understands the underlying implementation model, the programmer can code more efficiently and with greater confidence. Determining when to provide a copy constructor, and when not, is not something one should guess at or have adjudicated by some language guru. It should come from an understanding of the Object Model.

A second reason for writing this book is to dispel the various misunderstandings surrounding C++ and its support of object-oriented programming. For example, here is an excerpt from a letter I received from someone wishing to introduce C++ into his programming environment:

> I work with a couple of individuals who have not written and/or are completely unfamiliar with C++ and OO. One of the engineers who has been writing C code since 1985 feels very strongly that C++ is good only for user-type applications, but not server applications. What he is saying is to have a fast and efficient database level engine that it must be written in C compared to C++. He has identified that C++ is bulky and slow.

C++, of course, is not inherently bulky and slow, although I've found this to be a common assumption among many C programmers. However, just saying that is not very convincing, particularly if the person saying it is perceived as a C++ partisan. This book is partially an attempt to lay out as precisely as I can the kinds of overhead that are and are not inherent in the various Object facilities such as inheritance, virtual functions, and pointers to class members.

Rather than answering the individual myself, I forwarded his letter to Steve Vinoski of Hewlett-Packard, with whom I had previously corresponded regarding the efficiency of C++. Here is an excerpt from his response:

> I have heard a number of people over the years voice opinions similar to those of your colleagues. In every case, those opinions could be attributed to a lack of factual knowledge about the C++ language. Just last week I was chatting with an acquaintance who happens to work for an IC testing manufacturer, and he said they don't use C++ because "it does things behind your back." When I pressed him, he said that he understood that C++ calls `malloc()` and `free()` without the programmer knowing it. This is of course not true. It is this sort of "myth and legend" that leads to opinions such as those held by your colleagues....

> Finding the right balance [between abstraction and pragmatism] requires knowledge, experience, and above all, thought. Using C++ well requires effort, but in my experience the returns on the invested effort can be quite high.

I like to think of this book, then, as my answer to this individual, and, I hope, a repository of knowledge to help put to rest many of the myths and legends surrounding C++.

If the underlying mechanisms supporting the C++ Object Model vary both across implementations and over time, how can I possibly provide a general discussion of interest to any particular individual? Static initialization provides an interesting case in point.

Given a class X with a constructor, such as the following:

```
class X
{
    friend istream&
        operator>>( istream&, X& );
public:
    X( int sz = 1024 ) { ptr = new char[ sz ]; }
    ...
private:
    char *ptr;
};
```

and the declaration of a global object of class X, such as the following:

```
X buf;

int main()
{
    // buf must be constructed at this point
    cin >> setw( 1024 ) >> buf;
    ...
}
```

the C++ Object Model guarantees that the X constructor is applied to buf prior to the first user statement of main(). It does not, however, prescribe how that is to get done. The solution is called static initialization; the actual implementation depends on the degree of support provided by the environment.

The original cfront implementation not only presumed no environment support. It also presumed no explicit platform target. The only presumption was that of being under some variant of UNIX. Our solution, therefore, was specific only to UNIX: the presence of the **nm** command. The **CC** command (a UNIX shell script for portability) generated an executable, ran the **nm** command on the executable—thereby generating a new .c file—compiled the .c file, and then relinked the executable. (This was called the *munch* solution.) This did the job by trading compile-time efficiency for portability. Eventually, however, users chaffed under the compile-time overhead.

The next step was to provide a platform-specific solution: a COFF-based program (referred to as the *patch* solution) that directly examined and threaded the program executable, thus doing away with the need to run **nm**, compile, and relink. (COFF was the Common Object File Format for System V pre-Release 4 UNIX systems.) Both of these solutions are program-based, that is, within each *.c* file requiring static initialization cfront generated an `sti` function to perform the required initializations. Both munch and patch solutions searched for functions bearing an `sti` prefix and arranged for them to be executed in some undefined order by a `_main()` library function inserted as the first statement of `main()`.

In parallel with these releases of cfront, a System V COFF-specific C++ compiler was under development. Targeted for a specific platform and operating system, this compiler was able to effect a change in the System V link editor: a new initialize section that provided for the collection of objects needing static initialization. This extension of the link editor provides what I call an *environment-based* solution that is certainly superior to a program-based solution.

So any generalization based on the cfront program-based solution would be misleading. Why? Because as C++ has become a mainstream language, it has received more and more support for environment-based solutions. How is this book to maintain a balance, then? The book's strategy is as follows: If significantly different implementation models exist across C++ compilers, I present a discussion of at least two models. If subsequent implementation models evolved as an attempt to solve perceived problems with the original cfront model, as, for example, with support for virtual inheritance, I present a discussion of the historical evolution. Whenever I speak of the traditional implementation model, I mean, of course, Stroustrup's original design as reflected in cfront and which has provided a pattern of implementation that can still be seen today in all commercial implementations, even if only as a "reaction against."

Organization of This Book

Chapter 1, *Object Lessons*, provides background on the object-based and object-oriented programming paradigms supported by C++. It includes a brief tour of the Object Model, illustrating the current prevailing industry implementation without looking too closely at multiple or virtual inheritance. (This is fleshed out in Chapters 3 and 4.)

Chapter 2, *The Semantics of Constructors*, discusses in detail how constructors work. It discusses when constructors are synthesized by the compiler and what that means in practical terms for your program's performance.

Chapters 3 through 5 contain the primary material of the book. There, the details of the C++ Object Model are discussed. Chapter 3, *The Semantics of Data*, looks at the handling of data members. Chapter 4, *The Semantics of Function*, focuses on the varieties of member functions, with a detailed look at virtual function support. Chapter 5, *Semantics of Construction, Destruction, and Copy*, deals with support of the class model and object lifetime. Program test data is discussed within each of these chapters, where our performance expectations are compared against actual performance as the representations move from an object-based to object-oriented solution.

Chapter 6, *Runtime Semantics*, looks at some of the Object Model behavior at runtime, including the life and death of temporary objects and the support of operators **new** and **delete**.

Chapter 7, *On the Cusp of the Object Model*, focuses on exception handling, template support, and runtime type identification.

The Intended Audience

This book is primarily a tutorial, although it is aimed at the intermediate C++ programmer rather than the novice. I have attempted to provide sufficient context to make it understandable to anyone who has had some prior exposure to C++—for example, someone who has read my C++ *Primer*—and some experience in C++ programming. The ideal reader, however, has been programming in C++ for a few years and wants to better understand what is actually going on "under the hood." Portions of the material should be of interest even to the advanced C++ programmer, such as the generation of temporaries and the details of the named return value optimization. At least, this has proved to be so in the various public presentations of this material I have given as it has evolved.

A Note on Program Examples and Program Execution

The use of program code in this text serves two primary purposes:

1. To provide concrete illustrations of the various aspects of the C++ Object Model under discussion

2. To provide test cases by which to measure the relative cost of various language features

In neither case is the code intended to represent models of production-quality programming. I am not, for example, suggesting that a real 3D graphics library represents a 3D point using a virtual inheritance hierarchy (although one can be found in [POKOR94]).

All the test programs in the text were compiled and executed on an SGI Indigo2 XL (the R4400 MIPS RISC processor) running version 5.2 of SGI's UNIX operating system under both its CC and NCC compilers. CC is cfront Release 3.0.1 (it generates C code, which a C compiler then recompiles into an executable). NCC is version 2.19 of the Edison Design Group's C++ front-end with a code generator supplied by SGI. The times were measured as the average user time reported by the UNIX **timex** command and represent 10 million iterations of the test function or statement block.

While the use of these two compilers on the SGI hardware might strike the reader as somewhat esoteric, I feel doing so serves the book's purposes quite well. Both cfront and now the Edison Design Group's front-end (reportedly characterized by Bjarne as the *son of cfront)* are not platform specific. Rather, they are generic implementations licensed to over 34 computer manufacturers (including Cray, SGI, and Intel) and producers of software environments (including Centerline and Novell, which is the former UNIX Software Laboratories). Performance measurements are intended not to provide a benchmark of current compilation systems but to provide a measure of the relative costs of the various features of the C++ Object Model. Benchmark performance numbers can be found in nearly any "compiler shoot-out" product review in the trade press.

Acknowledgments

One reason people write books is to set down and share their expertise with others. A second, more selfish reason is to enlarge on and fine tune that expertise. A third is to provide for the public acknowledgment of those who provide the foundation for one's work.

I owe a deep debt of gratitude to many former colleagues at Bell Laboratories without whose encouragement and insight little or nothing of this work could have been accomplished. In particular, Barbara Moo, Andy Koenig, and Bjarne Stroustrup have challenged and supported me throughout the years. Warm appreciation also goes to the Grail gang—Steve Buroff, Martin Carroll, Rob Murray, and Judy Ward—which has been a foundation for many years.

Michael Ball, now at SunPro, generously shared his expertise both through e-mail exchanges and an in-depth review of the text. Doug Schmidt, Cay Horstmann, Greg Comeau, and Steve Clamage also provided

tough, thoughtful reviews of the manuscript that were invaluable in help-
ing me push the manuscript's development forward. Jonathan Shopiro
taught me a great deal while we worked together at Bell Laboratories;
nuggets of his insight are scattered throughout the text. Joseé Lajoie fielded
all too many questions about Standard C++ both with astounding patience
and fearful insight.

In addition, I'd like to acknowledge my current foundation here at Walt
Disney Feature Animation: Michael Blum, Nhi Casey, Shyh-Chyuan Huang,
Scott Dolim, Elena Driskill, Ed Leonard, David Remba, Cary Sandvig, and
Dave Tonnesen. Chyuan, Scott, and Elena provided thoughtful readings on
various versions of the text. Appreciation also goes to M. J. Turner, Kiran
Joshi, Scott Johnston, Marcus Hobbs, and, finally, to the Technology Division
management of Dean Schiller and Paul Yanover. They have all helped to
make my first year here at Disney sparkle a bit more brightly. A good deal of
thanks goes to Dr. Clouis Tondo for detailing errors in the first printing.
Thanks also goes to John Potter, Keulin Henny, and Francis Glassborow.

This material has been given at a great many public presentations during the more than two years I have worked on it. These include ACM-spon-
sored lectures in both Silicon Valley and Los Angeles; two presentations in
Tel Aviv sponsored by Sela (with particular thanks to Anna); talks at SIGS
Conferences: Object Expo London, Object Expo New York, and C++ World;
a tutorial at the 1994 ACM Sigplan Conference on Compiler Construction;
at the 1994 IBM-sponsored Cascon Conference; and as part of my C++ Short
Course sponsored by UCLA Extension. The resultant feedback has proved
of immense help in crafting and revising the material.

Deep thanks also goes to my editor, Debbie Lafferty, who provided both
sound counsel and unflagging support and always showed the good sense
to laugh at my jokes.

Finally, I'd like to extend my appreciation to Rick Friedman, founder
and President of Sigs Publications, publisher of the C++ *Report*, for his support and vision while I was editor of that magazine from mid-1992 through
1995. The C++ *Report* was and remains the best timely source of high-quality technical information on C++. Portions of this text were originally published as columns in the magazine while I was editor.

References

NOTE: *Many of the C++ Report articles have been collected on C++ Gems, edited by
Stanley Lippman, SIGS Books, New York, NY (1996).*

[BALL92] Ball, Michael, "Inside Templates," C++ *Report* (September 1992).

[BALL93a] Ball, Michael, "What Are These Things Called Templates,"
C++ *Report* (February 1993).

[BALL93b] Ball, Michael, "Implementing Class Templates," C++ *Report* (September 1993).

[BOOCH93] Booch, Grady and Michael Vilot, "Simplifying the Booch Components," C++ *Report* (June 1993).

[BORL91] *Borland Languages Open Architecture Handbook*, Borland International Inc., Scotts Valley, CA.

[BOX95] Box, Don, "Building C++ Components Using OLE2," C++ *Report* (March/April 1995).

[BUDD91] Budd, Timothy, *An Introduction to Object-Oriented Programming*, Addison-Wesley Publishing Company, Reading, MA (1991).

[BUDGE92] Budge, Kent G., James S. Peery, and Allen C. Robinson, "High Performance Scientific Computing Using C++," Usenix C++ Conference Proceedings, Portland, OR (1992).

[BUDGE94] Budge, Kent G., James S. Peery, Allen C. Robinson, and Michael K. Wong, "Management of Class Temporaries in C++ Translation Systems," *The Journal of C Language Translation* (December 1994).

[CARGILL95] Cargill, Tom, "STL Caveats," C++ *Report* (July/August 1993).

[CARROLL93] Carroll, Martin, "Design of the USL Standard Components," C++ *Report* (June 1993).

[CARROLL95] Carroll, Martin and Margaret A. Ellis, *Designing and Coding Reusable C++*, Addison-Wesley Publishing Company, Reading, MA (1995).

[CHASE94] Chase, David, "Implementation of Exception Handling, Part 1," *The Journal of C Language Translation* (June 1994).

[CLAM93a] Clamage, Stephen D., "Implementing New & Delete," C++ *Report* (May 1993).

[CLAM93b] Clamage, Stephen D., "Beginnings & Endings," C++ *Report* (September 1993).

[ELLIS90] Ellis, Margaret A. and Bjarne Stroustrup, *The Annotated C++ Reference Manual*, Addison-Wesley Publishing Company, Reading, MA (1990).

[GOLD94] Goldstein, Theodore C. and Alan D. Sloane, "The Object Binary Interface—C++ Objects for Evolvable Shared Class Libraries," Usenix C++ Conference Proceedings, Cambridge, MA (1994).

[HAM95] Hamilton, Jennifer, Robert Klarer, Mark Mendell, and Brian Thomson, "Using SOM with C++, " C++ *Report* (July/August 1995).

[HORST95] Horstmann, Cay S., "C++ Compiler Shootout," C++ *Report* (July/August 1995).

[KOENIG90a] Koenig, Andrew and Stanley Lippman, "Optimizing Virtual Tables in C++ Release 2.0," C++ *Report* (March 1990).

[KOENIG90b] Koenig, Andrew and Bjarne Stroustrup, "Exception Handling for C++ (Revised)," Usenix C++ Conference Proceedings (April 1990).

[KOENIG93] Koenig, Andrew, "Combining C and C++," *C++ Report* (July/August 1993).

[ISO-C++95] *C++ International Standard*, Draft (April 28, 1995).

[LAJOIE94a] Lajoie, Josee, "Exception Handling: Supporting the Runtime Mechanism," *C++ Report* (March/April 1994).

[LAJOIE94b] Lajoie, Joseé, "Exception Handling: Behind the Scenes," *C++ Report* (June 1994).

[LENKOV92] Lenkov, Dmitry, Don Cameron, Paul Faust, and Michey Mehta, "A Portable Implementation of C++ Exception Handling," Usenix C++ Conference Proceedings, Portland, OR (1992).

[LEA93] Lea, Doug, "The GNU C++ Library," *C++ Report* (June 1993).

[LIPP88] Lippman, Stanley and Bjarne Stroustrup, "Pointers to Class Members in C++," Implementor's Workshop, Usenix C++ Conference Proceedings (October 1988).

[LIPP91a] Lippman, Stanley, "Touring Cfront," *C++ Journal*, Vol. 1, No. 3 (1991).

[LIPP91b] Lippman, Stanley, "Touring Cfront: From Minutiae to Migraine," *C++ Journal,* Vol. 1, No. 4 (1991).

[LIPP91c] Lippman, Stanley, *C++ Primer*, Addison-Wesley Publishing Company, Reading, MA (1991).

[LIPP94a] Lippman, Stanley, "Default Constructor Synthesis," *C++ Report* (January 1994).

[LIPP94b] Lippman, Stanley, "Applying the Copy Constructor, Part 1: Synthesis," *C++ Report* (February 1994).

[LIPP94c] Lippman, Stanley, "Applying the Copy Constructor, Part 2," *C++ Report* (March/April 1994).

[LIPP94d] Lippman, Stanley, "Objects and Datum," *C++ Report* (June 1994).

[METAW94] *MetaWare High C/C++ Language Reference Manual*, Metaware Inc., Santa Cruz, CA (1994).

[MICRO92] Jones, David and Martin J. O'Riordan, *The Microsoft Object Mapping*, Microsoft Corporation, 1992.

[MOWBRAY95] Mowbray, Thomas J. and Ron Zahavi, *The Essential Corba*, John Wiley & Sons, Inc. (1995).

[NACK94] Nackman, Lee R., and John J. Barton *Scientific and Engineering C++, An Introduction with Advanced Techniques and Examples*, Addison-Wesley Publishing Company, Reading, MA (1994).

[PALAY92] Palay, Andrew J., "C++ in a Changing Environment," Usenix C++ Conference Proceedings, Portland, OR (1992).

[POKOR94] Pokorny, Cornel, *Computer Graphics*, Franklin, Beedle & Associates, Inc. (1994).

[PUGH90] Pugh, William and Grant Weddell, "Two-directional Record Layout for Multiple Inheritance," ACM SIGPLAN '90 Conference, White Plains, New York (1990).

[SCHMIDT94a] Schmidt, Douglas C., "A Domain Analysis of Network Daemon Design Dimensions," *C++ Report* (March/April 1994).

[SCHMIDT94b] Schmidt, Douglas C., "A Case Study of C++ Design Evolution," *C++ Report* (July/August 1994).

[SCHWARZ89] Schwarz, Jerry, "Initializing Static Variables in C++ Libraries," *C++ Report* (February 1989).

[STROUP82] Stroustrup, Bjarne, "Adding Classes to C: An Exercise in Language Evolution," *Software: Practices & Experience*, Vol. 13 (1983).

[STROUP94] Stroustrup, Bjarne, *The Design and Evolution of C++*, Addison-Wesley Publishing Company, Reading, MA (1994).

[SUN94a] *The C++ Application Binary Interface*, SunPro, Sun Microsystems, Inc.

[SUN94b] *The C++ Application Binary Interface Rationale*, SunPro, Sun Microsystems, Inc.

[VELD95] Veldhuizen, Todd, "Using C++ Template Metaprograms," *C++ Report* (May 1995).

[VINOS93] Vinoski, Steve, "Distributed Object Computing with CORBA," *C++ Report* (July/August 1993).

[VINOS94] Vinoski, Steve, "Mapping CORBA IDL into C++," *C++ Report* (September 1994).

[YOUNG95] Young, Douglas, *Object-Oriented Programming with C++ and OSF/Motif*, 2d ed., Prentice-Hall (1995).

Contents

1 Object Lessons 1

Layout Costs for Adding Encapsulation 5

1.1 The C++ Object Model 6
A simple object model 6/ A table-driven object model 7/
The C++ object model/ How the object model effects
programs

1.2 A Keyword Distinction 12
Keywords schmeewords 13/ The politically correct
struct 16

1.3 An Object Distinction 18
The type of a pointer 24/ Adding polymorphism 25

2 The Semantics of Constructors 31

2.1 Default Constructor Construction 32
Member class object with default constructor 34/ Base
class with default constructor 37/ Class with a virtual
function 37/ Class with a virtual base class 38/
Summary 39

2.2 Copy Constructor Construction 40
Default memberwise initialization 41/ Bitwise copy semantics 43/ Bitwise copy semantics—Not! 45/ Resetting
the Virtual Table Pointer 45/ Handling the Virtual Base
Class Subobject 47

2.3 Program Transformation Semantics 50
Explicit initialization 50/ Argument initialization 51/
Return value initialization 53/ Optimization at the user
level 54/ Optimization at the compiler level 55/
The copy constructor: to have or to have not? 59/
Summary 61

2.4 Member Initialization List 62

3 The Semantics of Data 69

3.1 The Binding of a Data Member 72

3.2 Data Member Layout **75**

3.3 Access of a Data Member **72**
Static data members 78/ Nonstatic data members 80

3.4 Inheritance and the Data Member **82**
Inheritance without polymorphism 83/ Adding polymorphism 87/ Multiple inheritance 91/ Virtual inheritance 95

3.5 Object Member Efficiency **101**

3.6 Pointer to Data Members **106**
Efficiency of pointers to members 109

4 The Semantics of Function 113

4.1 Varieties of Member Invocation **114**
Nonstatic member functions 114/ Virtual member functions 120/ Static member functions 121/

4.2 Virtual Member Functions **124**
Virtual functions under MI 131/ Virtual functions under
virtual inheritance 138

4.3 Function Efficiency **139**

4.4 Pointer-to-Member Functions **144**
Supporting pointer-to-virtual member functions 145/
Pointer-to-member functions under M1 147/ Pointer-to-
member efficiency 149

4.5 Inline Functions **151**
Formal arguments 154/ Local variables 155

5 Semantics of Construction, Destruction, and Copy 159
Presence of pure virtual destructor 160/ Presence of a virtual specification 161/ Presence of const within a virtual
specification 162/ A reconsidered class declaration 162

5.1 Object Construction without Inheritance **163**
Abstract data type 165/ Concrete base class 168

5.2 Object Construction under Inheritance **172**
Virtual inheritance 176/ The semantics of the vptr initialization 179

5.3 Object Copy Semantics **184**

5.4 Object Efficiency **190**

5.5 Semantics of Destruction **196**

6 Runtime Semantics 201

6.1 Object Construction and Destruction **203**
Global objects 205/ Local static objects 209/ Arrays of
objects 211/ Default constructors and arrays 214

6.2 Operators **new** and **delete** **215**
The semantics of new arrays 218

6.3 Temporary Objects **227**
A temporary myth 235

7 On the Cusp of the Object Model 239

7.1 Templates **239**
Template instantiation 241/ Error reporting within a template 244/ Member function instantiation 250

7.2 Exception Handling **254**
A quick review of exception handling 256/ Exception handling support 260

7.3 Runtime Type Identification **264**
Introducing a type safe downcast 266/ A type safe dy-
namic cast 267/ References are not pointers 269/ Typeid
Operator 270

7.4 Efficient, but Inflexible **272**
Dynamic Shared Libraries 272/ Shared Memory 272

Index 275

Chapter 1

Object Lessons

In C, a data abstraction and the operations that perform on it are declared separately—that is, there is no language-supported relationship between data and functions. We speak of this method of programming as procedural, driven by a set of algorithms divided into task-oriented functions operating on shared, external data. For example, if we declare a struct Point3d, such as the following:

```
typedef struct point3d
{
    float x;
    float y;
    float z;
} Point3d;
```

the operation to print a particular Point3d might be defined either as a function

```
void
Point3d_print( const Point3d *pd )
{
    printf("( %g, %g, %g )", pd->x, pd->y, pd->z );
}
```

or, for efficiency, as a preprocessor macro:

```
#define Point3d_print( pd )   \
    printf("( %g, %g, %g )", pd->x, pd->y, pd->z )
```

Or it may be directly implemented within individual code segments:

```
void
my_foo()
{
    Point3d *pd = get_a_point();
    ...
    /* print the point directly ... */
    printf("( %g, %g, %g )", pd->x, pd->y, pd->z );
}
```

Similarly, a particular coordinate member of a point is accessed either directly:

```
Point3d pt;
pt.x = 0.0;
```

or through a preprocessor macro:

```
#define X( p, xval ) (p.x) = (xval)
...
X( pt, 0.0 );
```

In C++, Point3d is likely to be implemented either as an independent abstract data type (ADT):

```
class Point3d
{
public:
   Point3d( float x = 0.0,
            float y = 0.0, float z = 0.0 )
        : _x( x ), _y( y ), _z( z ) {}

   float x() { return _x; }
   float y() { return _y; }
   float z() { return _z; }

   void x( float xval ) { _x = xval; }

   // ... etc ...
private:
   float _x;
   float _y;
   float _z;
};
```

```
inline ostream&
operator<<( ostream &os, const Point3d &pt )
{
    os << "( " << pt.x() << ", "
        << pt.y() << ", " << pt.z() << " )";
};
```

or as a two- or three-level class hierarchy:

```
class Point {
public:
    Point( float x = 0.0 ) : _x( x ) {}

    float x() { return _x; }
    void x( float xval ) { _x = xval; }
    // ...
protected:
    float _x;
};

class Point2d : public Point {
public:
    Point2d( float x = 0.0, float y = 0.0 )
        : Point( x ), _y( y ) {}

    float y() { return _y; }
    void y( float yval ) { _y = yval; }

    // ...
protected:
    float _y;
};

class Point3d : public Point2d {
public:
    Point3d( float x = 0.0, float y = 0.0, float z = 0.0 )
        : Point2d( x, y ), _z( z ) {}

    float z() { return _z; }
    void z( float zval ) { _z = zval; }

    // ...
protected:
    float _z;
};
```

Moreover, either of these implementations may be parameterized, either by the type of the coordinate:

```
template < class type >
class Point3d
{
public:
    Point3d( type x = 0.0,
              type y = 0.0, type z = 0.0 )
        : _x( x ), _y( y ), _z( z ) {}

    type x() { return _x; }
    void x( type xval ) { _x = xval; }

    // ... etc ...
private:
    type _x;
    type _y;
    type _z;
};
```

or by both the type and number of coordinates:

```
template < class type, int dim >
class Point
{
public:
    Point();
    Point( type coords[ dim ] ) {
        for ( int index = 0; index < dim; index++ )
            _coords[ index ] = coords[ index ];
    }

    type& operator[]( int index ) {
        assert( index < dim && index >= 0 );
        return _coords[ index ]; }

    type  operator[]( int index ) const
        { /* same as non-const instance */ }

    // ... etc ...
private:
    type _coords[ dim ];
};
```

```
inline
template < class type, int dim >
ostream&
operator<<( ostream &os, const Point< type, dim > &pt )
{
    os << "( ";
    for ( int ix = 0; ix < dim-1; ix++ )
        os << pt[ ix ] << ", " ;
    os << pt[ dim-1];
    os << " )";
}
```

These are obviously not only very different styles of programming, but
also very different ways of thinking about our programs. There are many
more or less convincing arguments for why the data encapsulation of an
ADT or class hierarchy is better (in the software engineering sense) than the
procedural use of global data such as that in C programs. Those arguments,
however, are often lost on programmers who are charged with getting an
application up and running quickly *and* efficiently. The appeal of C is both
its leanness and its relative simplicity.

The C++ implementations of a 3D point are more complicated than their
C counterpart, particularly the template instances. This doesn't mean they
are not also considerably more powerful or, again in a software engineering
sense, better. But being more powerful or better is not necessarily a convincing argument for their use.

Layout Costs for Adding Encapsulation

An obvious first question a programmer might ask while looking at the
transformed Point3d implementations under C++ concerns the layout costs
for adding encapsulation. The answer is that there are no additional layout
costs for supporting the class Point3d. The three coordinate data members
are directly contained within each class object, as they are in the C struct.
The member functions, although included in the class declaration, are not
reflected in the object layout; one copy only of each non-inline member
function is generated. Each inline function has either zero or one definition
of itself generated within each module in which it is used. The Point3d class
has no space or runtime penalty in supporting encapsulation. As you will
see, the primary layout and access-time overheads within C++ are associated with the *virtuals*, that is,

- the virtual function mechanism in its support of an efficient runtime binding, and

- a virtual base class in its support of a single, shared instance of a base
  class occurring multiple times within an inheritance hierarchy.

There is also additional overhead under multiple inheritance in the conversion between a derived class and its second or subsequent base class. In general, however, there is no inherent reason a program in C++ need be any larger or slower than its equivalent C program.

1.1 The C++ Object Model

In C++, there are two flavors of class data members—static and nonstatic—and three flavors of class member functions—static, nonstatic, and virtual. Given the following declaration of a class Point:

```
class Point
{
public:
    Point( float xval );
    virtual ~Point();

    float x() const;
    static int PointCount();

protected:
    virtual ostream&
        print( ostream &os ) const;

    float _x;
    static int _point_count;
};
```

how is the class Point to be represented within the machine? That is, how do we model the various flavors of data and function members?

A Simple Object Model

Our first object model is admittedly very simple. It might be used for a C++ implementation designed to minimize the complexity of the compiler at the expense of space and runtime efficiency. In this simple model, an object is a sequence of slots, where each slot points to a member. The members are

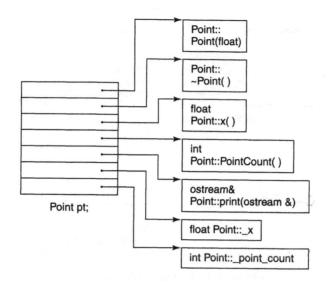

Figure 1.1   Simple Object Model

assigned a slot in the order of their declarations. There is a slot for each data or function member. This is illustrated in Figure 1.1.

In this simple model, the members themselves are not placed within the object. Only pointers addressing the members are placed within the object. Doing this avoids problems from members' being quite different types and requiring different amounts (and sometimes different types of) storage. Members within an object are addressed by their slot's index. For example, _x's index is 6 and _point_count's index is 7. The general size of a class object is the size of a pointer multiplied by the number of members declared by the class.

Although this model is not used in practice, this simple concept of an index or slot number is the one that has been developed into the C++ pointer-to-member concept (see [LIPP88]).

A Table-driven Object Model

For an implementation to maintain a uniform representation for the objects of all classes, an alternative object model might factor out all member specific information, placing it in a data member and member function pair of tables. The class object contains the pointers to the two member tables. The member function table is a sequence of slots, with each slot addressing a member. The data member table directly holds the data. This is shown in Figure 1.2 (on page 8).

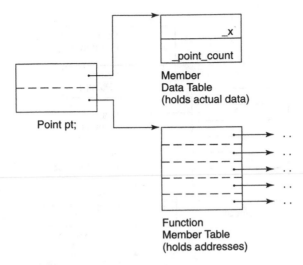

Figure 1.2 Member Table Object Model

Although this model is not used in practice within C++, the concept of a member function table has been the traditional implementation supporting efficient runtime resolution of virtual functions.[1]

The C++ Object Model

Stroustrup's original (and still prevailing) C++ Object Model is derived from the simple object model by optimizing for space and access time. Nonstatic data members are allocated directly within each class object. Static data members are stored outside the individual class object. Static and nonstatic function members are also hoisted outside the class object. Virtual functions are supported in two steps:

1. A table of pointers to virtual functions is generated for each class (this is called the *virtual table*).

2. A single pointer to the associated virtual table is inserted within each class object (traditionally, this has been called the *vptr*). The setting, resetting, and *not* setting of the vptr is handled automatically through code generated within each class constructor, destructor, and copy assignment operator (this is discussed in Chapter 5). The type_info object associated with each class in support of runtime type identification (RTTI) is also addressed within the virtual table, usually within the table's first slot.

---

[1] At least one implementation of the CORBA ORB has used a form of this two table model. The SOM object model also relies on this two table model [HAM95].

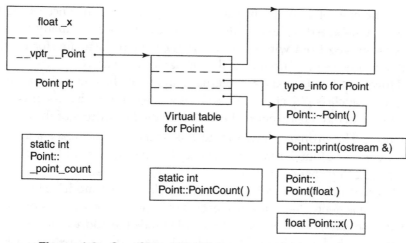

Figure 1.3 C++ Object Model

Figure 1.3 illustrates the general C++ Object Model for our Point class. The primary strength of the C++ Object Model is its space and runtime efficiency. Its primary drawback is the need to recompile unmodified code that makes use of an object of a class for which there has been an addition, removal, or modification of the nonstatic class data members. (The two table model, for example, offers more flexibility by providing an additional level of indirection. But it does this at the cost of space and runtime efficiency.)

Adding Inheritance

C++ supports both *single* inheritance:

```
class Library_materials { ... };
class Book : public Library_materials { ... };
class Rental_book : public Book { ... };
```

and *multiple* inheritance:

```
// original pre-Standard iostream implementation
class iostream:
   public istream,
   public ostream { ... };
```

Moreover, the inheritance may be specified as *virtual* (that is, shared):

```
class istream : virtual public ios { ... };
class ostream : virtual public ios { ... };
```

In the case of virtual inheritance, only a single occurrence of the base class is maintained (called a *subobject*) regardless of how many times the class is derived from within the inheritance chain. iostream, for example, contains only a single instance of the virtual ios base class.

How might a derived class internally model its base class instance? In a simple base class object model, each base class might be assigned a slot within the derived class object. Each slot holds the address of the base class subobject. The primary drawback to this scheme is the space and access-time overhead of the indirection. A benefit is that the size of the class object is unaffected by changes in the size of its associated base classes.

Alternatively, one can imagine a base class table model. Here, a base class table is generated for which each slot contains the address of an associated base class, much as the virtual table holds the address of each virtual function. Each class object contains a *bptr* initialized to address its base class table. The primary drawback to this strategy, of course, is both the space and access-time overhead of the indirection. One benefit is a uniform representation of inheritance within each class object. Each class object would contain a base class table pointer at some fixed location regardless of the size or number of its base classes. A second benefit would be the ability to grow, shrink, or otherwise modify the base class table without changing the size of the class objects themselves.

In both schemes, the degree of indirection increases with the depth of the inheritance chain; for example, a Rental_book requires two indirections to access an inherited member of its Library_materials class, whereas Book requires only one. A uniform access time could be gained by duplicating within the derived class a pointer to each base class within the inheritance chain. The tradeoff is in the additional space required to maintain the additional pointers.

The original inheritance model supported by C++ forgoes all indirection; the data members of the base class subobject are directly stored within the derived class object. This offers the most compact and most efficient access of the base class members. The drawback, of course, is that any change to the base class members, such as adding, removing, or changing a member's type, requires that all code using objects of the base class or any class derived from it be recompiled.

The introduction of virtual base classes into the language at the time of Release 2.0 required some form of indirect base class representation. The original model of virtual base class support added a pointer into the class object for each associated virtual base class. Alternative models have evolved that either introduce a virtual base class table or augment the existing virtual table to maintain the location of each virtual base class (see Section 3.4 for a discussion).

How the Object Model Effects Programs

In practice, what does this mean for the programmer? Support for the object model results in both modifications of the existing program code and the insertion of additional code. For example, given the following function, where class X defines a copy constructor, virtual destructor, and virtual function foo():

```
X foobar()
{
    X xx;
    X *px = new X;

    // foo() is virtual function
    xx.foo();
    px->foo();

    delete px;
    return xx;
}
```

the likely internal transformation of the function looks as follows:

```
// Probable internal transformation
// Pseudo C++ code
void foobar( X &_result )
{
    // construct _result
    // _result replaces local xx ...
    _result.X::X();

    // expand X *px = new X;
    px = _new( sizeof( X ));
    if ( px != 0 )
        px->X::X();

    // expand xx.foo(): suppress virtual mechanism
    // replace xx with _result
    foo( &_result );

    // expand px->foo() using virtual mechanism
    ( *px->_vtbl[ 2 ] )( px )
```

```
// expand delete px;
if ( px != 0 ) {
    ( *px->_vtbl[ 1 ] )( px ); // destructor
    _delete( px );
}

// replace named return statement
// no need to destroy local object xx
return;
};
```

Wow, that really is different, isn't it? Of course, you're not supposed to understand all these transformations at this point in the book. In the subsequent chapters, I look at the what and why of each of these, plus many more. Ideally, you'll look back, snap your fingers, and say, "Oh, yeah, sure," wondering why you were ever puzzled.

1.2   A Keyword Distinction

Because C++ strives to maintain (as close as possible) language compatibility with C, C++ is considerably more complicated than it would otherwise be. For example, overloaded function resolution would be a lot simpler if there were not eight flavors of integer to support. Similarly, if C++ were to throw off the C declaration syntax, lookahead would not be required to determine that the following is an invocation of pf rather than its definition:

```
// don't know if declaration or invocation
// until see the integer constant 1024
int ( *pf )( 1024 );
```

On the following declaration, lookahead does not even work:

```
// meta-language rule:
// declaration of pq, not invocation
int ( *pq )( );
```

A meta-language rule is required, dictating that when the language cannot distinguish between a declaration and an expression, it is to be interpreted as a declaration.

Similarly, the concept of a class could be supported by a single **class** keyword, if C++ were not required to support existing C code and, with that, the keyword **struct**. Surprisingly, one of the most-asked questions of C programmers moving to C++ (once the questions about performance have been put aside) is *when, if ever, should one use a struct declaration rather than a class declaration when writing a program using C++?*

In 1986, my answer to this question was an unequivocal "never." In both the first and second editions of my C++ *Primer*, the keyword **struct** does not appear in the text, except in Appendix C, which, logically enough, discusses the C language. At that time, this was one of those small philosophical points that one necessarily does not point out. However, it is one from which one gains some small (admittedly quite small) satisfaction when, well, when it is pointed out, usually as a question: "Hey, did you know? Struct. The keyword. It's not used anywhere...." But as a colleague of mine at Bell Laboratories indirectly pointed out to me, even the smallest philosophical point can have a human cost. For example, a C programmer in his group, anxious to learn C++, was quite distressed to find **struct** absent from my book. Apparently its inclusion would have provided a transitional lifeline to make the programmer's rocky ascent less bruising. So much, then, for philosophy.

Keywords, Schmeewords

One answer to the question of when, if ever, you should use a struct declaration rather than a class declaration, then, is *whenever it makes one feel better.*

Although this answer does not achieve a high technical level, it does point out an important distinction that it is important *not* to make: the keyword **struct** by itself does not necessarily signify anything about the declaration to follow. We can use **struct** in place of **class**, but still declare public, protected, and private sections and a full public interface, as well as specify virtual functions and the full range of single, multiple, and virtual inheritance. Back in the "early days," it seemed everyone would spend a full 10 minutes of a one-hour introductory talk on C++ distinguishing the nondistinction between

```
class cplus_plus_keyword {
public:
    // mumble ...
};
```

and its C equivalent

```
struct c_keyword {
    // the same mumble
};
```

When people and textbooks speak of a **struct**, they mean a data aggregate without private data or a set of operations associated with it, that is, its C usage. This usage should be distinguished from its more pedestrian use simply as a keyword introducing a user-defined type within C++. In the sense of its C usage, valid design reasons exist for its use. In the C++ sense, however, the reason for choosing between **struct** and **class** as a keyword with which to introduce an ADT is only so much sound and fury. This is much in the spirit of a discussion on the placement of braces within a function or whether to use an underscore within variable and type names (the infamous *isRight* versus *is_right* debate).

There is a significant conceptual distinction between a struct, as supported in C, and a class, as supported in C++. My point is simply that the keyword itself does not provide that distinction. That is, if one is provided with the following body of a user-defined type within C++, one simply says, "Oh, that's a class:"

```
// tag name is for the moment missing
{
public:
    operator int();
    virtual void foo();
    // ...
protected:
    static int object_count;
    // mumble;
};
```

regardless of the keyword used to introduce it. The use of the keywords **struct** and **class** are interchangeable in providing a tag name. The conceptual meaning of the two declarations is determined by an examination only of the body of the declaration.

In cfront, for example, the two keywords are replaced by the shared token AGGR in the parser. In the Foundation project, Rob Murray's ALF hierarchy did retain knowledge of the actual keyword used by the programmer. This information, however, was not used by the internal compiler. Rather it was used by the "unparser" when a user requested an ASCII representation of a program. Users became upset when the exact keyword they specified was not present in the "unparsed" instance, even when the program was otherwise equivalent.

I first stumbled across what I call the "passion of the keyword" around 1988 when a new member of our internal testing group issued a dead-in-the-water bug report against cfront itself. In cfront's original declaration of

its internal type hierarchy, the root node and each derived subtype was declared with the keyword **struct**. In a subsequent modification of the header
file, a forward declaration of one or another of the derived subtypes had
used the keyword **class:**

```
// illegal?  no ... simply inconsistent
class node;
...
struct node { ... };
```

The tester claimed this was a gross error, one that cfront failed to catch,
since, of course, cfront was used to compile itself.

The real issue, however, is not whether all declarations of a user-defined
type must use a consistent keyword. Rather the issue is whether the use of
the **class** or **struct** keyword makes any promise as to the internal declaration of the type. That is, if use of the **struct** keyword enforces the C concept
of a data abstraction, while use of the **class** keyword enforces the concept of
an ADT, then, of course, failure to be consistent is an incorrect usage of the
language. This would then be as incorrect as is, for example, the contrary
declaration of an object as static and extern:

```
// illegal?  yes
// declarations make contrary storage claims
static int foo;
...
extern int foo;
```

This set of declarations makes contrary storage claims on the object foo.
However, as you've seen, use of either the **struct** or **class** keyword makes
no such claims. The actual characteristics of the class are determined by the
body of the declaration. Enforcing a consistent usage is simply a question of
style.

The second time I stubbed my implementation toe on this issue was
during Release 3.0 with regard to the parameter lists of templates. Steve
Buroff, another Bell Laboratories colleague back then, walked into my office
one day pointing out that the following code:

```
// originally flagged as illegal
template < struct Type >
struct mumble { ... };
```

was flagged by the parser as illegal, while the following otherwise equivalent code was not:

```
// ok: explicit use of class keyword
template < class Type >
struct mumble { ... };
```

"Why?" he asked.

"Why not?" I cleverly countered, recounting the fact that templates did not present a backward C compatibility issue. Let's strike aside **struct**, I said, and be done with it. (I may even have then leaped atop my Sun 3/60 and brandished its mouse in my best Erroll Flynn manner. Honestly, I don't recall. However, I do recall changing the parser to accept both keywords. Changing it, in fact, without either first passing it by Bjarne or the fledgling ANSI C++ committee. Thus are language dialects born!)

One might argue, then, that a great deal of confusion could be removed if the language chose to support only one of the two keywords. It is impossible not to support **struct** if one wishes to support existing C code. And the language simply had to do that. Okay. Well, then was it necessary to introduce the additional keyword **class**? Really necessary? No, but it is certainly desirable, since the language introduces not only the keyword but the philosophy of encapsulation and inheritance that it supports. Imagine, for example, speaking of an abstract base struct or of the Zoo Animal struct hierarchy containing one or more virtual base structs.

In the preceding discussion, I distinguished between use of the keyword **struct** and the philosophical concept of a struct declaration. One might claim that use of the keyword accompanied by the declaration of a public interface (the philosophical underpinning of a class) is like the use of slang or diminutives in public discourse. One might even further claim that this use is simply the self-assertion of the C immigrant to the C++ community.

The Politically Correct Struct

A C program's trick is sometimes a C++ program's trap. One example of this is the use of a one-element array at the end of a struct to allow individual struct objects to address variable-sized arrays:

```
struct mumble {
   /* stuff */
   char pc[ 1 ];
};

// grab a string from file or standard input
// allocate memory both for struct & string
```

```
struct mumble *pmumbl = ( struct mumble* )
    malloc(sizeof(struct mumble)+strlen(string)+1);

strcpy( &mumble.pc, string );
```

This may or may not translate well when placed within a class declaration that

- specifies multiple access sections containing data,
- derives from another class or is itself the object of derivation, or
- defines one or more virtual functions.

The data members within a single access section are guaranteed within C++ to be laid out in the order of their declaration. The layout of data contained in multiple access sections, however, is left undefined. In the following declaration, for example, the C trick may or may not work, depending on whether the protected data members are placed before or after those declared private:

```
class stumble {
public:
    // operations ...
protected:
    // protected stuff
private:
    /* private stuff */
    char pc[ 1 ];
};
```

Similarly, the layout of data members of the base and derived classes is left undefined, thereby also negating any guarantee that the trick might work. The presence of a virtual function also places the trick's viability in question. The best advice is not to do it. (Chapter 3 discusses these layout issues in greater detail.)

If a programmer absolutely needs a data portion of an arbitrarily complex C++ class to have the look and feel of an equivalent C declaration, that portion is best factored out into an independent struct declaration. The original idiom for combining this C portion with its C++ part (see [KOENIG93]) was to derive the C++ part from the C struct:

```
struct C_point { ... };
class Point : public C_point { ... };
```

thus supporting both the C and C++ usage:

```
extern void draw_line( Point, Point );
extern "C" void draw_rect ( C_point, C_Point );

draw_line( Point( 0, 0 ), Point( 100, 100 ));
draw_rect( Point( 0, 0 ), Point( 100, 100 ));
```

This idiom is no longer recommended, however, because of changes to the class inheritance layout in some compilers (for example, the Microsoft C++ compiler) in support of the virtual function mechanism (see Section 3.4 for a discussion). Composition, rather than inheritance, is the only portable method of combining C and C++ portions of a class (the conversion operator provides a handy extraction method):

```
struct C_point { ... };

class Point {
public:
    operator C_point() { return _c_point; }
    // ...
private:
    C_point _c_point;
    // ...
};
```

One reasonable use of the C struct in C++, then, is when you want to pass all or part of a complex class object to a C function. This struct declaration serves to encapsulate that data and guarantees a compatible C storage layout. This guarantee, however, is maintained only under composition. Under inheritance, the compiler decides whether additional data members are inserted within the base struct subobject (again, see Section 3.4 for a discussion, as well as Figures 3.2a and 3.2b).

1.3   An Object Distinction

The C++ programming model directly supports three programming paradigms:

1. The *procedural model* as programmed in C, and, of course, supported within C++. An example of this is string manipulation using character arrays and the family of str* functions defined in the Standard C library:

```
char boy[] = "Danny";
char *p_son;

. . .

p_son = new char[ strlen( boy ) + 1 ];
strcpy( p_son, boy );

. . .

if ( !strcmp( p_son, boy ))
    take_to_disneyland( boy );
```

2. The *abstract data type (ADT) model* in which users of the abstraction are provided with a set of operations (the public interface), while the implementation remains hidden. An example of this is a String class:

```
String girl = "Anna";
String daughter;

. . .

// String::operator=();
daughter = girl;

. . .

// String::operator==();
if ( girl == daughter )
    take_to_disneyland( girl );
```

3. The *object-oriented (OO) model* in which a collection of related types are encapsulated through an abstract base class providing a common interface. An example of this is a Library_materials class from which actual subtypes such as Book, Video, Compact_Disc, Puppet, and Laptop are derived:

```
void
check_in( Library_materials *pmat )
{
    if ( pmat->late() )
        pmat->fine();
    pmat->check_in();
```

```
if ( Lender *plend = pmat->reserved() )
    pmat->notify( plend );
}
```

Programs written purely in the idiom of any one of these paradigms tend to be well behaved. Mixed paradigm programs, however, hold a greater potential for surprise, particularly when the mixing is inadvertent. The most common inadvertent mixing of idioms occurs when a concrete instance of a base class, such as

```
Library_materials thing1;
```

is used to program some aspect of polymorphism:

```
// class Book : public Library_materials { ... };
Book book;

// Oops: thing1 is not a Book!
// Rather, book is ``sliced'' -
// thing1 remains a Library_materials
thing1 = book;

// Oops: invokes
// Library_materials::check_in()
thing1.check_in();
```

rather than a pointer or reference of the base class:

```
// OK: thing2 now references book
Library_materials &thing2 = book;

// OK: invokes Book::check_in()
thing2.check_in();
```

Although you can manipulate a base class object of an inheritance hierarchy either directly or indirectly, only the indirect manipulation of the object through a pointer or reference supports the polymorphism necessary for OO programming. The definition and use of thing2 in the previous example is a well-behaved instance of the OO paradigm. The definition and use of thing1 falls outside the OO idiom; it reflects a well-behaved instance of the ADT paradigm. Whether the behavior of thing1 is good or bad depends on what the programmer intended. In this example, its behavior is very likely a surprise.

In the OO paradigm, the programmer manipulates an unknown instance of a bounded but infinite set of types. (The set of types is bounded by its inheritance hierarchy; in theory, however, there is no limit to the depth and breadth of that hierarchy.) The actual type of the object addressed is not resolved in principle until runtime at each particular point of execution. In C++, this is achieved only through the manipulation of objects through pointers and references. In contrast, in the ADT paradigm the programmer manipulates an instance of a fixed, singular type that is completely defined at the point of compilation. For example, given the following set of declarations:

```
// represent objects: uncertain type
Library_materials *px = retrieve_some_material();
Library_materials &rx = *px;

// represents datum: no surprise
Library_materials dx = *px;
```

it can never be said with certainty what the actual type of the object is that px or rx addresses. It can only be said that it is either a Library_materials object or a subtype rooted by the Library_materials class. dx, however, is and can only be an object of the Library_materials class. Later in this section, I discuss why this behavior, although perhaps unexpected, is well behaved.

Although the polymorphic manipulation of an object requires that the object be accessed either through a pointer or a reference, the manipulation of a pointer or reference in C++ does not in itself necessarily result in polymorphism! For example, consider

```
// no polymorphism
int *pi;

// no language supported polymorphism
void *pvi;

// ok: class x serves as a base class
x *px;
```

In C++, polymorphism exists only within individual public class hierarchies. px, for example, may address either an object of its own type or a type publicly derived from it (not considering ill-behaved casts). Nonpublic derivation and pointers of type void* can be spoken of as polymorphic, but they are without explicit language support; that is, they must be managed by the programmer through explicit casts. (One might say that they are not first-class polymorphic objects.)

The C++ language supports polymorphism in the following ways:

1. Through a set of implicit conversions, such as the conversion of a derived class pointer to a pointer of its public base type:

```
shape *ps = new circle();
```

2. Through the virtual function mechanism:

```
ps->rotate();
```

3. Through the **dynamic_cast** and **typeid** operators:

```
if ( circle *pc =
    dynamic_cast< circle* >( ps )) ...
```

The primary use of polymorphism is to effect type encapsulation through a shared interface usually defined within an abstract base class from which specific subtypes are derived. The Library_materials class, for example, defines an interface for a Book, Video, and Puppet subtype. This shared interface is invoked through the virtual function mechanism that resolves which instance of a function to invoke based on the actual type of the object at each point during execution. By our writing code such as

```
library_material->check_out();
```

user code is shielded from the variety and volatility of lending materials supported by a particular library. This not only allows for the addition, revision, or removal of types without requiring changes to user programs. It also frees the provider of a new Library_materials subtype from having to recode behavior or actions common to all types in the hierarchy itself.

Consider the following code fragment:

```
void rotate(
    X datum,
    const X *pointer,
    const X &reference )
{
    // cannot determine until run-time
    // actual instance of rotate() invoked
    (*pointer).rotate();
    reference.rotate();
```

```
        // always invokes X::rotate()
        datum.rotate();
    }

    main() {
        Z z; // a subtype of X

        rotate( z, &z, z );
        return 0;
    }
```

The two invocations through `pointer` and `reference` are resolved dynamically. In this example, they both invoke `Z::rotate()`. The invocation through `datum` may or may not be invoked through the virtual mechanism; however, it will always invoke `X::rotate()`. (This is what is called a "quality of compilation" issue: whether the invocation of a virtual function through `datum` circumvents or employs the virtual mechanism. Semantically, the results are equivalent. This is looked at in more detail in Section 4.2.)

The memory requirements to represent a class object in general are the following:

- The accumulated size of its nonstatic data members

- Plus any padding (between members or on the aggregate boundary itself) due to alignment constraints (or simple efficiency)

- Plus any internally generated overhead to support the virtuals

The memory requirement to represent a pointer,[2] however, is a fixed size regardless of the type it addresses. For example, given the following declaration of a ZooAnimal class:

```
class ZooAnimal {
public:
    ZooAnimal();
    virtual ~ZooAnimal();

    // ...

    virtual void rotate();
```

[2] Or to represent a reference; internally, a reference is generally implemented as a pointer and the object syntax transformed into the indirection required of a pointer.

```
protected:
    int loc;
    String name;
};

ZooAnimal za( "Zoey" );
ZooAnimal *pza = &za;
```

a likely layout of the class object za and the pointer pza is pictured in Figure 1.4. (I return to the layout of data members in Chapter 3.)

The Type of a Pointer

But how, then, does a pointer to a ZooAnimal differ from, say, a pointer to an integer or a pointer to a template Array instantiated with a String?

```
ZooAnimal *px;
int *pi;
Array< String > *pta;
```

In terms of memory requirements, there is generally no difference: all three need to be allocated sufficient memory to hold a machine address (usually a machine word). So the difference between pointers to different types rests neither in the representation of the pointer nor in the values (addresses) the pointers may hold. The difference lies in the type of object be-

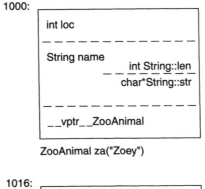

ZooAnimal za("Zoey")

ZooAnimal *pza = &za

Figure 1.4 Layout of Object and Pointer of Independent Class

ing addressed. That is, the type of a pointer instructs the compiler as to how to interpret the memory found at a particular address and also just how much memory that interpretation should span:

- An integer pointer addressing memory location 1000 on a 32-bit machine spans the address space 1000—1003.

- The `ZooAnimal` pointer, if we presume a conventional 8-byte String (a 4-byte character pointer and an integer to hold the string length), spans the address space 1000—1015.

Hmm. Just out of curiosity, what address space does a `void*` pointer that holds memory location 1000 span? That's right, we don't know. That's why a pointer of type `void*` can only hold an address and not actually operate on the object it addresses.

So a cast in general is a kind of compiler directive. In most cases, it does not alter the actual address a pointer contains. Rather, it alters only the interpretation of the size and composition of the memory being addressed.

Adding Polymorphism

Now, let's define a Bear as a kind of ZooAnimal. This is done, of course, through public inheritance:

```
class Bear : public ZooAnimal {
public:
   Bear();
   ~Bear();
   // ...
   void rotate();
   virtual void dance();
   // ...
protected:
   enum Dances { ... };

   Dances dances_known;
   int cell_block;
};

Bear b( "Yogi" );
Bear *pb = &b;
Bear &rb = *pb;
```

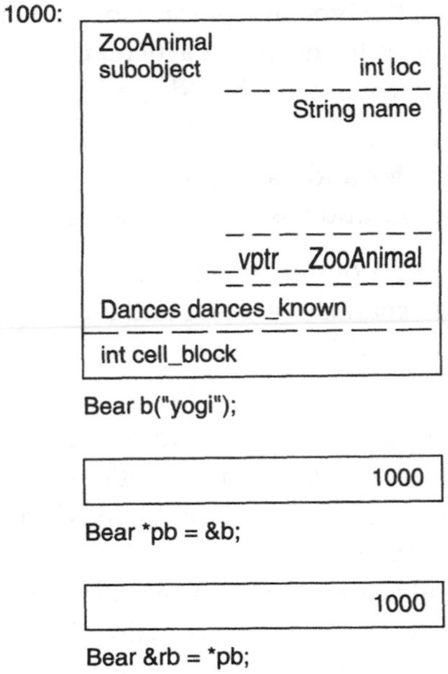

1000:

ZooAnimal	
subobject	int loc
- - - - -	String name
- - - - - - - -	
	__vptr__ZooAnimal
- - - - - - - -	
Dances dances_known	
int cell_block	

Bear b("yogi");

	1000

Bear *pb = &b;

	1000

Bear &rb = *pb;

Figure 1.5 Layout of Object and Pointer of Derived Class

What can we say about the memory requirements of b, pb, and rb? Both the pointer and reference require a single word of storage (4 bytes on a 32-bit processor). The Bear object itself, however, requires 24 bytes (the size of a ZooAnimal [16 bytes] plus the 8 bytes Bear introduces). A likely memory layout is pictured in Figure 1.5.

Okay, given that our Bear object is situated at memory location 1000, what are the real differences between a Bear and ZooAnimal pointer?

```
Bear b;
ZooAnimal *pz = &b;
Bear *pb = &b;
```

Each addresses the same first byte of the Bear object. The difference is that the address span of pb encompasses the entire Bear object, while the span of pz encompasses only the ZooAnimal subobject of Bear.

pz cannot directly access any members other than those present within the ZooAnimal subobject, except through the virtual mechanism:

```
// illegal: cell_block not a member
// of ZooAnimal, although we ``know''
// pz currently addresses a Bear object
pz->cell_block;
```

```
// okay: an explicit downcast
(static_cast< Bear* >( pz ))->cell_block;

// better: but a run-time operation
if ( Bear* pb2 = dynamic_cast< Bear* >( pz ))
    pb2->cell_block;

// ok: cell_block a member of Bear
pb->cell_block;
```

When we write

```
pz->rotate();
```

the type of pz determines the following at compile time:

- The fixed, available interface (that is, pz may invoke only the ZooAnimal public interface)

- The access level of that interface (for example, rotate() is a public member of ZooAnimal)

The type of the object that pz addresses at each point of execution determines the instance of rotate() invoked. The encapsulation of the type information is maintained not in pz but in the *link* between the object's vptr and the virtual table the vptr addresses (see Section 4.2 for a full discussion of virtual functions).

So, then, why is it that, given

```
Bear b;
ZooAnimal za = b;

// ZooAnimal::rotate() invoked
za.rotate();
```

the instance of rotate() invoked is the ZooAnimal instance and not that of Bear? Moreover, if memberwise initialization copies the values of one object to another, why is za's vptr not addressing Bear's virtual table?

The answer to the second question is that the compiler intercedes in the initialization and assignment of one class object with another. The compiler must ensure that if an object contains one or more vptrs, those vptr values are not initialized or changed by the source object.

The answer to the first question is that za is not (and can never be) a Bear; it is (and can never be anything but) a ZooAnimal. Polymorphism, the potential to be of more than one type, is not physically possible in directly accessed objects. Paradoxically, direct object manipulation is not supported under OO programming. For example, given the following set of definitions:

```
{
    ZooAnimal  za;
    ZooAnimal  *pza;

    Bear  b;
    Panda  *pp = new Panda;

    pza = &b;
}
```

one possible memory layout is pictured in Figure 1.6.

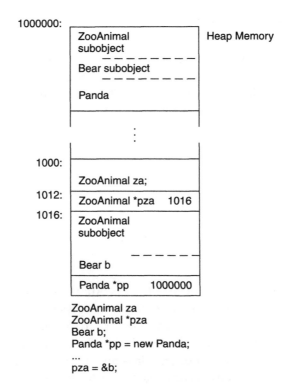

Figure 1.6   Memory Layout of Sequence of Definitions

Assigning pz the address of either za, b, or that contained by pp is obviously not a problem. A pointer and a reference support polymorphism because they do not involve any type-dependent commitment of resources. Rather, all that is altered is the interpretation of the size and composition of the memory they address.

Any attempt to alter the actual size of the object za, however, violates the contracted resource requirements of its definition. Assign the entire Bear object to za and the object overflows its allocated memory. As a result, the executable is, literally, corrupted, although the corruption may not manifest itself as a core dump.

When a base class object is directly initialized or assigned with a derived class object, the derived object is *sliced* to fit into the available memory resources of the base type. There is nothing of the derived type remaining. Polymorphism is not present, and an observant compiler can resolve an invocation of a virtual function through the object at compile time, thus bypassing the virtual mechanism. This can be a significant performance win if the virtual function is defined as inline.

To summarize, polymorphism is a powerful design mechanism that allows for the encapsulation of related types behind an abstract public interface, such as our Library_materials hierarchy. The cost is an additional level of indirection, both in terms of memory acquisition and type resolution. C++ supports polymorphism through class pointers and references. This style of programming is called *object-oriented*.

C++ also supports a concrete ADT style of programming now called *object-based (OB)*—nonpolymorphic data types, such as a String class. A String class exhibits a nonpolymorphic form of encapsulation; it provides a public interface and private implementation (both of state and algorithm) but does not support type extension. An OB design can be faster and more compact than an *equivalent* OO design. Faster because all function invocations are resolved at compile time and object construction need not set up the virtual mechanism, and more compact because each class object need not carry the additional overhead traditionally associated with the support of the virtual mechanism. However, an OB design also is less flexible.

Both OO and OB design strategies have their proponents and critics. An interesting point/counterpoint discussion of these two strategies can be found in [BOOCH93], [CARROLL93], and [LEA93]. These articles discuss, in turn, the design decisions of the C++ Booch Components library, the Bell Laboratories' Standard C++ Components library, and the GNU g++ library. The trade-off usually boils down to one of flexibility (OO) versus efficiency (OB). Before one can effectively choose between the two, however, one needs to clearly understand the behavior of each and the requirements of the application domain.

Chapter 2

The Semantics of Constructors

One of the most often heard complaints about C++ is that the compiler does things behind the programmer's back. Conversion operators are the example most often cited. There's a story that Jerry Schwarz, the architect of the iostream library, tells about his first attempt to support a scalar test of an iostream class object such as

```
if ( cin ) ...
```

For `cin` to evaluate to a true/false scalar value, Jerry first defined an `operator int()` conversion operator. This worked fine in well-behaved instances such as this example, but it behaved in a somewhat surprising manner under the following programmer error:

```
// oops: meant cout, not cin
cin << intVal;
```

The programmer, of course, meant `cout` not `cin`. The type-safe nature of the class hierarchy is supposed to catch this misapplication of the output operator. The compiler, however, in a somewhat maternalistic way, prefers to find a correct interpretation, if there is one, rather than flag the program as bad. In this case, the built-in left-shift operator can be applied if only `cin` is convertible to an integral value. The compiler checks the available conversion operators. It finds the `operator int()` instance, the very thing it was looking for. The left-shift operator can now be applied—if not successfully, at least legally:

```
// oops: not quite what the programmer intended
int temp = cin.operator int();
temp << intVal;
```

Jerry resolved this unexpected behavior by replacing the `operator int()` instance with `operator void*()`. This kind of error is still sometimes referred to jokingly as a Schwarz Error. While errors of this sort are an embarrassment, the absence of an implicit class conversion facility would be sorely missed. The example of the original String class is cited in [STROUP94], p. 83, as motivation: Without implicit conversion support, the String library would have had to replicate all the C library functions that were expecting a string.[1]

Among many programmers, the uneasy feeling persists that a user-defined conversion operator applied implicitly by the compiler is as likely as not to result in a Schwarz Error. The keyword **explicit**, in fact, was introduced into the language in order to give the programmer a method by which to suppress application of a single argument constructor as a conversion operator. Although it is easy (from a distance, anyway) to be amused by tales of the Schwarz Error, conversion operators in practice are difficult to use in a predictable, well-behaved manner. In this case, programmers are, I think, warranted in their concern. Introduction of conversion operators should be made judiciously, tested rigorously, and, at the first sign of unusual program activity, brought in for questioning.

The problem, however, is more in the nature of the compiler's taking your intentions far too literally than of its actually doing something behind your back—although it is often difficult to convince a programmer bitten by a Schwarz Error of this. "Behind the back" type of activities are much more likely to occur in support of memberwise initialization or in the application of what is referred to as the *named return value optimization (NRV)*. In this chapter, I look at compiler "meddlings" in terms of object construction and the impact that has on the form and performance of our programs.

2.1 Default Constructor Construction

The C++ Annotated Reference Manual (ARM) [ELLIS90] (Section 12.1) tells us that "default constructors...are generated (by the compiler) where needed...." The crucial word here is *needed*—needed by whom and to do what? Consider, for example, the following program fragment:

---

[1] Interestingly enough, the standard C++ library string class does not provide an implicit conversion operator; rather, it provides a named instance the user must explicitly invoke.

```
class Foo { public: int val; Foo *pnext; };

void foo_bar()
{
    // Oops:  program needs bar's members zeroed out
    Foo bar;
    if ( bar.val || bar.pnext )
        // ... do something
    // ...
}
```

In this example, correct program semantics requires of Foo a default constructor that initializes its two members to zero. Does this fragment, then, fulfill the requirement of *needed* as stated in the ARM? The short answer is no. The distinction is that between the needs of the program and the needs of the implementation. A program's need for a default constructor is the responsibility of the programmer; in this case, the individual who designed class Foo.[2] A default constructor is not *synthesized* for this code fragment.

When is a default constructor synthesized, then? Only when the implementation needs it. Moreover, the synthesized constructor performs only those activities required by the implementation. That is, even if there were a need to synthesize a default constructor for class Foo, that constructor would not include code to zero out the two data members val and pnext. For the previous program fragment to execute correctly, the designer of class Foo needs to provide an explicit default constructor that properly initializes the class's two members.

The Standard has refined the discussion in the ARM, although the behavior, in practice, remains the same. The Standard states [ISO-C++95] (also Section 12.1) the following:

> If there is no user-declared constructor for class X, a default constructor is implicitly declared.... A constructor is *trivial* if it is an implicitly declared default constructor....

The standard then goes on to iterate the conditions under which the implicit default constructor is considered trivial. A nontrivial default constructor is one that in the ARM's terminology is needed by the implementation and, if necessary, is synthesized by the compiler. The next four sections look at the four conditions under which the default constructor is nontrivial.

---

[2] Global objects are guaranteed to have their associated memory "zeroed out" at program start-up. Local objects allocated on the program stack and heap objects allocated on the free-store do not have their associated memory zeroed out; rather, the memory retains the arbitrary bit pattern of its previous use.

Member Class Object with Default Constructor

If a class without any constructors contains a member object of a class with
a default constructor, the implicit default constructor of the class is nontrivial and the compiler needs to synthesize a default constructor for the containing class. This synthesis, however, takes place only if the constructor
actually needs to be invoked.

An interesting question, then: Given the separate compilation model of
C++, how does the compiler prevent synthesizing multiple default constructors, for example, one for file A.C and a second for file B.C? In practice,
this is solved by having the synthesized default constructor, copy constructor, destructor, and/or assignment copy operator defined as inline. An inline function has static linkage and is therefore not visible outside the file
within which it is synthesized. If the function is too complex to be inlined
by the implementation, an explicit non-inline static instance is synthesized.
(Inline functions are discussed in more detail in Section 4.5.)

For example, in the following code fragment, the compiler synthesizes a
default constructor for class Bar:

```
class Foo { public: Foo(); Foo( int ); ... };

class Bar { public: Foo foo; char *str; };

void foo_bar() {
    Bar bar; // Bar::foo must be initialized here
    if ( bar.str ) { } ...
}
```

The synthesized default constructor contains the code necessary to invoke the class Foo default constructor on the member object Bar::foo, but
it does not generate any code to initialize Bar::str. Initialization of
Bar::foo is the compiler's responsibility; initialization of Bar::str is the
programmer's. The synthesized default constructor might look as follows: [3]

```
// possible synthesis of Bar default constructor
// invoke Foo default constructor for member foo
inline
Bar::Bar()
{
    // Pseudo C++ Code
    foo.Foo::Foo();
}
```

---

[3] To simplify our discussion, these examples ignore the insertion of the implicit **this** pointer.

Again, note that the synthesized default constructor meets only the needs of the implementation, not the needs of the program. For the program fragment to execute correctly, the character pointer str also needs to be initialized. Let's assume the programmer provides for the initialization of str via the following default constructor:

```
// programmer defined default constructor
Bar::Bar() { str = 0; }
```

Now the program need is fulfilled, but the implementation need to initialize the member object foo still remains. Because the default constructor is explicitly defined, the compiler cannot synthesize a second instance to do its work. *Oh, bother*, as Winnie the Pooh might say. What's an implementation to do?

Consider the case of each constructor defined for a class containing one or more member class objects for which a default constructor must be invoked. In this case, the compiler augments the existing constructors, inserting code that invokes the necessary default constructors prior to the execution of the user code. In the previous example, the resulting augmented constructor might look as follows:

```
// Augmented default constructor
// Pseudo C++ Code
Bar::Bar()
{
    foo.Foo::Foo();  // augmented compiler code
    str = 0;         // explicit user code
}
```

What happens if there are multiple class member objects requiring constructor initialization? The language requires that the constructors be invoked in the order of member declaration within the class. This is accomplished by the compiler. It inserts code within each constructor, invoking the associated default constructors for each member in the order of member declaration. This code is inserted just prior to the explicitly supplied user code. For example, say we have the following three classes:

```
class Dopey   { public: Dopey(); ... };
class Sneezy  { public: Sneezy( int ); Sneezy(); ... };
class Bashful { public: Bashful(); ... };
```

and a containing class Snow_White:

```
class Snow_White {
public:
    Dopey dopey;
    Sneezy sneezy;
    Bashful bashful;
    // ...
private:
    int mumble;
};
```

If Snow_White does not define a default constructor, a nontrivial default constructor is synthesized that invokes the three default constructors of Dopey, Sneezy, and Bashful in that order. If, on the other hand, Snow_White defines the following default constructor:

```
// programmer coded default constructor
Snow_White::Snow_White() : sneezy( 1024 )
{
    mumble = 2048;
}
```

it is augmented as follows:

```
// Compiler augmented default constructor
// Pseudo C++ Code
Snow_White::Snow_White()
{
    // insertion of member class object
    // constructor invocations
    dopey.Dopey::Dopey();
    sneezy.Sneezy::Sneezy( 1024 );
    bashful.Bashful::Bashful();

    // explicit user code
    mumble = 2048;
}
```

The interaction of invoking implicit default constructors with that of invoking constructors explicitly listed within the member initialization list is discussed in Section 2.4.

Base Class with Default Constructor

Similarly, if a class without any constructors is derived from a base class containing a default constructor, the default constructor for the derived class is considered nontrivial and so needs to be synthesized. The synthesized default constructor of the derived class invokes the default constructor of each of its immediate base classes in the order of their declaration. To a subsequently derived class, the synthesized constructor appears no different than that of an explicitly provided default constructor.

What if the designer provides multiple constructors but no default constructor? The compiler augments each constructor with the code necessary to invoke all required default constructors. However, it does not synthesize a default constructor because of the presence of the other user-supplied constructors. If member class objects with default constructors are also present, these default constructors are also invoked—after the invocation of all base class constructors.

Class with a Virtual Function

There are two additional cases in which a synthesized default constructor is needed:

1. The class either declares (or inherits) a virtual function

2. The class is derived from an inheritance chain in which one or more base classes are virtual

In both cases, in the absence of any declared constructors, implementation bookkeeping necessitates the synthesis of a default constructor. For example, given the following code fragment:

```
class Widget {
public:
   virtual void flip() = 0;
   // ...
};

void flip( const Widget& widget ) { widget.flip(); }

// presuming Bell and Whistle are derived from Widget
void foo() {
   Bell b;   Whistle w;
```

```
     flip( b );
     flip( w );
   }
```

the following two class "augmentations" occur during compilation:

1. A virtual function table (referred to as the class *vtbl* in the original cfront implementation) is generated and populated with the addresses of the active virtual functions for that class.

2. Within each class object, an additional pointer member (the vptr) is synthesized to hold the address of the associated class vtbl.

In addition, the virtual invocation of widget.flip() is rewritten to make use of widget's vptr and flip()'s entry into the associated vtbl:

```
// simplified transformation of virtual invocation: widget.flip()
( * widget.vptr[ 1 ] ) ( &widget )
```

where

*   1 represents flip()'s fixed index into the virtual table, and

*   &widget represents the **this** pointer to be passed to the particular invocation of flip().

For this mechanism to work, the compiler must initialize the vptr of each Widget object (or the object of a class derived from Widget) with the address of the appropriate virtual table. For each constructor the class defines, the compiler inserts code that does just that (this is illustrated in Section 5.2). In classes that do not declare any constructors, the compiler synthesizes a default constructor in order to correctly initialize the vptr of each class object.

Class with a Virtual Base Class

Virtual base class implementations vary widely across compilers. However, what is common to each implementation is the need to make the virtual base class location within each derived class object available at runtime. For example, in the following program fragment:

```
class X { public: int i; };
class A : public virtual X   { public: int j; };
class B : public virtual X   { public: double d; };
class C : public A, public B { public: int k; };
```

```
// cannot resolve location of pa->X::i at compile-time
void foo( const A* pa ) { pa->i = 1024; }

main() {
    foo( new A );
    foo( new C );
    // ...
}
```

the compiler cannot fix the physical offset of X::i accessed through pa within foo(), since the actual type of pa can vary with each of foo()'s invocations. Rather, the compiler must transform the code doing the access so that the resolution of X::i can be delayed until runtime. In the original cfront implementation, for example, this is accomplished by inserting a pointer to each of the virtual base classes within the derived class object. All reference and pointer access of a virtual base class is achieved through the associated pointer. In our example, foo() might be rewritten as follows under this implementation strategy:

```
// possible compiler transformation
void foo( const A* pa ) { pa->__vbcX->i = 1024; }
```

where __vbcX represents the compiler-generated pointer to the virtual base class X.

As you've no doubt guessed by now, the initialization of __vbcX (or whatever implementation mechanism is used) is accomplished during the construction of the class object. For each constructor the class defines, the compiler inserts code that permits runtime access of each virtual base class. In classes that do not declare any constructors, the compiler needs to synthesize a default constructor.

Summary

There are four characteristics of a class under which the compiler needs to synthesize a default constructor for classes that declare no constructor at all. The Standard refers to these as implicit, nontrivial default constructors. The synthesized constructor fulfills only an implementation need. It does this by invoking member object or base class default constructors or initializing the virtual function or virtual base class mechanism for each object. Classes that do not exhibit these characteristics and that declare no constructor at all are said to have implicit, trivial default constructors. In practice, these trivial default constructors are not synthesized.

Within the synthesized default constructor, only the base class subobjects and member class objects are initialized. All other nonstatic data members, such as integers, pointers to integers, arrays of integers, and so on, are not initialized. These initializations are needs of the program, not of the implementation. If there is a program need for a default constructor, such as initializing a pointer to 0, it is the programmer's responsibility to provide it in the course of the class implementation.

Programmers new to C++ often have two common misunderstandings:

1. That a default constructor is synthesized for every class that does not define one

2. That the compiler-synthesized default constructor provides explicit default initializers for each data member declared within the class

As we have seen, neither of these is true.

2.2   Copy Constructor Construction

There are three program instances in which a class object is initialized with another object of its class. The most obvious instance, of course, is an object's explicit initialization, such as

```
class X { ... };
X x;

// explicit initialization of one class object with
another
    X xx = x;
```

The other two are when an object is passed as an argument to a function, such as

```
extern void foo( X x );

void bar()
{
    X xx;

    // implicit initialization of foo()'s
    // first argument with xx
    foo( xx );

    // ...
}
```

and when a function returns a class object, such as

```
X
foo_bar()
{
    X xx;
    // ...;
    return xx;
}
```

Say the class designer explicitly defines a copy constructor (a constructor requiring a single argument of its class type), such as either of the following:

```
// examples of user defined copy constructors
// may be multi-argument provided each second
// and subsequent argument is provided with a
// default value

X::X( const X& x );
Y::Y( const Y& y, int = 0 );
```

In this case, that constructor is invoked, under most circumstances, in each program instance where initialization of one class object with another occurs. This may result in the generation of a temporary class object or the actual transformation of program code (or both).

Default Memberwise Initialization

What if the class does not provide an explicit copy constructor? Each class object initialized with another object of its class is initialized by what is called *default memberwise initialization*. Default memberwise initialization copies the value of each built-in or derived data member (such as a pointer or an array) from the one class object to another. A member class object, however, is not copied; rather, memberwise initialization is recursively applied. For example, consider the following class declaration:

```
class String {
public:
    // ... no explicit copy constructor
private:
    char *str;
    int   len;
};
```

The default memberwise initialization of one String object with another, such as

```
String noun( "book" );
String verb = noun;
```

is accomplished *as if* each of its members was individually initialized in turn:

```
// semantic equivalent of memberwise initialization
verb.str = noun.str;
verb.len = noun.len;
```

If a String object is declared as a member of another class, such as the following:

```
class Word {
public:
    // ...no explicit copy constructor
private:
    int     _occurs;
    String  _word;
};
```

then the default memberwise initialization of one Word object with another copies the value of its built-in member _occurs and then recursively applies memberwise initialization to its class String member object _word.

How is this operation in practice carried out? The original ARM tells us:

> Conceptually, for a class X [this operation is] implemented by...a copy constructor.

The operative word here is *conceptually*. The commentary that follows explains:

> In practice, a good compiler can generate bitwise copies for most class objects since they have bitwise copy semantics....

That is, a copy constructor is not automatically generated by the compiler for each class that does not explicitly define one. Rather, as the ARM tells us,

Default constructors and copy constructors...are generated (by the compiler) where needed.

Needed in this instance means when the class does not exhibit bitwise copy semantics. The Standard retains the meaning of the ARM, while formalizing its discussion (my comments are inserted within parentheses) as follows:

A class object can be copied in two ways, by initialization (what we are concerned with here)...and by assignment (treated in Chapter 5). *Conceptually* (my italics), these two operations are implemented by a copy constructor and copy assignment operator.

As with the default constructor, the Standard speaks of an *implicitly declared* and *implicitly defined* copy constructor if the class does not declare one. As before, the Standard distinguishes between a trivial and nontrivial copy constructor. It is only the nontrivial instance that in practice is synthesized within the program. The criteria for determining whether a copy constructor is trivial is whether the class exhibits bitwise copy semantics. In the next section, I look at what it means to say that a class exhibits bitwise copy semantics.

Bitwise Copy Semantics

In the following program fragment:

```
#include "Word.h"

Word noun( "block" );

void foo()
{
   Word verb = noun;
   // ...
}
```

it is clear that verb is initialized with noun. But without looking at the declaration of class Word, it is not possible to predict the program behavior of that initialization. If the designer of class Word defines a copy constructor, the initialization of verb invokes it. If, however, the class is without an explicit copy constructor, the invocation of a compiler-synthesized instance depends on whether the class exhibits bitwise copy semantics. For example, given the following declaration of class Word:

```
// declaration exhibits bitwise copy semantics
class Word {
public:
    Word( const char* );
    ~Word() { delete [] str; }
    // ...
private:
    int    cnt;
    char *str;
};
```

a default copy constructor need not be synthesized, since the declaration exhibits bitwise copy semantics, and the initialization of verb need not result in a function call.[4] However, the following declaration of class Word does not exhibit bitwise copy semantics:

```
// declaration does not exhibit bitwise copy semantics
class Word {
public:
    Word( const String& );
    ~Word();
    // ...
private:
    int     cnt;
    String str;
};
```

where String declares an explicit copy constructor:

```
class String {
public:
    String( const char* );
    String( const String& );
    ~String();
    // ...
};
```

---

[4] Of course, the program fragment will execute disastrously given this declaration of class Word. (Both the local and global object now address the same character string. Prior to exiting foo(), the destructor is applied to the local object, thus the character string is deleted. The global object now addresses garbage.) The aliasing problem with regard to member str can be solved only by overriding default memberwise initialization with an explicit copy constructor implemented by the designer of the class (or by disallowing copying altogether). This, however, is independent of whether a copy constructor is synthesized by the compiler.

In this case, the compiler *needs* to synthesize a copy constructor in order to invoke the copy constructor of the member class String object:

```
// A synthesized copy constructor
// Pseudo C++ Code
inline Word::Word( const Word& wd )
{
    str.String::String( wd.str );
    cnt = wd.cnt;
}
```

It is important to note that in the case of the synthesized copy constructor, the nonclass members of types such as integers, pointers, and arrays are also copied, as one would expect.

Bitwise Copy Semantics—Not!

When are bitwise copy semantics not exhibited by a class? There are four instances:

1. When the class contains a member object of a class for which a copy constructor exists (either explicitly declared by the class designer, as in the case of the previous String class, or synthesized by the compiler, as in the case of class Word)

2. When the class is derived from a base class for which a copy constructor exists (again, either explicitly declared or synthesized)

3. When the class declares one or more virtual functions

4. When the class is derived from an inheritance chain in which one or more base classes are virtual

In instances 1 and 2, the implementation needs to insert invocations of the member or base class copy constructors inside the synthesized copy constructor. The synthesized copy constructor for class Word in the previous section illustrates case 1. Cases 3 and 4 are slightly more subtle. I briefly look at those next.

Resetting the Virtual Table Pointer

Recall that two program "augmentations" occur during compilation whenever a class declares one or more virtual functions.

- A virtual function table that contains the address of each active virtual function associated with that class (the vtbl) is generated.

- A pointer to the virtual function table is inserted within each class object (the vptr).

Obviously, things would go terribly wrong if the compiler either failed to initialize or incorrectly initialized the vptr of each new class object. Hence, once the compiler introduces a vptr into a class, the affected class *no longer exhibits bitwise semantics*. Rather, the implementation now needs to synthesize a copy constructor in order to properly initialize the vptr. Here's an example.

First, I define a two-class hierarchy of ZooAnimal and Bear:

```
class ZooAnimal {
public:
   ZooAnimal();
   virtual ~ZooAnimal();

   virtual void animate();
   virtual void draw();
   // ...
private:
   // data necessary for ZooAnimal's
   // version of animate() and draw()
};

class Bear : public ZooAnimal {
public:
   Bear();

   void animate();
   void draw();
   virtual void dance();
   // ...
private:
   // data necessary for Bear's version
   // of animate(), draw(), and dance()
};
```

The initialization of one ZooAnimal class object with another or one Bear class object with another is straightforward and could actually be implemented with bitwise copy semantics (apart from possible pointer member aliasing, which for simplicity is not considered). For example, given

```
Bear yogi;
Bear winnie = yogi;
```

yogi is initialized by the default Bear constructor. Within the constructor, yogi's vptr is initialized to address the Bear class virtual table with code inserted by the compiler. It is safe, therefore, to simply copy the value of yogi's vptr into winnie's. The copying of an object's vptr value, however, ceases to be safe when an object of a base class is initialized with an object of a class derived from it. For example, given

```
ZooAnimal franny = yogi;
```

the vptr associated with franny must not be initialized to address the Bear class virtual table (which would be the result if the value of yogi's vptr were used in a straightforward bitwise copy). Otherwise the invocation of draw() in the following program fragment would blow up when franny were passed to it:[5]

```
void draw( const ZooAnimal& zoey ) { zoey.draw(); }
void foo() {
    // franny's vptr must address the ZooAnimal virtual table
    // not the Bear virtual table yogi's vptr addresses
    ZooAnimal franny = yogi;

    draw( yogi );    // invoke Bear::draw()
    draw( franny ); // invoke ZooAnimal::draw()

}
```

That is, the synthesized ZooAnimal copy constructor explicitly sets the object's vptr to the ZooAnimal class virtual table rather than copying it from the right-hand class object.

Handling the Virtual Base Class Subobject

The presence of a virtual base class also requires special handling. The initialization of one class object with another in which there is a virtual base class subobject also invalidates bitwise copy semantics.

---

[5] The draw() virtual function call through franny must invoke the ZooAnimal instance rather than the Bear instance, even though franny is initialized with the Bear object yogi because franny is a ZooAnimal object. In effect, the Bear portion of yogi is sliced off when franny is initialized. Were franny declared a reference (or were it a pointer initialized with the address of yogi), then invocations of draw() through franny would invoke the Bear instance. This is discussed in Section 1.3.

Each implementation's support of virtual inheritance involves the need to make each virtual base class subobject's location within the derived class object available at runtime. Maintaining the integrity of this location is the compiler's responsibility. Bitwise copy semantics could result in a corruption of this location, so the compiler must intercede with its own synthesized copy constructor. For example, in the following declaration, ZooAnimal is derived as a virtual base class of Raccoon:

```
class Raccoon : public virtual ZooAnimal {
public:
   Raccoon() { /* private data initialization */ }
   Raccoon( int val ) { /* private data initialization */ }
   // ...
private:
   // all necessary data
};
```

Compiler-generated code to invoke ZooAnimal's default constructor, initialize Raccoon's vptr, and locate the ZooAnimal subobject within Raccoon is inserted as a prefix within the two Raccoon constructors.

What about memberwise initialization? *The presence of a virtual base class invalidates bitwise copy semantics.* Again, the problem is not when one object of a class is initialized with a second object of the same exact class. It is when an object is initialized with an object of one of its derived classes. For example, consider the case in which a Raccoon object is initialized with a RedPanda object, where RedPanda is declared as follows:

```
class RedPanda : public Raccoon {
public:
   RedPanda() { /* private data initialization */ }
   RedPanda( int val ) { /* private data initialization */ }
   // ...
private:
   // all necessary data
};
```

Again, in the case of initializing one Raccoon object with another, simple bitwise copy is sufficient:

```
// simple bitwise copy is sufficient
Raccoon rocky;
Raccoon little_critter = rocky;
```

However, an attempt to initialize `little_critter` with a RedPanda object requires the compiler to intercede if subsequent programmer attempts to access its ZooAnimal subobject are to execute properly (not an unreasonable programmer expectation!):

```
// simple bitwise copy is not sufficient
// compiler must explicitly initialize little_critter's
// virtual base class pointer/offset

RedPanda    little_red;
Raccoon     little_critter = little_red;
```

In this case, to achieve the correct initialization of `little_critter`, the compiler must synthesize a copy constructor, inserting code to initialize the virtual base class pointer/offset (or simply being sure that it not be reset), performing the necessary memberwise initializations of its members, and other memory tasks. (Virtual base classes are discussed in more detail in Section 3.4.)

In the following case, the compiler cannot know whether bitwise copy semantics hold, since it cannot know (without flow analysis) whether the Raccoon pointer addresses an actual Raccoon object or an object of a derived class:

```
// simple bitwise copy may or may not be sufficient
Raccoon *ptr;
// ...
Raccoon little_critter = *ptr;
```

Here's an interesting question: Should a compiler, in the presence of an initialization in which bitwise copy semantics hold, optimize its code generation by suppressing the invocation of the copy constructor if it can guarantee the correct equivalent initialization of the object? At least in the case of a synthesized copy constructor, the possibility of program side effects is nil and the optimization would seem to make good sense. What about in the case of a copy constructor explicitly provided by the class designer? (This is actually a rather contentious issue. I return to it at the end of the next section.)

To summarize: We have looked at the four conditions under which bitwise copy semantics do not hold for a class and the default copy constructor, if undeclared, is considered nontrivial. Under these conditions, the compiler, in the absence of a declared copy constructor, must synthesize a copy constructor in order to correctly implement the initialization of one class object with another. In the next section, the implementation strategies for invoking the copy constructor and how those strategies affect our programs are discussed.

2.3   Program Transformation Semantics

Given the following program fragment:

```
#include "X.h"

X foo()
{
    X xx;
    // ...
    return xx;
}
```

one might be tempted to categorically assert that

1. every invocation of `foo()` returns xx by value, and

2. if class X defines a copy constructor, that copy constructor is guaranteed to be invoked with each invocation of `foo()`.

The truth of assertion 1, however, depends on the definition of class X. The truth of assertion 2, although partly dependent on the definition of class X, primarily depends on the degree of aggressive optimization provided by your C++ compiler. To turn things on their heads, one might even assert that in a high-quality C++ implementation, both assertions are always false for nontrivial definitions of class X. The rest of this subsection explains why.

Explicit Initialization

Given the definition

```
    X x0;
```

the following three definitions each explicitly initialize its class object with x0:

```
void foo_bar() {
    X x1( x0 );
    X x2 = x0;
    X x3 = X( x0 );
    // ...
}
```

The required program transformation is two-fold:

1. Each definition is rewritten with the initialization stripped out.

2. An invocation of the class copy constructor is inserted.

For example, `foo_bar()` might look as follows after this straightforward, two-fold transformation:

```
// Possible program transformation
// Pseudo C++ Code
void foo_bar() {
    X x1;
    X x2;
    X x3;

    // compiler inserted invocations
    // of copy constructor for X
    x1.X::X( x0 );
    x2.X::X( x0 );
    x3.X::X( x0 );
    // ...
}
```

where the call

```
x1.X::X( x0 );
```

represents a call of the copy constructor

```
X::X( const X& xx );
```

Argument Initialization

The Standard states (Section 8.5) that passing a class object as an argument to a function (or as that function's return value) is equivalent to the following form of initialization:

```
X xx = arg;
```

where xx represents the formal argument (or return value) and arg represents the actual argument. Therefore, given the function

```
void foo( X x0 );
```

an invocation of the form

```
X xx;
// ...
foo( xx );
```

requires that the local instance of x0 be memberwise initialized with xx.
One implementation strategy is to introduce a temporary object, initialize it
with a call of the copy constructor, and then pass that temporary object to
the function. For example, the previous code fragment would be transformed as follows:

```
// Pseudo C++ code
// compiler generated temporary
X __temp0;

// compiler invocation of copy constructor
__temp0.X::X ( xx );

// rewrite function call to take temporary
foo( __temp0 );
```

This transformation, however, is only half complete as presented. Do
you see the remaining problem? It is that given foo()'s declaration, the
temporary object is first correctly initialized with the class X copy constructor and then is bitwise copied into the local instance of x0! Oh, bother. The
declaration of foo() therefore must also be transformed, with the formal
argument from an object changed to a reference of class X as follows:

```
void foo( X& x0 );
```

Were class X to declare a destructor, that destructor would be invoked on
the temporary object following the call of foo().

An alternative implementation is to copy construct the actual argument
directly onto its place within the function's activation record on the
program stack. Prior to the return of the function, the local object's destructor, if defined, is applied to it. The Borland C++ compiler, for example,

implements this strategy, although it provides a compiler option to employ
the first strategy previously described for backward compatibility with earlier versions of the compiler.

Return Value Initialization

Given the following definition of bar ():

```
X bar()
{
    X xx;
    // process xx ...
    return xx;
}
```

you may ask how might bar ()'s return value be copy constructed from its
local object xx? Stroustrup's solution in cfront is a two-fold transformation:

1. Add an additional argument of type reference to the class object.
   This argument will hold the copy constructed "return value."

2. Insert an invocation of the copy constructor prior to the return
   statement to initialize the added argument with the value of the
   object being returned.

What about the actual return value, then? A final transformation
rewrites the function to have it *not* return a value. The transformation of
bar (), following this algorithm, looks like this:

```
// function transformation to reflect
// application of copy constructor
// Pseudo C++ Code
void
bar( X& __result )
{
    X xx;

    // compiler generated invocation
    // of default constructor
    xx.X::X();

    // ... process xx
```

```
// compiler generated invocation
// of copy constructor
__result.X::X( xx );

return;
}
```

Given this transformation of bar (), the compiler is now required to transform each invocation of bar () to reflect its new definition. For example,

```
X xx = bar();
```

is transformed into the following two statements:

```
// note: no default constructor applied
X xx;
bar( xx );
```

while an invocation such as

```
bar().memfunc();
```

might be transformed into

```
// compiler generated temporary
X __temp0;
( bar( __temp0 ), __temp0 ).memfunc();
```

Similarly, if the program were to declare a pointer to a function, such as

```
X ( *pf )();
pf = bar;
```

that declaration, too, would need to be transformed:

```
void ( *pf )( X& );
pf = bar;
```

Optimization at the User Level

It was Jonathan Shopiro, I believe, who first noticed a programmer optimization of a function such as bar () by defining a "computational" constructor. That is, rather than the programmer's writing

```
X bar( const T &y, const T &z )
{
    X xx;
    // ... process xx using y and z
    return xx;
}
```

which requires xx to be memberwise copied into the compiler-generated __result, Jonathan defined an auxiliary constructor that computed the value of xx directly:

```
X bar( const T &y, const T &z )
{
    return X( y, z );
}
```

This definition of bar(), when transformed, is more efficient:

```
// Pseudo C++ Code
void
bar( X &__result )
{
    __result.X::X( y, z );
    return;
}
```

since __result is directly computed, rather than copied through an invocation of the copy constructor. One criticism of this solution, however, is the possible proliferation of specialized computational constructors. (Class design on this level becomes driven more by efficiency concerns than by the underlying abstraction the class is intended to support.)

Optimization at the Compiler Level

In a function such as bar(), where all return statements return the same named value, it is possible for the compiler itself to optimize the function by substituting the result argument for the named return value. For example, given the original definition of bar():

```
X bar()
{
    X xx;
    // ... process xx
    return xx;
}
```

__result is substituted for xx by the compiler:

```
void
bar( X &__result )
{
    // default constructor invocation
    // Pseudo C++ Code
    __result.X::X();

    // ... process in __result directly

    return;
}
```

This compiler optimization, sometimes referred to as the Named Return Value (NRV) optimization, is described in Section 12.1.1c of the ARM (pages 300–303). The NRV optimization is now considered an obligatory Standard C++ compiler optimization, although that requirement, of course, falls outside the formal Standard. To get a sense of the performance gain, consider the following class:

```
class test {
    friend test foo( double );
public:
    test()
        { memset( array, 0, 100*sizeof( double )); }
private:
    double array[ 100 ];
};
```

Consider also the following function, which creates, modifies, and returns a test class object:

```
test
foo( double val )
{
    test local;

    local.array[ 0 ] = val;
    local.array[ 99 ] = val;

    return local;
}
```

and a main() routine that calls the function 10 million times:

```
main()
{
    for ( int cnt = 0; cnt < 10000000; cnt++ )
        { test t = foo( double( cnt )); }
    return 0;
}
```

This first version of the program does not apply the NRV optimization because of the absence of a copy constructor for the test class. The second version adds an inline copy constructor:

```
inline
test::test( const test &t )
{
    memcpy( this, &t, sizeof( test ));
}
```

The presence of the copy constructor "turns on" the NRV optimization within the C++ compiler. (The optimization is not performed by a separate optimizer. In this case, the optimizer's effect on the performance is negligible.) Here are the timings.

```
Named Return Value (NRV) Optimization
- - - - - - - - - - - - - - - - - - -
```

	NRV Not Applied	NRV Applied	NRV Applied + -O
CC	1:48.52	46.73	46.05
NCC	3:00.57	1:33.48	1.32.36

Although the NRV optimization provides significant performance improvement, there are several criticisms of this approach. One is that because the optimization is done silently by the compiler, whether it was actually performed is not always clear (particularly since few compilers document the extent of its implementation or whether it is implemented at all).[6] A second is that as the function becomes more complicated, the optimization becomes more difficult to apply. In cfront, for example, the optimization is applied only if all the named return statements occur at the top level of the function. Introduce a nested local block with a return statement, and cfront quietly turns off the optimization. Programmers arguing this case recommend the specialized constructor strategy instead.

These two criticisms concern the compiler's possibly failing to apply the optimization. A third criticism takes the opposite position: Some programmers actually criticize the application of the optimization. Can you see what

[6] The NCC compiler is currently without NRV support. Support for it is promised in future releases.

their complaint might be? For example, imagine you had instrumented your copy constructor such that your application depended on the symmetry of its invocation for each destructor invoked on an object initialized by copying; for example,

```
void foo()
{
    // copy constructor expected here
    X xx = bar();
    // ...
    // destructor invoked here
}
```

In this case, the symmetry is broken by the optimization, and the program, albeit faster, fails. Is the compiler at fault here for suppressing the copy constructor invocation? That is, must the copy constructor be invoked in every program situation in which the initialization of an object is achieved through copying?

Such a requirement would levy a possibly severe performance penalty on a great many programs. For example, although the following three initializations are semantically equivalent:

```
X xx0( 1024 );
X xx1 = X( 1024 );
X xx2 = ( X ) 1024;
```

in the second and third instances, the syntax explicitly provides for a two-step initialization:

1. Initialize a temporary object with 1024.

2. Copy construct the explicit object with the temporary object.

That is, whereas xx0 is initialized by a single constructor invocation

```
// Pseudo C++ Code
xx0.X::X( 1024 );
```

a strict implementation of either xx1 or xx2 results in two constructor invocations, a temporary object, and a call to the destructor of class X on that temporary object:

```
// Pseudo C++ Code
X __temp0;
__temp0.X::X( 1024 );
xx1.X::X( __temp0 );
__temp0.X::~X();
```

The Standards committee has been debating the legality of eliminating the copy constructor invocation. As of this writing, it has not reached a final decision.[7] However, according to Josée Lajoie, vice chairperson of the committee and chairperson of the Core Language group, the NRV optimization is considered too important to disallow. Apparently the debate has wound its way down to two somewhat esoteric cases: whether the elimination of the copy constructor should also be allowed in the copying of static and local objects. For example, given the following code fragment:

```
Thing outer;
{
    // can inner be eliminated?
    Thing inner( outer );
}
```

should `inner` be copy constructed from `outer` or can `inner` simply be eliminated? (The question can similarly be asked regarding the copy initialization of static with `extern` objects.) According to Josée, the elimination of the copy constructor for static objects is almost certainly not to be allowed. The outcome for automatic objects such as `inner`, however, remains unresolved.

In general, then, the language permits the compiler a great deal of leeway regarding the initialization of one class object with another. The benefit of this, of course, is significantly more efficient code generation. The drawback is that you cannot safely program side effects into your copy constructor and depend on their being executed.

The Copy Constructor: To Have or To Have Not?

Given the following straightforward 3D point class:

```
class Point3d {
public:
    Point3d( float x, float y, float z );
    // ...
private:
    float _x, _y, _z;
};
```

should the class designer provide an explicit copy constructor?

The default copy constructor is considered trivial. There are no member or base class objects with a copy constructor that need to be invoked. Nor is there a virtual base class or virtual function associated with the class. So, by

---

[7] The NRV optimization was voted into the standard in the summer 1996 meeting.

default, a memberwise initialization of one Point3d class object with another results in a bitwise copy. This is efficient. But is it safe?

The answer is yes. The three coordinate members are stored by value. Bitwise copy results in neither a memory leak nor address aliasing. Thus it is both safe and efficient.

So, how would you answer the question, should the class designer provide an explicit copy constructor? The obvious answer, of course, is no. There is no reason to provide an instance of the copy constructor, as the compiler automatically does the best job for you. The more subtle answer is to ask whether you envision the class's requiring a good deal of memberwise initialization, in particular, returning objects by value? If the answer is yes, then it makes excellent sense to provide an explicit inline instance of the copy constructor—that is, provided your compiler provides the NRV optimization.

For example, the Point3d class supports the following set of functions:

```
Point3d operator+( const Point3d&, const Point3d& );
Point3d operator-( const Point3d&, const Point3d& );
Point3d operator*( const Point3d&, int );
etc.
```

all of which fit nicely into the NRV template

```
{
    Point3d result;
    // compute result
    return result;
}
```

The simplest method of implementing the copy constructor is as follows:

```
Point3d::Point3d( const Point3d &rhs )
{
    _x = rhs._x;
    _y = rhs._y;
    _z = rhs._z;
};
```

This is okay, but use of the C library memcpy() function would be more efficient:

```
Point3d::Point3d( const Point3d &rhs )
{
```

```
    memcpy( this, &rhs, sizeof( Point3d ) );
}
```

Use of both memcpy() and memset(), however, works only if the classes do not contain any compiler-generated internal members. If the Point3d class declares one or more virtual functions or contains a virtual base class, use of either of these functions will result in overwriting the values the compiler set for these members. For example, given the following declaration:

```
class Shape {
public:
    // oops: this will overwrite internal vptr!
    Shape() { memset( this, 0, sizeof( Shape )); }
    virtual ~Shape();
    // ...
};
```

the compiler augmentation for the constructor generally looks like this:

```
// Expansion of constructor
// Pseudo C++ Code

Shape::Shape()
{
    // vptr must be set before user code executes
    __vptr__Shape = __vtbl__Shape;

    // oops: memset zeros out value of vptr
    memset( this, 0, sizeof( Shape ));
}
```

As you can see, correct use of the memset() and memcpy() functions requires some knowledge of the C++ Object Model semantics!

Summary

Application of the copy constructor requires the compiler to more or less transform portions of your program. In particular, consider a function that returns a class object by value for a class in which a copy constructor is either explicitly defined or synthesized. The result is profound program transformations both in the definition and use of the function. Also, the compiler optimizes away the copy constructor invocation where possible, replacing the NRV with an additional first argument within which the value is stored directly. Programmers who understand these transformations and the likely conditions for copy constructor optimization can better control the runtime performance of their programs.

2.4   Member Initialization List

When you write a constructor, you have the option of initializing class members either through the member initialization list or within the body of the constructor. Except in four cases, which one you choose is not significant.

In this section, I first clarify when use of the initialization list is "significant" and then explain what actually gets done with that list internally. I then look at a number of possible, subtle pitfalls.

You *must* use the member initialization list in the following cases in order for your program to compile:

1. When initializing a reference member

2. When initializing a const member

3. When invoking a base or member class constructor with a set of arguments

In the fourth case, the program compiles and executes correctly. But it does so inefficiently. For example, given

```
class Word {
    String _name;
    int    _cnt;
public:
    // not wrong, just naive ...
    Word() {
        _name = 0;
        _cnt = 0;
    }
};
```

this implementation of the Word constructor initializes _name once, then overrides the initialization with an assignment, resulting in the creation and the destruction of a temporary String object. Was this intentional? Unlikely. Does the compiler generate a warning? I'm not aware of any that does. Here is the likely internal augmentation of this constructor:

```
// Pseudo C++ Code
Word::Word( /* this pointer goes here */ )
{
    // invoke default String constructor
    _name.String::String();

    // generate temporary
    String temp = String( 0 );

    // memberwise copy _name
    _name.String::operator=( temp );

    // destroy temporary
    temp.String::~String();

    _cnt = 0;
}
```

Had the code been reviewed by the project and corrected, a significantly more efficient implementation would have been coded:

```
// preferred implementation
Word::Word : _name( 0 )
{
    _cnt = 0;
}
```

This expands to something like this:

```
// Pseudo C++ Code
Word::Word( /* this pointer goes here */ )
{
    // invoke String( int ) constructor
    _name.String::String( 0 );
    _cnt = 0;
}
```

This pitfall, by the way, is most likely to occur in template code of this form:

```
template < class type >
foo< type >::foo( type t )
{
    // may or may not be a good idea
    // depending on the actual type of type
    _t = t;
}
```

This has led some programmers to insist rather aggressively that all member initialization be done within the member initialization list, even the initialization of a well-behaved member such as _cnt:

```
// some insist on this coding style
Word::Word()
    : _cnt( 0 ), _name( 0 )
    {}
```

A reasonable question to ask at this point is, what actually happens to the member initialization list? Many people new to C++ confuse the syntax of the initialization list with that of a set of function calls, which of course it is not.

The compiler iterates over the initialization list, inserting the initializations in the proper order within the constructor prior to any explicit user code. For example, the previous Word constructor is expanded as follows:

```
// Pseudo C++ Code
Word::Word( /* this pointer goes here */ )
{
    _name.String::String( 0 );
    _cnt = 0;
}+
```

Hmm-m-m. It looks exactly the same as when _cnt was assigned within the body of the constructor. Actually, there is a subtlety to note here: The order in which the list entries are set down is determined by the declaration order of the members within the class declaration, not the order within the initialization list. In this case, _name is declared before _cnt in Word and so is placed first.

This apparent anomaly between initialization order and order within the initialization list can lead to the following nasty pitfall:

```
class X {
    int i;
    int j;
public:
    // oops!   do you see the problem?
    X( int val )
        : j( val ), i( j )
        {}
    ...
};
```

The difficulty with this bug is how difficult it is even to see it. Compilers should issue a warning, yet there is only one that I am aware of that does (g++, the GNU C++ compiler).[6] I recommend always placing the initialization of one member with another (if you really feel it is necessary) within the body of the constructor, as follows:

```
// preferred idiom
X::X( int val )
    : j( val )
{
    i = j;
}
```

Here is an interesting question: Are the entries in the initialization list entered such that the declaration order of the class is preserved? That is, given

```
// An interesting question is asked:
X::X( int val )
    : j( val )
{
    i = j;
}
```

is the initialization of j inserted before or after the explicit user assignment of j to i? If the declaration order is preserved, this code fails badly. The code is correct, however, because the initialization list entries are placed before explicit user code.

Another common question is whether you can invoke a member function to initialize a member, such as

---

[8] Unfortunately, the person who wrote telling me of the warning's generation also told me that his group had never actually understood what the warning's warning was about until he had read the above few paragraphs in a column I wrote for the C++ *Report*.

```
// is the invocation of X::xfoo() ok?
X::X( int val )
   : i( xfoo( val )),
     j( val )
   {}
```

where `xfoo()` is a member function of X. The answer is yes, but.... To answer the "but" first, I reiterate my advice to initialize one member with another inside the constructor body, not in the member initialization list. You don't know the dependencies `xfoo()` has regarding the state of the X object to which it is bound. By placing `xfoo()` within the constructor body, you can ensure there is no ambiguity about which members are initialized at the point of its invocation.

The use of the member function is valid (apart from the issue of whether the members it accesses have been initialized). This is because the **this** pointer associated with the object being constructed is well formed and the expansion simply takes a form like the following:

```
// Pseudo C++ Code: constructor augmentation
X::X( /* this pointer, */ int val )
{
   i = this->xfoo( val );
   j = val;
}
```

Finally, then, what about this, in which a derived class member function is invoked to pass an argument to the base class constructor:

```
// is the invocation of FooBar::fval() ok?
class FooBar : public X {
   int _fval;
public:
   int fval() { return _fval; }
   FooBar( int val )
      : _fval( val ),
        X( fval() )
      {}
   ...
};
```

What do you think? A good idea or not? Here is its probable expansion:

```
// Pseudo C++ Code
FooBar::FooBar( /* this pointer goes here */ )
{
```

```
    // Oops: definitely not a good idea

    X::X( this, this->fval() );
    _fval = val;
};
```

It's definitely not a good idea. (In later chapters, base and virtual base class initialization within the member initialization list is detailed.)

In summary, the compiler iterates over and possibly reorders the initialization list to reflect the declaration order of the members. It inserts the code within the body of the constructor prior to any explicit user code.

Chapter 3

The Semantics of Data

Some while back I received e-mail from someone in France who was both mystified and a might upset. He had either volunteered or been drafted to provide a persistence library for his project group. In preparation for his work, he coded and then printed out the result of applying the **sizeof** operator to the following seemingly trivial class hierarchy:

```
class X {};
class Y : public virtual X {};
class Z : public virtual X {};
class A : public Y, public Z {};
```

None of these classes contains any explicit data—any anything, in fact, except an inheritance relationship—so he apparently believed the size of each class should be 0. It wasn't, of course—not even the apparently benign class X:

```
sizeof X yielded 1
sizeof Y yielded 8
sizeof Z yielded 8
sizeof A yielded 12
```

Let's look at each declaration in turn and see what's going on. An empty class, such as

```
// sizeof X == 1
class X {};
```

in practice is never empty. Rather it has an associated size of 1 byte—a char member inserted by the compiler. This allows two objects of the class, such as

```
X a, b;
if ( &a == &b ) cerr << "yipes!" << endl;
```

to be allocated unique addresses in memory.

What surprised (and dismayed) my correspondent even more, I suspect, was the result of applying the **sizeof** operator to the empty declaration of both classes Y and Z:

```
// sizeof Y == sizeof Z == 8
class Y : public virtual X{};
class Z : public virtual X{};
```

On his machine, the size of both classes Y and Z is 8. This size, however, is partially machine dependent. It also depends in part on the compiler implementation being used. The given size of both class Y and class Z on any machine is the interplay of three factors:

1. *Language support overhead.* There is an associated overhead incurred in the language support of virtual base classes. Within the derived class, this overhead is reflected as some form of pointer, either to the virtual base class subobject or to an associated table within which either the address or offset to the virtual base class subobject is stored. On my correspondent's machine, the pointer is 4 bytes. (Virtual base classes are discussed in Section 3.4.)

2. *Compiler optimization of recognized special cases.* There is the 1 byte size of the virtual base class X subobject also present within Y (and Z). Traditionally, this is placed at the end of the "fixed" (that is, invariant) portion of the derived class. Some compilers now provide special support for an empty virtual base class (the paragraph following item 3 discusses this in more detail). Our correspondent's compiler, however, did not provide this special handling.

3. *Alignment constraints.* The size of class Y (and Z) at this point is 5 bytes. On most machines, aggregate structures have an alignment constraint so that they can be efficiently loaded from and stored to memory. On my correspondent's machine, alignment of an aggregate is on a 4-byte boundary. So class Y (and Z) requires 3 bytes of padding. The result is a final size of 8.

The empty virtual base class has become a common idiom of OO design under C++ (it provides a virtual interface without defining any data). In response, some recent compilers provide special handling of the empty virtual base class (see [SUN94a]). Under this strategy, an empty virtual base class is treated as being coincident with the beginning of the derived class object; that is, it takes up no additional space. This saves the 1 byte associated with item 2. This savings in turn removes the need for the 3 bytes of padding required in item 3. The overhead to support the virtual derivation (item 1), however, remains: The size of both Y and Z under this model is 4 bytes, not 8.

This potential difference between compilers illustrates the evolutionary nature of the C++ Object Model. The model provides for the general case. As special cases are recognized over time, this or that heuristic is introduced to provide optimal handling. If successful, the heuristic is raised to common practice and becomes incorporated across implementations. It becomes thought of as standard, although it is not prescribed by the Standard, and over time it is likely to be thought of as part of the language. The virtual function table is a good example of this. Another is the named return value (NRV) optimization discussed in Chapter 2.

What, then, would you expect the size of class A to be? Obviously, in part that depends on the compiler being used. First, consider the compiler without special handling of the empty virtual base class. If we forget that both Y and Z are derived virtually from class X, we might answer 16 for the size of class A. After all, Y and Z are both 8 bytes each. However, when we apply the **sizeof** operator to class A, we discover that it has a size of 12 bytes. What is going on?

A virtual base class subobject occurs only once in the derived class regardless of the number of times it occurs within the class inheritance hierarchy. The size of class A is determined by the following:

- The size of the single shared instance of class X: 1 byte

- The size of its base classes Y and Z minus the storage allocated for class X: 4 bytes each (8 bytes total)

- The size of class A itself: in this case, 0 bytes

- The alignment requirement of class A, if any. The size without alignment is 9 bytes. Class A must align on a 4-byte boundary, thus it requires 3 bytes of padding. This results in a total size of 12 bytes.

What about under the special handling of the empty virtual base class? As before, the additional 1 byte for the empty instance of class X is removed and, with that, the additional 3 bytes of padding. Thus the size of Class A under this special handling is 8 bytes. Note that had we ourselves introduced one or more data members into the virtual base class X, the two compilers would have generated essentially equivalent object layouts.

The C++ standard does not mandate details such as the ordering of either base class subobjects or of data members across access levels. Neither does it mandate the implementation of either virtual functions or virtual base classes; rather, it declares them to be implementation dependent. In my discussion both in this chapter and in the rest of the book, I will distinguish between what the Standard mandates and what the current standard practice is.

In this chapter, the data members of the class and class hierarchy take center stage. The data members of a class, in general, represent the state of the class at some point in the program execution. Nonstatic data members hold the values of individual class objects; static data members hold values of interest to the class as a whole.

The C++ object model representation for nonstatic data members optimizes for space and access time (and to preserve compatibility with the C language layout of the C struct) by storing the members directly within each class object. This is also true for the inherited nonstatic data members of both virtual and nonvirtual base classes, although the ordering of their layout is left undefined. Static data members are maintained within the global data segment of the program and do not affect the size of individual class objects. Only one instance of a static data member of a class exists within a program regardless of the number of times that class is an object of direct or indirect derivation. (The static data members of a template class behave slightly differently. See Section 7.1 for a discussion.)

Each class object, then, is exactly the size necessary to contain the nonstatic data members of its class. This size may at times surprise you as being larger than necessary, as it did my correspondent from France. This girth comes about in two ways:

1. Additional data members added by the compilation system to support some language functionality (primarily the virtuals)

2. Alignment requirements on the data members and data structures as a whole

3.1   The Binding of a Data Member

Consider the following program fragment:

```
// A third party foo.h header file
// pulled in from somewhere
extern float x;

// the programmer's Point3d.h file
class Point3d
{
public:
    Point3d( float, float, float );
```

```
   // question:   which x is returned and set?
   float X() const { return x; }
   void X( float new_x ) { x = new_x; }
   // ...
private:
   float x, y, z;
};
```

If I were to ask which x the Point3d member X() returns—the class instance or the extern instance—everyone today would answer the class instance, and everyone would be right. Most everyone, however, would probably be surprised to learn that this answer was not always correct.

In the original implementation of C++, the references to x within the two instances of Point3d::X() actually resolved to the global x object! This binding was nearly universally unexpected and led to two styles of defensive programming in the early use of C++:

1. Placing all data members first in the class declaration to ensure the right binding:

```
class Point3d
{
   // defensive programming style #1
   // place all data first ...
   float x, y, z;
public:
   float X() const { return x; }
   // ... etc. ...
};
```

2. Placing all inline functions, regardless of their size, outside the class declaration:

```
class Point3d
{
public:
   // defensive programming style #2
   // place all inlines outside the class
   Point3d();
   float X() const;
   void X( float );
   // ... etc. ...
};
```

```
inline float
Point3d::
X() const
{
    return x;
}

// ... etc. ...
```

These styles still persist, in fact, although the necessity for their use was explicitly removed from the language with Release 2.0 and the accompanying revised C++ Reference Manual. The language rule back then was referred to as the "member rewriting rule" and stated generally that the body of an inline function is not evaluated until after the entire class declaration is seen. The Standard refined the rewriting rule with a tuple of member scope resolution rules. The effect is still to evaluate the body of an inline member function as if it had been defined immediately following the class declaration. That is, when one writes

```
extern int x;

class Point3d
{
public:
    ...
    // analysis of function body delayed until
    // closing brace of class declaration seen.
    float X() const { return x; }
    ...
private:
    float x;
    ...
};

// in effect, analysis is done here
```

the analysis of the member function's body is delayed until the entire class declaration is seen. Thus the binding of a data member within the body of an inline member function does not occur until after the entire class declaration is seen.

This is not true of the argument list of the member function, however. Names within the argument list are still resolved in place at the point they are first encountered. Nonintuitive bindings between extern and nested type names, therefore, can still occur. In the following code fragment, for example, the type of `length` in both member function signatures resolves to that of the global typedef—that is, to **int**. When the subsequent declaration of the nested typedef of `length` is encountered, the Standard requires that the earlier bindings be flagged as illegal:

```
typedef int length;

class Point3d
{
public:
    // oops: length resolves to global
    // ok: _val resolves to Point3d::_val
    mumble( length val ) { _val = val; }
    length mumble() { return _val; }
    // ...

private:
    // length must be seen before its first
    // reference within the class.  This
    // declaration makes the prior reference illegal.
    typedef float length;
    length _val;
    // ...
};
```

This aspect of the language still requires the general defensive programming style of always placing nested type declarations at the beginning of the class. In our example, placing the nested typedef defining `length` above any of its uses within the class corrects the nonintuitive binding.

3.2 Data Member Layout

Given the following set of data members:

```
class Point3d {
public:
    // ...
private:
    float x;
    static List<Point3d*> *freeList;
    float y;
    static const int chunkSize = 250;
    float z;
};
```

the nonstatic data members are set down in the order of their declaration within each class object (any intervening static data members, such as `freeList` and `chunkSize`, are ignored). In our example, then, each Point3d object consists of three **float** members in order: x, y, z. The static data members are stored in the program's data segment independent of individual class objects.

The Standard requires within an access section (the private, public, or protected section of a class declaration) only that the members be set down such that "later members have higher addresses within a class object" (Section 9.2 of the Standard). That is, the members are not required to be set down contiguously. What might intervene between the declared members? Alignment constraints on the type of a succeeding member may require padding. This is true both of C and C++, and in this case, the member layout of the two languages is in current practice the same.

Additionally, the compiler may synthesize one or more additional internal data members in support of the Object Model. The vptr, for example, is one such synthesized data member that all current implementations insert within each object of a class containing one or more virtual functions. Where should the vptr be placed within the class object? Traditionally, it has been placed after all the explicitly declared members of the class. More recently, it has been placed at the beginning of the class object. The Standard, by phrasing the layout requirement as it does, allows the compiler the freedom to insert these internally generated members anywhere, even between those explicitly declared by the programmer.

The Standard also allows the compiler the freedom to order the data members within multiple access sections within a class in whatever order it sees fit. That is, given the following class declaration:

```
class Point3d {
public:
    // ...
private:
    float x;
    static List<Point3d*> *freeList;
private:
    float y;
    static const int chunkSize = 250;
private:
    float z;
};
```

the size and composition of the resultant class object is the same as our earlier declaration, but the order of members is now implementation dependent. The implementation is free to place y first, or z, or whatever. However, I am not aware currently of any compilation system that does.

In practice, multiple access sections are concatenated together into one contiguous block in the order of declaration. No overhead is incurred by the access section specifier or the number of access levels. For example, declaring eight members in one access section or eight separate access sections in practice results in the same-sized objects.

The following template function, given two data members, identifies which occurs first within the class layout. If the two members are the first members declared in two different access sections, it identifies which section occurs first (if you are not familiar with pointers to class members, see Section 3.6):

```
template< class class_type,
          class data_type1,
          class data_type2 >
char*
access_order(
   data_type1 class_type::*mem1,
   data_type2 class_type::*mem2 )
{  //this ignores access privilege
   assert ( mem1 != mem2 );
   return
      mem1 < mem2
         ? "member 1 occurs first"
         : "member 2 occurs first";
}
```

This function could then be invoked as follows:

```
access_order( &Point3d::z, &Point3d::y );
```

where class-type binds to Point3d and data_type1 and data_type2 bind to **float**.

3.3   Access of a Data Member

Given the following pair of program statements:

```
Point3d origin;
origin.x = 0.0;
```

you may reasonably ask what is the cost of accessing the x data member? The answer depends both on how x and the Point3d class are declared. x can be either a static or nonstatic member. Point3d can be an independent class or be derived from a single base class. Less likely, but still possible, it can be either multiply or virtually derived. The following sections examine each of these possibilities in turn, including the first detailed look at virtual base classes.

Before I begin, however, let me pose a question. If we have the two definitions, origin and pt,

```
Point3d origin, *pt = &origin;
```

is the access of the coordinate data members, such as

```
origin.x = 0.0;
pt->x = 0.0;
```

ever *significantly* different when accessed through the object origin and the pointer pt? If your answer is yes, describe the characteristics of both the class Point3d and the data member x that result in the difference. I revisit this question and provide an answer at the end of this section.

Static Data Members

Static data members are literally lifted out of their class, as we saw in Section 1.1 and treated as if each were declared as a global variable (but with visibility limited to the scope of the class). Each member's access permission and class association is maintained without incurring any space or runtime overhead either in the individual class objects or in the static data member itself.

A single instance of each class static data member is stored within the data segment of the program. Each reference to the static member is internally translated to be a direct reference of that single extern instance. For example,

```
// origin.chunkSize == 250;
Point3d::chunkSize == 250;

// pt->chunkSize == 250;
Point3d::chunkSize == 250;
```

This is the only case in the language where the access of a member through a pointer and through an object are exactly equivalent in terms of the instructions actually executed. This is because the access of a static data member through the member selection operators is a syntactic convenience only. The member is not within the class object, and therefore the class object is not necessary for the access.

What if chunkSize were an inherited member of a complex inheritance hierarchy, perhaps the member of a virtual base class of a virtual base class, or some other equally complex hierarchy? It doesn't matter. There is still only a single instance of the member within the program, and its access is direct.

What if the access of the static data member is through a function call or some other form of expression? For example, if we write

```
foobar().chunkSize == 250;
```

what happens to the invocation of foobar()? In the pre-Standard language, one didn't know what would happen: It was left unspecified in the ARM whether foobar() had to be evaluated. In cfront, for example, it was simply discarded. Standard C++ explicitly requires that foobar() be evaluated, although no use is made of its result. A probable translation looks as follows:

```
// foobar().chunkSize == 250;

// evaluate expression, discarding result
(void) foobar();
Point3d::chunkSize == 250;
```

Taking the address of a static data member yields an ordinary pointer of its data type, not a pointer to class member, since the static member is not contained within a class object. For example,

```
&Point3d::chunkSize;
```

yields an actual memory address of type

```
const int*
```

If two classes each declare a static member freeList, then placing both of them in the program data segment is going to result in a name conflict. The compiler resolves this by internally encoding the name of each static data member—it's affectionately called *name-mangling*—to yield a unique program identifier. There are as many name-mangling schemes as there are implementations, it seems, each one described in more or less rigorous detail with tables, grammars, and so on. The two important aspects of any name-mangling scheme are that

1. the algorithm yields unique names, and

2. those unique names can be easily recast back to the original name in case the compilation system (or environment tool) needs to communicate with the user.

Nonstatic Data Members

Nonstatic data members are stored directly within each class object and cannot be accessed except through an explicit or implicit class object. An implicit class object is present whenever the programmer directly accesses a nonstatic data member within a member function. For example, in the following code:

```
Point3d
Point3d::translate( const Point3d &pt ) {
    x += pt.x;
    y += pt.y;
    z += pt.z;
}
```

the seemingly direct access of x, y, and z is actually carried out through an implicit class object represented by the **this** pointer. Internally, the function is augmented as follows:

```
// internal augmentation of member function
Point3d
Point3d::translate( Point3d *const this, const Point3d &pt ) {
    this->x += pt.x;
    this->y += pt.y;
    this->z += pt.z;
}
```

Member functions are examined in more detail in Chapter 4.

Access of a nonstatic data member requires the addition of the beginning address of the class object with the offset location of the data member. For example, given

```
origin.y = 0.0;
```

the address of

```
&origin.y;
```

is equivalent to the addition of

```
&origin + ( &Point3d::y - 1 );
```

(Notice the peculiar "subtract by one" expression applied to the pointer-to-data-member offset value. Offset values yielded by the pointer-to-data-member syntax are always bumped up by one. Doing this permits the compilation system to distinguish between a pointer to data member that is addressing the first member of a class and a pointer to data member that is addressing no member. Pointers to data members are discussed in more detail in Section 3.6.)

The offset of each nonstatic data member is known at compile time, even if the member belongs to a base class subobject derived through a single or multiple inheritance chain. Access of a nonstatic data member, therefore, is equivalent in performance to that of a C struct member or the member of a nonderived class.

Virtual inheritance introduces an additional level of indirection in the access of its members through a base class subobject. Thus

```
Point3d *pt3d;
pt3d->x = 0.0;
```

performs equivalently if x is a member of a struct, class, single inheritance hierarchy, or multiple inheritance hierarchy, but it performs somewhat slower if it is a member of a virtual base class. In the next sections, I examine the effect of inheritance on member layout. Before I turn to that, however, recall the question at the beginning of this section: When, if ever, is the access of the coordinate data members, such as

```
origin.x = 0.0;
pt->x = 0.0;
```

ever *significantly* different when accessed through the object `origin` or the pointer `pt`? The answer is the access is significantly different when the Point3d class is a derived class containing a virtual base class within its inheritance hierarchy and the member being accessed, such as x, is an inherited member of that virtual base class. In this case, we cannot say with any certainty which class type pt addresses (and therefore we cannot know at compile time the actual offset location of the member), so the resolution of the access must be delayed until runtime through an additional indirection. This is not the case with the object `origin`. Its type is that of a Point3d class, and the offset location of even inherited virtual base class members are fixed at compile time. An aggressive compiler can therefore resolve the access of x through `origin` statically.

3.4   Inheritance and the Data Member

Under the C++ inheritance model, a derived class object is represented as the concatenation of its members with those of its base class(es). The actual ordering of the derived and base class parts is left unspecified by the Standard. In theory, a compiler is free to place either the base or the derived part first in the derived class object. In practice, the base class members always appear first, except in the case of a virtual base class. (In general, the handling of a virtual base class is an exception to all generalities, even, of course, this one.)

Given this inheritance model, one can ask: What is the difference in providing two abstract data types for the representation of two- and three-dimensional points, such as

```
// supporting abstract data types
class Point2d {
public:
    // constructor(s)
    // operations
    // access functions
private:
    float x, y;
};

class Point3d {
public:
    // constructor(s)
    // operations
    // access functions
private:
    float x, y, z;
};
```

and providing a two- or three-level hierarchy in which each additional dimension is a class derived from the lower dimension? In the following subsections, the effects of single inheritance without the support of virtual

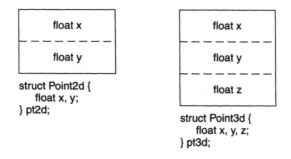

Figure 3.1(a) Data Layout: Independent Structs

functions, single inheritance with virtual functions, multiple inheritance, and virtual inheritance are examined. Figure 3.1(a) pictures the layout of Point2d and Point3d objects. (In the absence of virtual functions, they are equivalent to C struct declarations.)

Inheritance without Polymorphism

Imagine that the programmer wishes to share an implementation but continue to use type-specific instances of either the two- or three-dimensional point. One design strategy is to derive Point3d from our Point2d class, with Point3d inheriting all the operations and maintenance of the *x*- and *y*-coordinates. The effect is to localize and share data and the operations upon that data among two or more related abstractions. In general, concrete inheritance adds no space or access-time overhead to the representation.

```
class Point2d {
public:
    Point2d( float x = 0.0, float y = 0.0 )
        : _x( x ), _y( y ) {}

    float x() { return _x; }
    float y() { return _y; }

    void x( float newX ) { _x = newX; }
    void y( float newY ) { _y = newY; }

    void operator+=( const Point2d& rhs ) {
        _x += rhs.x();
        _y += rhs.y();
    }
```

```
    // ... more members
protected:
    float _x, _y;
};

// inheritance from concrete class
class Point3d : public Point2d {
public:
    Point3d( float x = 0.0, float y = 0.0, float z = 0.0 )
        : Point2d( x, y ), _z( z ) {}

    float z() { return _z; }
    void z( float newZ ) { _z = newZ; }

    void operator+=( const Point3d& rhs ) {
        Point2d::operator+=( rhs );
        _z += rhs.z();
    }
    // ... more members
protected:
    float _z;
};
```

The benefit of this design strategy is the localization of the code to manage the *x*- and *y*-coordinates. In addition, the design clearly indicates the
tight coupling of the two abstractions. The declaration and use of both
Point2d and Point3d class objects do not change from when the two classes
were independent, so clients of these abstractions need not be aware of
whether the objects are independent class types or related through inheritance. Figure 3.1(b) shows the layout of the Point2d and Point3d inheritance
layout without the declaration of a virtual interface.

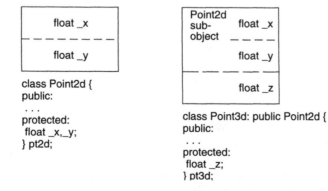

Figure 3.1(b) Data Layout: Single Inheritance without Virtual
Functions

What are the possible pitfalls of transforming two independent classes into a type/subtype relationship through inheritance? A naive design might, in fact, double the number of function calls to perform the same operations. That is, say the constructor or operator+=() in our example were not made inline (or the compiler could not for some reason support the inlining of the member functions). The initialization or addition of a Point3d object would be the cost of the partial Point2d and Point3d instances. In general, choosing candidate functions for inlining is an important, if unglamorous, aspect of class design. Confirming that they are in fact inlined is necessary before final release of the implementation.

A second possible pitfall in factoring a class into a two-level or deeper hierarchy is a possible bloating of the space necessary to represent the abstraction as a class hierarchy. The issue is the language guarantee of the integrity of the base class subobject within the derived class. It's slightly subtle. A walk-through of an example might best explain it. Let's begin with a concrete class:

```
class Concrete {
public:
    // ...
private:
    int val;
    char c1;
    char c2;
    char c3;
};
```

On a 32-bit machine, the size of each Concrete class object is going to be 8 bytes, broken down as follows:

1. 4 bytes for val

2. 1 byte each for c1, c2, and c3

3. 1 byte for the alignment of the class on a word boundary

Say, after some analysis, we decide that a more logical representation splits Concrete into a three-level inheritance hierarchy as follows:

```
class Concrete1 {
public:
    // ...
protected:
    int val;
    char bit1;
};
```

```
class Concrete2 : public Concrete1 {
public:
   // ...
protected:
   char bit2;
};

class Concrete3 : public Concrete2 {
public:
   // ...
protected:
   char bit3;
};
```

From a design standpoint, this representation may make more sense. From an implementation standpoint, however, we may be distressed to find that a Concrete3 class object now has a size of 16 bytes—double its previous size.

What's going on? Recall that the issue is the integrity of the base class subobject within the derived class. Let's walk through the layout of the inheritance hierarchy to see what is going on.

The Concrete1 class contains the two members—val and bit1—that together take up 5 bytes. The size of a Concrete1 class object, however, is 8 bytes: the 5 bytes of actual size plus 3 bytes of padding to align the object on a machine word boundary. That's as true in C as it is in C++; generally, alignment constraints are determined by the underlying processor.

Nothing necessarily to complain about so far. It's the layout of the derived class that typically drives the unwary programmer into fits of either perplexity or angry indignation. Concrete2 adds a single nonstatic data member, bit2, of type char. Our unwary programmer expects it to be packed into the base Concrete1 representation, taking up one of the bytes otherwise wasted as alignment padding. This layout strategy makes the Concrete2 class object also of size 8 bytes, with 2 bytes of padding.

The layout of the Concrete2 class, however, instead preserves the 3 bytes of padding within the Concrete1 base class subobject. The bit2 member is set down after that, followed by an additional 3 bytes of padding. The size of a Concrete2 class object is 12 bytes, not 8, with 6 bytes wasted for padding. The same layout algorithm results in a Concrete3 class object's being 16 bytes, 9 of which are wasted on padding.

"That's stupid," is the unwary programmer's judgment, which more than one has chosen to share with me over e-mail, on the phone, and in person. Do you see why the language behaves as it does?

Let's declare the following set of pointers:

```
Concrete2 *pc2;
Concrete1 *pc1_1, *pc2_2;
```

Both pc1_1 and pc2_2 can address objects of either three classes. The following assignment

```
*pc1_1 = *pc2_2;
```

should perform a default memberwise copy of the Concrete1 portion of the object addressed. If pc1_1 addresses a Concrete2 or Concrete3 object, that should not be of consequence to the assignment of its Concrete1 subobject.

However, if the language were to pack the derived class members Concrete2::bit2 or Concrete3::bit3 into the Concrete1 subobject, these language semantics could not be preserved. An assignment such as

```
pc1_1 = pc2;

// oops: derived class subobject is overridden
// its bit2 member now has an undefined value
*pc1_1 = *pc2_2;
```

would overwrite the values of the packed inherited members. It would be an enormous effort on the user's part to debug this, to say the least.

Adding Polymorphism

If we want to operate on a point independent of whether it is a Point2d or Point3d instance, we need to provide a virtual function interface within our hierarchy. Let's see how things change when we do that:

```
class Point2d {
public:
    Point2d( float x = 0.0, float y = 0.0 )
        : _x( x ), _y( y ) {}

    // access functions for x & y same as above
    // invariant across type: not made virtual

    // add placeholders for z - do nothing ...
    virtual float z(){ return 0.0;  }
    virtual void z( float ) {}
```

```
// turn type explicit operations virtual
virtual void
operator+=( const Point2d& rhs ) {
    _x += rhs.x(); _y += rhs.y(); }

// ... more members
protected:
    float _x, _y;
};
```

It makes sense to introduce a virtual interface into our design only if we intend to manipulate two- and three-dimensional points polymorphically, that is, to write code such as

```
void foo( Point2d &p1, Point2d &p2 ) {
    // ...
    p1 += p2;
    // ...
}
```

where p1 and p2 may be either two- or three-dimensional points. This is not something that any of our previous designs supported. This flexibility, of course, is at the heart of OO programming. Support for this flexibility, however, does introduce a number of space and access-time overheads for our Point2d class:

- Introduction of a virtual table associated with Point2d to hold the address of each virtual function it declares. The size of this table in general is the number of virtual functions declared plus an additional one or two slots to support runtime type identification.

- Introduction of the vptr within each class object. The vptr provides the runtime link for an object to efficiently find its associated virtual table.

- Augmentation of the constructor to initialize the object's vptr to the virtual table of the class. Depending on the aggressiveness of the compiler's optimization, this may mean resetting the vptr within the derived and each base class constructor. (This is discussed in more detail in Chapter 5.)

- Augmentation of the destructor to reset the vptr to the associated virtual table of the class. (It is likely to have been set to address the virtual table of the derived class within the destructor of the derived class. Remember, the order of destructor calls is in reverse:

derived class and then base class.) An aggressive optimizing compiler can suppress a great many of these assignments.

The impact of these overheads depends on the number and lifetime of the Point2d objects being manipulated and the benefits gained in programming the objects polymorphically. If an application knows its use of point objects is limited to either (but not both) two- or three-dimensional points, the overheads of this design may become unacceptable.[1]

Here is our new Point3d derivation:

```
class Point3d : public Point2d {
public:
    Point3d( float x = 0.0, float y = 0.0, float z = 0.0 )
        : Point2d( x, y ), _z( z ) {}
    float z() { return _z; }
    void z( float newZ ) { _z = newZ; }

    void operator+=( const Point2d& rhs ) {
        Point2d::operator+=( rhs );
        _z += rhs.z();
    }
    // ... more members
protected:
    float _z;
};
```

Although the syntax of the class's declaration has not changed, everything about it is now different: The two z() member functions and the operator+=() operator are virtual instances. Each Point3d class object contains an additional vptr member object (the instance inherited from Point2d). There is also a Point3d virtual table. The invocation of each member function made virtual is also more complex (this is covered in Chapter 4).

One current topic of debate within the C++ compiler community concerns where best to locate the vptr within the class object. In the original cfront implementation, it was placed at the end of the class object in order to support the following inheritance pattern, shown in Figure 3.2(a):

```
struct no_virts {
    int d1, d2;
};
```

---

[1] I am not aware of any production system actually making use of a polymorphic Point hierarchy.

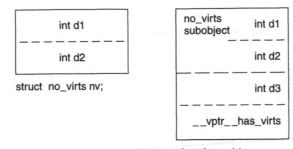

struct no_virts nv;

class has_virts:
    public no_virts hv;

Figure 3.2(a)   Vptr Placement at End of Class

```
class has_virts: public no_virts {
public:
    virtual void foo();
    // ...
private:
    int d3;
};

no_virts *p = new has_virts;
```

Placing the vptr at the end of the class object preserves the object layout of the base class C struct, thus permitting its use within C code. This inheritance idiom is believed by many to have been more common when C++ was first introduced than currently.

Subsequent to Release 2.0, with its addition of support for multiple inheritance and abstract base classes, and the general rise in popularity of the OO paradigm, some implementations began placing the vptr at the start of the class object. (For example, Martin O'Riordan, who led Microsoft's original C++ compiler effort, persuasively argues for this implementation model.) See Figure 3.2(b) for an illustration.

Placing the vptr at the start of the class is more efficient in supporting some virtual function invocations through pointers to class members under multiple inheritance (see Section 4.4). Otherwise, not only must the offset to the start of the class be made available at runtime, but also the offset to the location of the vptr of that class must be made available. The trade-off, however, is a loss in C language interoperability. How significant a loss? What percentage of programs derive a polymorphic class from a C-language struct? There are currently no empirical numbers to support either position.

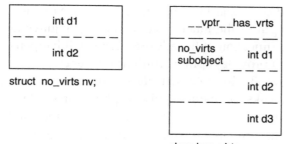

struct no_virts nv;

class has_virts:
    public no_virts hv;

Figure 3.2(b)   Vptr Placement at Front of Class

Figure 3.3 shows the Point2d and Point3d inheritance layout with the addition of virtual functions. (*Note:* The figure shows the vptr placement at the end of the base class.)

Multiple Inheritance

Single inheritance provides a form of "natural" polymorphism regarding the conversion between base and derived types within the inheritance hierarchy. Look at Figures 3.1(b), 3.2(a), or 3.3, where you can see that the base and derived class objects both begin at the same address. They differ in that the derived object extends the length of its nonstatic data members. The assignment, such as

```
Point3d p3d;
Point2d *p = &p3d;
```

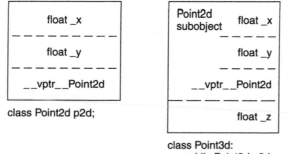

class Point2d p2d;

class Point3d:
    public Point2d p3d;

Figure 3.3   Data Layout: Single Inheritance with Virtual Inheritance

of the derived class object to a pointer or reference to the base class (regardless of the depth of the inheritance hierarchy) requires no compiler intervention or modification of the address. Instead, it happens "naturally," and in that sense, it provides optimal runtime efficiency.

From Figure 3.2(b), note that placing the vptr at the beginning of the class object breaks the natural polymorphism of single inheritance in the special case of a base class without virtual functions and a derived class with them. The conversion of the derived object to the base in this case requires the intervention of the compiler in order to adjust the address being assigned by the size of the vptr. Under both multiple and virtual inheritances, the need for compiler intervention is considerably more pronounced.

Multiple inheritance is neither as well behaved nor as easily modeled as single inheritance. The complexity of multiple inheritance lies in the "unnatural" relationship of the derived class with its second and subsequent base class subobjects. Consider, for example, the following multiply derived class, Vertex2d:

```
class Point2d {
public:
    // ...
protected:
    float _x, _y;
};

class Vertex {
public:
    // ...
protected:
    Vertex *next;
};

class Vertex2d :
    public Point2d, public Vertex {
public:
    //...
protected:
    float mumble;
};
```

The problem of multiple inheritance primarily affects conversions between the derived and second or subsequent base class objects, either directly

```
extern void mumble( const Vertex& );
Vertex2d v;
...
// conversion of a Vertex2d to Vertex is ``unnatural''
mumble( v );
```

or through support for the virtual function mechanism. The problems with supporting virtual function invocation are discussed in Section 4.2.

The assignment of the address of a multiply derived object to a pointer of its leftmost (that is, first) base class is the same as that for single inheritance, since both point to the same beginning address. The cost is simply the assignment of that address (Figure 3.4 shows the multiple inheritance layout). The assignment of the address of a second or subsequent base class, however, requires that that address be modified by the addition (or subtraction in the case of a downcast) of the size of the intervening base class subobject(s). For example, with

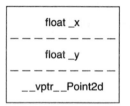

class Point2d pt2d;

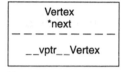

Vertex v;

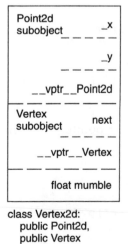

class Vertex2d:
    public Point2d,
    public Vertex
    { } v2d;

Figure 3.4 Data Layout: Multiple Inheritance

```
Vertex2d v2d;
Vertex  *pv;
Point *pp;
Point2d *p2d;
```

the assignment

```
pv = &v2d;
```

requires a conversion of the form

```
// Pseudo C++ Code
pv = (Vertex*)(((char*)&v2d) + sizeof( Point2d ));
```

whereas the assignments

```
pp  = &v2d;
p2d = &v2d;
```

both simply require a copying of the address. With

```
Vertex2d *p2d;
Vertex   *pv;
```

the assignment

```
pv = p2d;
```

cannot simply be converted into

```
// Pseudo C++ Code
pv = (Vertex*)((char*)p2d) + sizeof( Point2d );
```

since, if p2d were set to 0, pv would end up with the value
sizeof(Point2d). So, for pointers, the internal conversion requires a
conditional test:

```
// Pseudo C++ Code
pv = p2d
   ? (Vertex*)((char*)p2d) + sizeof( Point2d )
   : 0;
```

Conversion of a reference need not defend itself against a possible 0
value, since the reference cannot refer to no object.

The Standard does not require a specific ordering of the Point2d and Vertex base classes of Vertex2d. The original cfront implementation always placed them in the order of declaration. A Vertex2d object under cfront, therefore, consisted of the Point2d subobject (which itself consisted of a Point subobject), followed by the Vertex subobject and finally by the Vertex2d part. In practice, this is still how all implementations lay out the multiple base classes (with the exception of virtual inheritance).

An optimization under some compilers, however, such as the MetaWare compiler, switch the order of multiple base classes if the second (or subsequent) base class declares a virtual function and the first does not. This shuffling of the base class order saves the generation of an additional vptr within the derived class object. There is no universal agreement among implementations about the importance of this optimization, and use of this optimization is not (at least currently) widespread.

What about access of a data member of a second or subsequent base class? Is there an additional cost? No. The member's location is fixed at compile time. Hence its access is a simple offset the same as under single inheritance regardless of whether it is a pointer, reference, or object through which the member is being accessed.

Virtual Inheritance

A semantic side effect of multiple inheritance is the need to support a form of shared subobject inheritance. The classic example of this is the original iostream library implementation:

```
//pre-standard iostream implementation
class ios { ... };
class istream : public ios { ... };
class ostream : public ios { ... };
class iostream :
    public istream, public ostream { ... };
```

Both the istream and ostream classes contain an ios subobject. In the layout of iostream, however, we need only a single ios subobject. The language level solution is the introduction of virtual inheritance:

```
class ios { ... };
class istream : public virtual ios { ... };
class ostream : public virtual ios { ... };
class iostream :
    public istream, public ostream { ... };
```

As complicated as the semantics of virtual inheritance may seem, its support within the compiler has proven even more complicated. In our iostream example, the implementational challenge is to find a reasonably efficient method of collapsing the two instances of an ios subobject maintained by the istream and ostream classes into a single instance maintained by the iostream class, while still preserving the polymorphic assignment between pointers (and references) of base and derived class objects.

The general implementation solution is as follows. A class containing one or more virtual base class subobjects, such as istream, is divided into two regions: an invariant region and a shared region. Data within the invariant region remains at a fixed offset from the start of the object regardless of subsequent derivations. So members within the invariant region can be accessed directly. The shared region represents the virtual base class subobjects. The location of data within the shared region fluctuates with each derivation. So members within the shared region need to be accessed indirectly. What has varied among implementations is the method of indirect access. The following example illustrates the three predominant strategies. Here is the data portion of a virtual Vertex3d inheritance hierarchy: [2]

```
class Point2d {
public:
    ...
protected:
    float _x, _y;
};

class Vertex : public virtual Point2d {
public:
    ...
protected:
    Vertex *next;
};

class Point3d : public virtual Point2d {
public:
    ...
protected:
    float _z;
};
```

---

[2] This hierarchy is suggested by [POKOR94], an excellent 3D Graphics textbook using C++.

```
class Vertex3d :
   public Point3d, public Vertex {
public:
   ...
protected:
   float mumble;
};
```

The general layout strategy is to first lay down the invariant region of the derived class and then build up the shared region.

However, one problem remains: How is the implementation to gain access to the shared region of the class? In the original cfront implementation, a pointer to each virtual base class is inserted within each derived class object. Access of the inherited virtual base class members is achieved indirectly through the associated pointer. For example, if we have the following Point3d operator:

```
void
Point3d::
operator+=( const Point3d &rhs )
{
   _x += rhs._x;
   _y += rhs._y;
   _z += rhs._z;
}
```

under the cfront strategy, this is transformed internally into

```
// Pseudo C++ Code
__vbcPoint2d->_x += rhs.__vbcPoint2d->_x;
__vbcPoint2d->_y += rhs.__vbcPoint2d->_y;
_z += rhs._z;
```

A conversion between the derived and base class instances, such as

```
Vertex *pv = pv3d;
```

under the cfront implementation model becomes

```
// Pseudo C++ code
Vertex *pv = pv3d ? pv3d->__vbcPoint2d : 0;
```

There are two primary weaknesses with this implementation model:

1. An object of the class carries an additional pointer for each virtual base class. Ideally, we want a constant overhead for the class object that is independent of the number of virtual base classes within its inheritance hierarchy. Think of how you might solve this.

2. As the virtual inheritance chain lengthens, the level of indirection increases to that depth. This means that three levels of virtual derivation requires indirection through three virtual base class pointers. Ideally, we want a constant access time regardless of the depth of the virtual derivation.

MetaWare and other compilers still using cfront's original implementation model solve the second problem by promoting (by copying) all nested virtual base class pointers into the derived class object. This solves the constant access time problem, although at the expense of duplicating the nested virtual base class pointers. MetaWare provides a compile-time switch to allow the programmer to choose whether to generate the duplicate pointers. Figure 3.5(a) illustrates the pointer-to-base-class implementation model.

There are two general solutions to the first problem. Microsoft's compiler introduced the virtual base class table. Each class object with one or more virtual base classes has a pointer to the virtual base class table inserted within it. The actual virtual base class pointers, of course, are placed within the table. Although this solution has been around for many years, I am not aware of any other compiler implementation that employs it. (It may be that Microsoft's patenting of their virtual function implementation effectively prohibits its use.)

The second solution, and the one preferred by Bjarne (at least while I was working on the Foundation project with him), is to place not the address but the offset of the virtual base class within the virtual function table. (Figure 3.5(b) on page 100 shows the base class offset implementation model.) I implemented this in the Foundation research project, interweaving the virtual base class and virtual function entries. In the recent Sun compiler, the virtual function table is indexed by both positive and negative indices. The positive indices, as previously, index into the set of virtual functions; the negative indices retrieve the virtual base class offsets. Under this strategy, the Point3d operator is translated into the following general form (leaving off casts for readability and not showing the more efficient precalculation of the addresses):

```
// Pseudo C++ Code
(this + __vptr__Point3d[-1])->_x +=
    (&rhs + rhs.__vptr__Point3d[-1])->_x;
```

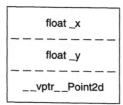

Point2d pt2d;

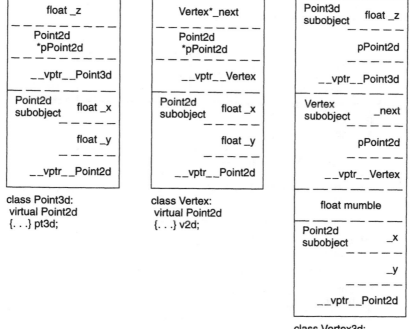

Figure 3.5(a)   Data Layout: Virtual Inheritance with Pointer Strategy

```
(this + __vptr__Point3d[-1])->_y +=
    (&rhs + rhs.__vptr__Point3d[-1])->_y;
_z += rhs._z;
```

Although the actual access of the inherited member is more expensive under this strategy, the cost of that access is localized to a use of the member. A conversion between the derived and base class instances, such as

```
Vertex *pv = pv3d;
```

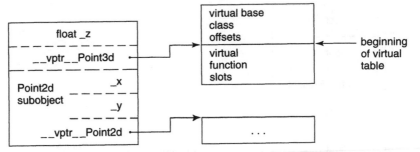

class Point3d: virtual Point2d {. . .} pt3d;

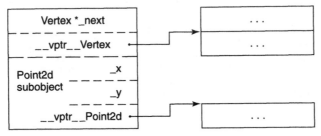

class Vertex: virtual Point2d {. . .} v2d;

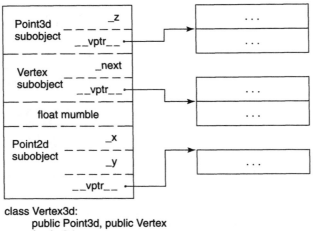

class Vertex3d:
   public Point3d, public Vertex
   {. . .} v3d;

Figure 3.5(b)   Data Layout: Virtual Inheritance with Virtual Table Offset Strategy

under this implementation model becomes

```
// Pseudo C++ code
Vertex *pv = pv3d
   ? pv3d + pv3d->__vptr__Point3d[-1])
   : 0;
```

Each of these are implementation models; they are not required by the Standard. Each solves the problem of providing access to a shared subobject whose location is likely to fluctuate with each derivation. Because of the overhead and complexity of virtual base class support, each implementation is somewhat different and likely to continue to evolve over time.

Access of an inherited virtual base class member through a nonpolymorphic class object, such as

```
Point3d origin;
...
origin._x;
```

can be optimized by an implementation into a direct member access, much as a virtual function call through an object can be resolved at compile time. The object's type cannot change between one program access and the next, so the problem of the fluctuating virtual base class subobject in this case does not hold.

In general, the most efficient use of a virtual base class is that of an abstract virtual base class with no associated data members.

3.5   Object Member Efficiency

The following sequence of tests attempts to measure the overhead associated with using aggregation, encapsulation, and inheritance. The case against which all the tests are measured is the access cost of assigning, adding, and subtracting individual local variables:

```
float pA_x = 1.725, pA_y = 0.875, pA_z = 0.478;
float pB_x = 0.315, pB_y = 0.317, pB_z = 0.838;
```

The actual expression loop, iterated over 10 million times, looks as follows (of course, the syntax changes as the point representation changes):[3]

```
for ( int iters = 0; iters < 10000000; iters++ )
{
    pB_x = pA_x - pB_z;
    pB_y = pA_y + pB_x;
    pB_z = pA_z + pB_y;
}
```

The first test against the use of individual variables is that of a local array of three float elements:

---

[3] Note that neither compiler, with the optimizer turned on, hoisted these expressions out of the loop. Has that happened, I would have added iters%12 to each.

```
enum fussy { x, y, z };

for ( int iters = 0; iters < 10000000; iters++ )
{
    pB[ x ] = pA[ x ] - pB[ z ];
    pB[ y ] = pA[ y ] + pB[ x ];
    pB[ z ] = pA[ z ] + pB[ y ];
}
```

The second test converted the homogeneous array elements into a C-struct data abstraction with named float members x, y, and z:

```
for ( int iters = 0; iters < 10000000; iters++ )
{
    pB.x = pA.x - pB.z;
    pB.y = pA.y + pB.x;
    pB.z = pA.z + pB.y;
}
```

The next rung of the abstraction ladder is the introduction of data encapsulation and the use of inline access functions. The point representation becomes an independent Point3d class. I tried two forms of access functions. First, I defined an inline instance that returns a reference, allowing it to appear on both sides of the assignment operator:

```
class Point3d {
public:
    Point3d( float xx = 0.0, float yy = 0.0, float zz = 0.0 )
        : _x( xx ), _y( yy ), _z( zz ) {}

    float& x() { return _x; }
    float& y() { return _y; }
    float& z() { return _z; }

private:
    float _x, _y, _z;
};
```

The actual access of each coordinate element then looked as follows:

```
for ( int iters = 0; iters < 10000000; iters++ )
{
    pB.x() = pA.x() - pB.z();
    pB.y() = pA.y() + pB.x();
    pB.z() = pA.z() + pB.y();
}
```

The second form of access function I defined provided a pair of get and set functions:

```
float x() { return _x; }
void x( float newX )
   { _x = newX; }
```

The assignment of each coordinate value took the form

```
pB.x( pA.x() - pB.z() );
```

Table 3.1 lists the results of running the tests for both compilers. (I break out the times for the two compilers only when their performances differ from each other's significantly.)

Table 3.1 Data Access under Increasing Abstraction

	Optimized	Non-optimized
Individual Local Variables	0.80	1.42
Local Array		
CC	0.80	2.55
NCC	0.80	1.42
Struct with Public Members	0.80	1.42
Class with Inline Get Method		
CC	0.80	2.56
NCC	0.80	3.10
Class with Inline Get & Set Method		
CC	0.80	1.74
NCC	0.80	2.87

In terms of actual program performance, the important point here is that with optimization turned on, no runtime performance cost for encapsulation and the use of inline access functions was exhibited.

I was curious why the array access under CC is nearly twice as slow as that for NCC, particularly as the array access involves access only of the C language array and not of any "complex" C++ feature. A code generation expert dismissed the anomaly as a "quirk of code generation . . . unique to a particular compiler." True enough, perhaps, but it happens to be the compiler I currently use to develop software. Call me Curious George, if you will. If you're not interested, please skip the next few paragraphs.

In the following assembler output, 1.s means load a single-precision floating-point value; s.s means store a single-precision floating-point value; and sub.s means subtract two single-precision floating-point values. In the following assembler output for the two compilers, both sequences load the two values, subtract one from the other, and store the result. In the less efficient CC output, the address of each local variable is computed and placed within a register (the addu means add unsigned):

```
// CC assembler output
#   13  pB[ x ] = pA[ x ] - pB[ z ];
    addu $25, $sp, 20
    1.s   $f4, 0($25)
    addu $24, $sp, 8
    1.s   $f6, 8($24)
    sub.s $f8, $f4, $f6
    s.s   $f8, 0($24)
```

while in the NCC sequence, the load step computes the address directly:

```
// NCC assembler output
#   13  pB[ x ] = pA[ x ] - pB[ z ];
    1.s   $f4, 20($sp)
    1.s   $f6, 16($sp)
    sub.s $f8, $f4, $f6
    s.s   $f8, 8($sp)
```

If the local variables had been accessed multiple times, the CC strategy would probably be more efficient. For a single access, however, the otherwise reasonable strategy of placing the variable's address within a register significantly adds to the cost of the expression. In any case, with the optimizer turned on, both code sequences are transformed into the same set of statements in which all operations within the loop are performed on values placed within registers.

An obvious observation is that without the optimizer turned on, it is extremely difficult to guess at the performance characteristics of a program, since the code is potentially hostage to the "quirk(s) of code generation...unique to a particular compiler." Before one begins source level "optimizations" to speed up a program, one should always do actual performance measurements rather than relying on speculation and common sense.

In the next sequence of tests, I introduced first a three-level single inheritance representation of the Point abstraction and then a virtual inheritance representation of the Point abstraction. I tested both direct and inline access (multiple inheritance did not fit naturally into the model, so I decided to forego it.) The general hierarchy is

```
class Point1d {...};                    // maintains x
class Point2d : public Point1d {...};   // maintains y
class Point3d : public Point2d {...};   // maintains z
```

The one-level virtual inheritance derived Point2d virtually from Point1d. The two-level virtual inheritance additionally derived Point3d virtually from Point2d. Table 3.2 lists the results of running the tests for both compilers. (Again, I break out the times for the two compilers only when their performances differ significantly from each other's.)

Table 3.2 Data Access under Inheritance Models

	Optimized	Non-optimized
Single Inheritance		
Direct Access	0.80	1.42
Inline Methods		
CC	0.80	2.55
NCC	0.80	3.10
Virtual Inheritance – 1-Level		
Direct Access	1.60	1.94
Inline Methods		
CC	1.60	2.75
NCC	1.60	3.30
Virtual Inheritance – 2-Level		
Direct Access		
CC	2.25	2.74
NCC	3.04	3.68
Inline Methods		
CC	2.25	3.22
NCC	2.50	3.81

Single inheritance should not affect the test performance, since the members are stored contiguously within the derived class object and their offsets are known at compile time. The results, as expected, were exactly the same as those of the independent abstract data type. (The same should be true under multiple inheritance, but I didn't confirm that.)

Again, it is worth noting that with the optimizer off, performance, which common sense says should be the same (direct member access versus inline access), is in practice slower in the case of inline functions. The lesson again is that the programmer concerned with efficiency must actually measure the performance of his or her program and not leave the measurement of the program to speculation and assumption. It is also worth noting that optimizers don't always work. I've more than once had compilations fail with an optimizer turned on that compiled fine "normally."

The virtual inheritance performance is disappointing in that neither compiler recognized that the access of the inherited data member `pt1d::_x` is through a nonpolymorphic class object and that therefore indirect runtime access is unnecessary. Both compilers generate indirect access of `pt1d::_x` (and `pt1d::y` in the case of two levels of virtual inheritance), even though its location within the two Point3d objects is fixed at compile time. The indirection significantly inhibited the optimizer's ability to move all the operations within registers. The indirection did not affect the non-optimized executables significantly.

3.6 Pointer to Data Members

Pointers to data members are a somewhat arcane but useful feature of the language, particularly if you need to probe at the underlying member layout of a class. One example of such a probing might be to determine if the vptr is placed at the beginning or end of the class. A second use, presented in Section 3.2, might be to determine the ordering of access sections within the class. As I said, it's an arcane, although potentially useful, language feature.

Consider the following Point3d class declaration. It declares a virtual function, a static data member, and three coordinate values:

```
class Point3d {
public:
    virtual ~Point3d();
    // ...
protected:
    static Point3d origin;
    float x, y, z;
};
```

The member layout for each Point3d class object contains the three coordinate values in the order x, y, z and a vptr. (Recall that origin, the static data member, is hoisted outside the individual class object.) The only implementation aspect of the layout is the placement of the vptr. The Standard permits the vptr to be placed anywhere within the object: at the beginning, at the end, or in between either of the three members. In practice, all implementations place it either at the beginning or at the end.

What does it mean, then, to take the address of one of the coordinate members? For example, what value should the following yield?

```
& 3d_point::z;
```

It is going to yield the z-coordinate's offset within the class object. Minimally, this has to be the size of the x and y members, since the language requires the members within an access level be set down in the order of declaration.

At the compiler's discretion, however, the vptr may be placed either before, in-between, or after the coordinate members. Again, in practice, the vptr is either placed at the beginning or at the end of the class object. On a 32-bit machine, floats are 4 bytes each, so we would expect the value to be either 8 bytes without an intervening vptr or 12 bytes with it. (The vptr, and pointers in general, use 4 bytes on a 32-bit architecture.)

That expectation, however, is off by one—a somewhat traditional error for both C and C++ programmers.

The physical offset of the three coordinate members within the class layout are, respectively, either 0, 4, and 8 if the vptr is placed at the end or 4, 8, and 12 if the vptr is placed at the start of the class. The value returned from taking the member's address, however, is traditionally bumped up by 1. Thus the actual values are 1, 5, and 9, and so on. Do you see why Bjarne decided to do that?

The problem is distinguishing between a pointer to no data member and a pointer to the first data member. Consider for example:

```
float Point3d::*p1 = 0;
float Point3d::*p2 = &Point3d::x;

// oops: how to distinguish?
if ( p1 == p2 ) {
   cout << " p1 & p2 contain the same value — ";
   cout << " they must address the same member!" << end
}
```

To distinguish between p1 and p2, each actual member offset value is bumped up by 1. Hence, both the compiler (and the user) must remember to subtract 1 before actually using the value to address a member.

Given what we now know about pointers to data members, we find that explaining the difference between

```
& 3d_point::z;
```

and

```
& origin.z
```

is straightforward. Whereas taking the address of a nonstatic data member yields its offset within the class, taking the address of a data member bound to an actual class object yields the member's actual address in memory. The result of

```
& origin.z
```

adds the offset of z (minus 1) to the beginning address of origin. The value returned is of type

```
float*
```

not

```
float Point3d::*
```

because it refers to an specific single instance, much the same as taking the address of a static data member.

Under multiple inheritance, the combination of a second (or subsequent) base class pointer to a member bound to a derived class object is complicated by the offset that needs to be added. For example, if we have

```
struct Base1 { int val1; };
struct Base2 { int val2; };
struct Derived : Base1, Base2 { ... };

void func1( int Derived::*dmp, Derived *pd )
{
    // expects a derived pointer to member
    // what if we pass it a base pointer?
    pd->*dmp;
}
```

```
void func2( Derived *pd )
{
    // assigns bmp 1
    int Base2::*bmp = &base2::val2;

    // oops: bmp == 1,
    // but in Derived, val2 == 5
    func1( bmp, pd )
}
```

bmp must be adjusted by the size of the intervening Base1 class when passed as the first argument to func1(). Otherwise, the invocation of

```
pd->*dmp;
```

within func1() will access Base1::val1, not Base2::val2 as the programmer intended. The specific solution in this case is

```
// internal transformation by compiler
func1( bmp + sizeof( Base1 ), pd );
```

In general, however, we cannot guarantee that bmp is not 0 and so must guard against it:

```
// internal transformation
// guarding against bmp == 0
func1( bmp ? bmp + sizeof( Base1 ) : 0, pd );
```

Efficiency of Pointers to Members

The following sequence of tests attempts to gain some measure of the overhead associated with using pointers to members under the various class representations of the 3D point. In the first two cases, there is no inheritance. The first case takes the address of a bound member:

```
float *ax = &pA.x;
```

for the three coordinate members of points pA and pB. The assignment, addition, and subtraction look as follows:

```
*bx = *ax - *bz;
*by = *ay + *bx;
*bz = *az + *by;
```

The second case takes the address of a pointer to data member:

```
float pt3d::*ax = &pt3d::x;
```

for the three coordinate members. The assignment, addition, and subtraction use the pointer to data member syntax, binding the values to the objects pA and pB:

```
pB.*bx = pA.*ax - pB.*bz;
pB.*by = pA.*ay + pB.*bx;
pB.*bz = pA.*az + pB.*by;
```

Recall that the direct data member exercise of this function, executed in Section 3.5, ran with an average user time of 0.80 with optimization turned on and 1.42 with optimization turned off for both compilers. The results of running these two tests, coupled with the results of the direct data access, are shown in Table 3.3:

Table 3.3 Nonstatic Data Member Access

	Optimized	Non-optimized
Direct Access	0.80	1.42
Pointer to		
Bound Member	0.80	3.04
Pointer to		
Data Member		
CC	0.80	5.34
NCC	4.04	5.34

The non-optimized results conform to expectations. That is, the addition of one indirection per member access through the bound pointer more than doubles the execution time. The pointer-to-member access again nearly doubles the execution time. The binding of the pointer to data member to the class object requires the addition of the offset minus 1 to the address of the object. More important, of course, the optimizer is able to bring the performance of all three access strategies into conformance, except the anomalous behavior of the NCC optimizer. (It is interesting to note here that the appalling performance of the NCC executable under optimization reflects a poor optimization of the generated assembly code and not an attribute of the source-level C++ code. An examination of the generated non-optimized assembly for both CC and NCC showed the two outputs to be identical.)

The next set of tests looks at the impact of inheritance on the performance of pointers to data members. In the first case, the independent Point class is redesigned into a three-level single inheritance hierarchy with one coordinate value as a member of each class:

```
class Point { ... }; // float x;
class Point2d : public Point   { ... }; // float y;
class Point3d : public Point2d { ... }; // float z;
```

The next representation retains the three-level single inheritance hierarchy but introduces one level of virtual inheritance: the Point2d class is virtually derived from Point. As a result, each access of Point::x is now accessing a virtual base class data member. Then, more out of curiosity than need, the final representation added a second level of virtual inheritance, that of Point3d being virtually derived from Point2d. Table 3.4 shows the results. (*Note*: The poor performance of the NCC optimizer was consistent across the tests, so I've left it off the listing.)

Table 3.4 Pointer to Data Member Access

	Optimized	%	Non-optimized
No Inheritance	0.80		5.34
SI (3 levels)	0.80		5.34
VI (1 level)	1.60		5.44
VI (2 level)	2.14		5.51
SI: Single Inheritance		VI: Virtual Inheritance	

Because inherited data members are stored directly within the class object, the introduction of inheritance does not affect the performance of the code at all. The major impact of introducing virtual inheritance is to impede the effectiveness of the optimizer. Why? In these two implementations, each level of virtual inheritance introduces an additional level of indirection. Under both implementations, each access of Point::x, such as

```
pB.*bx
```

is translated into

```
&pB->__vbcPoint + ( bx - 1 )
```

rather than the more direct

```
&pB + ( bx - 1 )
```

The additional indirection reduced the ability of the optimizer to move all the processing into registers.

Chapter 4

The Semantics of Function

If we have a Point3d pointer and object:

```
Point3d obj;
Point3d *ptr = &obj;
```

the question is, what actually happens when we write

```
obj.normalize();
ptr->normalize();
```

where `Point3d::normalize()` is implemented as

```
Point3d
Point3d::normalize() const
{
    register float mag = magnitude();
    Point3d normal;

    normal._x = _x/mag;
    normal._y = _y/mag;
    normal._z = _z/mag;

    return normal;
}
```

and `Point3d::magnitude()` is implemented as

```
float
Point3d::magnitude() const
{
```

```
return sqrt(
    _x * _x + _y * _y + _z * _z
);
}
```

The answer is, we don't yet know. C++ supports three flavors of member functions: static, nonstatic, and virtual. Each is invoked differently; those differences are the topic of the next section. (A short quiz: Although we cannot say with certainty whether normalize() and magnitude() are virtual or nonvirtual members, we can safely discount the functions as being static, since both (a) directly access the nonstatic coordinate data and (b) are declared to be **const** members. Static member functions may not do either.)

4.1   Varieties of Member Invocation

Historically, the original C with Classes supported only nonstatic member functions (see [STROUP82] for the first public description of the language). Virtual functions were added in the mid-1980s, and apparently to much skepticism (some of which still persists within the C community). In [STROUP94], Bjarne writes:

> A common opinion was that virtual functions were simply a kind of crippled pointer to function and thus redundant.... Therefore, the argument went, virtual functions were simply a form of inefficiency.

Static member functions were the last to be introduced. They were formally proposed for the language at the Implementor's Workshop of the 1987 Usenix C++ Conference and introduced with cfront, Release 2.0.

Nonstatic Member Functions

One C++ design criterion is that a nonstatic member function at a minimum must be as efficient as its analogous nonmember function. That is, if we are given a choice between

```
float magnitude3d( const Point3d *_this ){ ... }
float Point3d::magnitude() const { ... }
```

there should be no additional overhead for choosing the member function instance. This is achieved by internally transforming the member instance into the equivalent nonmember instance.

For example, here is a nonmember implementation of `magnitude()`:

```
float magnitude3d( const Point3d *_this ){
    return sqrt( _this->_x * _this->_x +
                 _this->_y * _this->_y +
                 _this->_z * _this->_z );
}
```

By visual inspection, we can see that the nonmember instance seems less efficient. It accesses the coordinate members indirectly through its argument, while the member instance accesses the coordinate members directly. In practice, however, the member function is transformed internally to be equivalent to the nonmember instance. Following are the steps in the transformation of a member function:

1. Rewrite the signature to insert an additional argument to the member function that provides access to the invoking class object. This is called the implicit **this** pointer:

   ```
   // non-const nonstatic member augmentation
   float
   Point3d::magnitude( Point3d *const this )
   ```

   If the member function is **const**, the signature becomes

   ```
   // const nonstatic member augmentation
   float
   Point3d::magnitude( const Point3d *const this )
   ```

2. Rewrite each direct access of a nonstatic data member of the class to access the member through the **this** pointer:

   ```
   {
       return sqrt(
           this->_x * this->_x +
           this->_y * this->_y +
           this->_z * this->_z );
   }
   ```

3. Rewrite the member function into an external function, *mangling* its name so that it's lexically unique within the program:

   ```
   extern float magnitude__7Point3dFv(
       register Point3d *const this );
   ```

Now that the function has been transformed, each of its invocations must also be transformed. Hence

```
obj.magnitude();
```

becomes

```
magnitude__7Point3dFv( &obj );
```

and

```
ptr->magnitude();
```

becomes

```
magnitude__7Point3dFv( ptr );
```

The normalize() function is internally transformed into something like the following. This presumes a Point3d copy constructor is declared and the named returned value (NRV) optimization is applied (see Section 2.3 for a discussion of the NRV optimization).

```
// Representing internal transformation
// with application of named return value
// Pseudo C++ Code

void
normalize__7Point3dFv( register const Point3d *const this,
                       Point3d &__result )
{
    register float mag = this->magnitude();

    // default constructor
    __result.Point3d::Point3d();

    __result._x = this->_x/mag;
    __result._y = this->_y/mag;
    __result._z = this->_z/mag;

    return;
}
```

A slightly more efficient implementation is to directly construct the normal, as follows:

```
// slightly more efficient user implementation
Point3d
Point3d::normalize() const
{
    register float mag = magnitude();
    return Point3d( _x/mag, _y/mag, _z/mag );
}
```

This instance is transformed into something like the following (again presuming a Point3d copy constructor is declared and the NRV optimization is applied):

```
// Representing internal transformation
// Pseudo C++ Code
void
normalize__7Point3dFv( register const Point3d *const this,
                       Point3d &__result )
{
    register float mag = this->magnitude();

    // __result substituted for return value
    __result.Point3d::Point3d(
        this->_x/mag, this->_y/mag, this->_z/mag );

    return;
}
```

This saves the overhead of the default constructor initialization that is then overwritten.

Name Mangling

In general, member names are made unique by concatenating the name of the member with that of the class. For example, given the declaration

```
class Bar { public: int ival; ... };
```

ival becomes something like

```
// a possible member name-mangling
ival__3Bar
```

Why does the compiler do that? Consider this derivation:

```
class Foo : public Bar { public: int ival; ... };
```

Remember that the internal representation of a Foo object is the concatenation of its base and derived class members:

```
// Pseudo C++ Code
// internal representation of Foo
class Foo { public:
    int ival__3Bar;
    int ival__3Foo;
    ...
};
```

Unambiguous access of either `ival` member is achieved through name mangling. Member functions, because they can be overloaded, require a more extensive mangling to provide each with a unique name. Transforming

```
class Point { public:
    void  x( float newX );
    float x();
    ...
};
```

into

```
class Point { public:
    void  x__5Point( float newX );
    float x__5Point();
    ...
};
```

ends up generating the same name for the two overloaded instances. What makes these instances unique are their argument lists (referred to as the function signature). Function names are made unique by internally encoding the signature types and concatenating those to the name (use of the **extern "C"** declaration suppresses mangling of nonmember functions). This yields a more workable transformation of our pair of `x()` member functions:

```
class Point { public:
    void  x__5PointFf( float newX );
    float x__5PointFv();
    ...
};
```

Having shown you a specific encoding scheme (that used within cfront), I now have to confess that there is currently no conformity of encoding schemes across compilers, although there is a periodic rise and fall of activity to arrive at an industry standard. However, although the details differ across implementations, name mangling itself is a necessary part of every C++ compiler.

By encoding the argument list with the function name, the compiler achieves a limited form of type checking across separately compiled modules. For example, if a print function was defined as

```
void print( const Point3d& ){ ... }
```

but was accidentally declared and invoked as

```
// oops: suppose to be const Point3d&
void print( const Point3d );
```

the unique name mangling of the two instances would cause any invocation of the incorrect instance to fail to be resolved at link time—sometimes optimistically referred to as *type-safe linkage*. I say "optimistically" because the process catches function signature errors only; a misdeclared return type still goes unnoticed.

In current compilation systems, "demangling" tools intercept and convert these names; the user remains blissfully unaware of the actual internal names. However, life was not always so accommodating for the user. With Release 1.1, our system was considerably less sophisticated. cfront always tucked away both names, and its error messages referenced the source level function name. Not so the linker, however; it echoed the internally mangled names handed to it.

I still remember the anguished and half-furious red-haired, freckled developer who late one afternoon staggered into my office demanding to know what cfront had done to his program. I was somewhat new to this kind of user interaction, so my first thought was to answer, "Nothing, of course. Well, nothing, that is, that isn't for your own good. Well, anyway, I don't know. Why don't you go ask Bjarne?" My second thought was to quietly ask him what the problem was. (Thus is a reputation made. :-))

"This," he nearly shouted, shoving a print-out of the compilation into my hand. An abomination, he implied: The link editor had reported an unresolved function:

```
_oppl_mat44rcmat44
```

or some such admittedly less-than-user-friendly mangling of a 4-x-4 matrix class addition operator:

```
mat44::operator+( const mat44& );
```

The programmer had declared and invoked this operator but had forgotten to define it. "Oh," he said. "Hmmm," he added. He then strongly suggested that in the future we not display the internal name to the user. Generally speaking, we've followed his advice.

Virtual Member Functions

If normalize() were a virtual member function, the call

```
ptr->normalize();
```

would be internally transformed into

```
( * ptr->vptr[ 1 ])( ptr );
```

where the following holds:

- vptr represents the internally generated virtual table pointer inserted within each object whose class declares or inherits one or more virtual functions. (In practice, its name is mangled. There may be multiple vptrs within a complex class derivation.)

- **1** is the index into the virtual table slot associated with normal-ize().

- ptr in its second occurrence represents the **this** pointer.

Similarly, if magnitude() were a virtual function, its invocation within normalize() would be transformed as follows:

```
// register float mag = magnitude();
register float mag = ( *this->vptr[ 2 ] )( this );
```

In this case, because Point3d::magnitude() is being invoked within Point3d::normalize() (which has already been resolved through the virtual mechanism), explicitly invoking the Point3d instance (and thereby suppressing the unnecessary reinvocation through the virtual mechanism) is more efficient:

```
// explicit invocation suppresses virtual mechanism
register float mag = Point3d::magnitude();
```

This is *significantly* more efficient if `magnitude()` is declared inline. The explicit invocation of a virtual function using the class scope operator is resolved in the same way as a nonstatic member function:

```
register float mag = magnitude__7Point3dFv( this );
```

Although it is semantically correct, it is unnecessary, given the call

```
// Point3d obj;
obj.normalize();
```

for the compiler to transform it internally into

```
// unnecessary internal transformation!
( * obj.vptr[ 1 ])( &obj );
```

Recall that objects do not support polymorphism (see Section 1.3). So the instance invoked through `obj` can only be the Point3d instance of `normalize()`. The invocation of a virtual function through a class object should always be resolved by your compiler as an ordinary nonstatic member function:

```
normalize__7Point3dFv( &obj );
```

An additional benefit of this optimization is that an inline instance of the virtual function can then be expanded, thus providing significant performance benefit.

Virtual functions, particularly their behavior under inheritance, are discussed in more detail in Section 4.2.

Static Member Functions

If `Point3d::normalize()` were a static member function, both its invocations

```
obj.normalize();
ptr->normalize();
```

would be internally transformed into "ordinary" nonmember function calls such as

```
// obj.normalize();
normalize__7Point3dSFv();
```

```
// ptr->normalize();
normalize__7Point3dSFv();
```

Prior to the introduction of static member functions, it was not uncommon to see the following admittedly bizarre idiom in the code of advanced users:[1]

```
(( Point3d* ) 0 )->object_count();
```

where `object_count()` does nothing more than return the `_object_count` static data member. How did this idiom evolve?

Before the introduction of static member functions, the language required all member functions to be invoked through an object of that class. In practice, the class object is necessary only when one or more nonstatic data members are directly accessed within the member function. The class object provides the **this** pointer value for the call. The **this** pointer binds the nonstatic class members accessed within the member function to the members contained within the object. If no member is directly accessed, there is, in effect, no need of the **this** pointer. There then is no need to invoke the member function with a class object. The language at the time, however, did not recognize this case.

This created an anomaly in terms of accessing static data members. If the designer of the class declared the static data member nonpublic, as is taught to be good style, then the designer would also have to provide one or more member functions for read and write access of the member. Thus, although one could access a static data member independent of a class object, invocation of its access member function(s) required that those functions be bound to an object of the class.

Access independent of a class object is particularly important when, as in the case of `object_count()`, the class designer wants to support the condition of there being no class objects. The programming solution is the peculiar idiom of casting 0 to a class pointer, thereby providing the unnecessary but required **this** pointer instance:

```
// internal transformation of call
object_count(( Point3d* ) 0 );
```

---

[1] Jonathan Shopiro, formerly of Bell Laboratories, was the first person I'm aware of to use this idiom and was the primary advocate of the introduction of static member functions into the language. The first *formal* presentation of static member functions occurred during a floundering talk I was giving at the Usenix C++ Conference Implementor's Workshop in 1988 on pointer-to-member functions. I had, perhaps not surprisingly, failed to convince Tom Cargill that multiple inheritance was not *too* complicated and somehow introduced Jonathan and his idea of static member functions. He thankfully leaped onto the podium and lectured us on his idea while I caught my wind. (In [STROUP94], Bjarne mentions first hearing a proposal for static member functions from Martion O'Riordan.)

The language solution was the introduction of static member functions within the official cfront Release 2.0. The primary characteristic of a static member function is that it is without a **this** pointer. The following secondary characteristics all derive from that primary one:

- It cannot directly access the nonstatic members of its class.

- It cannot be declared **const, volatile,** or **virtual**.

- It does not need to be invoked through an object of its class, although for convenience, it may.

The use of the member selection syntax is a notational convenience; it is transformed internally into a direct invocation:

```
if ( Point3d::object_count() > 1 ) ...
```

What if the class object is obtained as a side effect of some expression, such as a function call:

```
if ( foo().object_count() > 1 ) ...
```

The expression still needs to be evaluated:

```
// transformation to preserve side-effects
(void) foo();
if ( Point3d::object_count() > 1 ) ...
```

A static member function, of course, is also lifted out of the class declaration and given a suitably mangled name. For example,

```
unsigned int
Point3d::
object_count()
{
    return _object_count;
}
```

under cfront is transformed internally into

```
// internal transformaton under cfront
unsigned int
object_count__7Point3dSFv()
{
```

```
      return _object_count__7Point3d;
   }
```

where SFv indicates it is a static member function with an empty (**void**) argument list.

Taking the address of a static member function always yields the value of its location in memory, that is, its address. Because the static member function is without a **this** pointer, the type of its address value is not a pointer to class member function but the type of a nonmember pointer to function. That is,

```
   &Point3d::object_count();
```

yields a value of type

```
   unsigned int (*)();
```

not of type

```
   unsigned int ( Point3d::* )();
```

Static member functions, by being **this**-less and therefore of the same type as an equivalent nonmember function, also provide an unexpected solution to the problem of mixing C++ with the C-based X Window system with regard to the use of callback functions (see [YOUNG95] for a discussion). They have also been used to successfully interface C++ with C APIs for threading (see [SCHMIDT94a]).

4.2   Virtual Member Functions

We've already seen the general virtual function implementation model: the class-specific virtual table that contains the addresses of the set of active virtual functions for the class and the vptr that addresses that table inserted within each class object. In this section, I walk through a set of possible designs evolving to that model and then step through that model in detail under single, multiple, and virtual inheritance.

To support a virtual function mechanism, some form of runtime type resolution applied to polymorphic objects must be supported. That is, if we have the call

```
   ptr->z();
```

there needs to be some information associated with `ptr` available at runtime such that the appropriate instance of `z()` can be identified, found, and invoked.

Perhaps the most straightforward but costly solution is to add the required information to `ptr`. Under this strategy, a pointer (and, implicitly, a reference as well) holds two pieces of information:

1. The address of the object it refers to (this is what it holds now, of course)

2. Some encoding of the object's type or the address of a structure containing that information (this is what is needed to resolve the correct instance of `z()`)

The problem with this solution is two-fold. First, it adds significant space overhead to the use of pointers regardless of whether the program makes use of polymorphism. Second, it breaks link compatibility with C.

If this additional information cannot be placed within the pointer, a next logical place in which to store it is in the object itself. This localizes the storage to those objects that need it. But which objects actually need this information? Should we place the information within every aggregate that may potentially be inherited from? Perhaps. But consider the following C struct declaration:

```
struct date { int m, d, y; };
```

Strictly speaking, this meets the criterion. In practice, it will never have need of that information. Adding that information would bloat the C struct and again break link compatibility without providing any obvious compensatory benefits.

"Okay," you might say, "the additional runtime information should be added only when a class declaration explicitly uses the keyword **class**." Doing this retains language compatibility, but it is still a policy without smarts. For example, the following class declaration meets the new criterion:

```
class date { public: int m, d, y; };
```

But again, in practice, it doesn't need this information. Moreover, the following class declaration using the keyword **struct** fails to meet our new criterion, but it does have need of this information:

```
struct geom { public: virtual ~geom(); ... };
```

What we need is a better criterion—one that is based on the use of the class—and not simply on the presence or absence of the **class** or **struct** keywords (see Section 1.2). If the class intrinsically needs the information, it is there; if it does not, it is not there. Then when exactly is this information needed? Obviously, when some form of runtime polymorphic operation needs to be supported.

In C++, polymorphism "exhibits" itself as the potential addressing of a derived class object through a pointer or reference of a public base class. For example, given the declaration

```
Point *ptr;
```

we can assign `ptr` to address either a Point2d object

```
ptr = new Point2d;
```

or a Point3d object

```
ptr = new Point3d;
```

`ptr`'s polymorphism functions primarily as a transport mechanism by which we can carry the set of types publicly derived from it throughout our program. This form of polymorphic support can be characterized as *passive* and, except in the case of a virtual base class, is accomplished during compilation.

Polymorphism becomes *active* when the object being addressed is actually used. An invocation of a virtual function is one such use:

```
// familiar example of active polymorphism
ptr->z();
```

Until the introduction of runtime type identification (RTTI) into the language in 1993, the only support C++ provided for active polymorphism was the resolution of a virtual function call. With RTTI, the runtime query of a polymorphic pointer or reference is also supported (RTTI is discussed in detail in Section 7.3):

```
// second example of active polymorphism
if ( Point3d *p3d =
     dynamic_cast< Point3d * >( ptr ))
   return p3d->_z;
```

So the problem has been isolated to that of identifying the set of classes that exhibits polymorphism and that therefore requires additional runtime information. As we saw, the keywords **class** and **struct** by themselves don't help us. In the absence of introducing a new keyword—perhaps polymorphic—the only certain way of identifying a class intended to support polymorphism is the presence of one or more virtual functions. So the presence of at least one virtual function is the criterion for identifying those classes requiring additional runtime information.

The next obvious question is, what additional information, exactly, do we need to store? That is, if we have the call

```
ptr->z();
```

where z() is a virtual function, what information is needed to invoke the correct runtime instance of z()? We need to know

- the actual type of the object addressed by ptr. This allows us to choose the correct instance of z(); and

- the location of that instance of z() in order to invoke it.

A first implementation might be to add two members to each polymorphic class object:

1. A string or numeric representation of the type

2. A pointer to some table holding the runtime locations of the program's virtual functions

How might the table containing the virtual function addresses be constructed? In C++, the set of virtual functions capable of being invoked through an object of its class is known at compile time. Moreover, this set is invariant. It cannot be added to nor can a virtual instance be replaced at runtime. The table, therefore, serves only as a passive repository. Since neither its size nor its contents change during program execution, its construction and access can be completely handled by the compiler. No runtime intervention is necessary.

Having the address available at runtime, however, is only half the solution. The other half is finding the address. This is accomplished in two steps:

1. To find the table, an internally generated virtual table pointer is inserted within each class object.

2. To find the function's address, each virtual function is assigned a fixed index within the table.

This is all set up by the compiler. All that is left to do at runtime is invoke the function addressed within the particular virtual table slot.

The virtual table is generated on a per-class basis. Each table holds the addresses of all the virtual function instances "active" for objects of the table's associated class. These active functions consist of the following:

- An instance defined within the class, thus overriding a possible base class instance

- An instance inherited from the base class, should the derived class choose not to override it

- A pure_virtual_called() library instance that serves as both a placeholder for a pure virtual function and a runtime exception should the instance somehow be invoked

Each virtual function is assigned a fixed index in the virtual table. This index remains associated with the particular virtual function throughout the inheritance hierarchy. In our Point class hierarchy, for example,

```
class Point {
public:
    virtual ~Point();

    virtual Point& mult( float ) = 0;
    // ... other operations ...

    float x() const { return _x; }
    virtual float y() const { return 0; }
    virtual float z() const { return 0; }
    // ...

protected:
    Point( float x = 0.0 );
    float _x;
};
```

the virtual destructor is likely to be assigned slot 1 and mult() assigned slot 2. (In this case, there is no mult() definition, so the address of the library function pure_virtual_called() is placed within the slot. If that instance should by some accident get invoked, generally it would terminate the program.) y() is assigned slot 3 and z() slot 4. What slot is x() as-

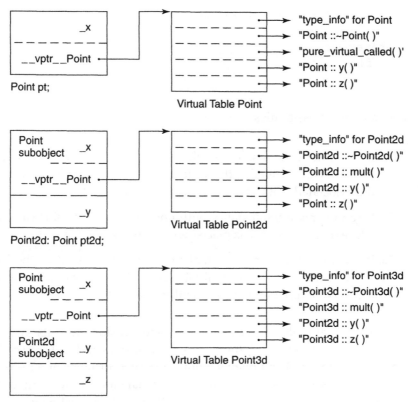

Figure 4.1 Virtual Table Layout: Single Inheritance

signed? None because it is not declared to be virtual. Figure 4.1 shows the class layout and virtual table of the Point class.

What happens when a class is subsequently derived from Point, such as class Point2d:

```
class Point2d : public Point {
public:
   Point2d( float x = 0.0, float y = 0.0 )
      : Point( x ), _y( y ) {}
   ~Point2d();

   // overridden base class virtual functions
   Point2d& mult( float );
   float y() const { return _y; }
```

```
   // ... other operations ...

protected:
   float _y;
};
```

There are three possibilities:

1. It can inherit the instance of the virtual function declared within the base class. Literally, the address of that instance is copied into the associated slot in the derived class's virtual table.

2. It can override the instance with one of its own. In this case, the address of its instance is placed within the associated slot.

3. It can introduce a new virtual function not present in the base class. In this case, the virtual table is grown by a slot and the address of the function is placed within that slot.

Point2d's virtual table addresses its destructor in slot 1 and its instance of mult() in slot 2 (replacing the pure virtual instance). It addresses its instance of y() in slot 3 and retains Point's inherited instance of z() in slot 4. Figure 4.1 also shows the class layout and virtual table of the Point2d class.

Similarly, a derivation of Point3d from Point2d looks as follows:

```
class Point3d: public Point2d {
public:
   Point3d( float x = 0.0,
            float y = 0.0, float z = 0.0 )
      : Point2d( x, y ), _z( z ) {}
   ~Point3d();

   // overridden base class virtual functions
   Point3d& mult( float );
   float z() const { return _z; }

   // ... other operations ...

protected:
   float _z;
};
```

generates a virtual table with Point3d's destructor in slot 1 and Point3d's instance of mult() in slot 2. It places Point2d's inherited instance of y() in slot 3 and Point3d's instance of z() in slot 4. Figure 4.1 shows the class layout and virtual table of the Point3d class.

So if we have the expression

```
ptr->z();
```

how do we know enough at compile time to set up the virtual function call?

- In general, we don't know the exact type of the object ptr addresses at each invocation of z(). We do know, however, that through ptr we can access the virtual table associated with the object's class.

- Although we again, in general, don't know which instance of z() to invoke, we know that each instance's address is contained in slot 4.

This information allows the compiler to internally transform the call into

```
( *ptr->vptr[ 4 ] )( ptr );
```

In this transformation, vptr represents the internally generated virtual table pointer inserted within each class object and 4 represents z()'s assigned slot within the virtual table associated with the Point hierarchy. The only thing we don't know until runtime is the address of which instance of z() is actually contained in slot 4.

Within a single inheritance hierarchy, the virtual function mechanism is well behaved; it is both efficient and easily modeled. Support for virtual functions under multiple and virtual inheritance is somewhat less well behaved.

Virtual Functions under MI

The complexity of virtual function support under multiple inheritance revolves around the second and subsequent base classes and the need to adjust the **this** pointer at runtime. With the following simple class hierarchy

```
// hierarchy to illustrate MI complications
// of virtual function support
```

```
class Base1 {
public:
    Base1();
    virtual ~Base1();
    virtual void speakClearly();
    virtual Base1 *clone() const;
protected:
    float data_Base1;
};

class Base2 {
public:
    Base2();
    virtual ~Base2();
    virtual void mumble();
    virtual Base2 *clone() const;
protected:
    float data_Base2;
};

class Derived : public Base1, public Base2 {
public:
    Derived();
    virtual ~Derived();
    virtual Derived *clone() const;
protected:
    float data_Derived;
};
```

all the complexity of virtual function support within the Derived class rests with the Base2 subobject. There are three primary cases that require support. These are represented in the example by (1) the virtual destructor, (2) the inherited Base2::mumble() instance, and (3) the set of clone() instances. I'll look at each in turn.

First, let's assign a Base2 pointer the address of a Derived class object allocated on the heap:

```
Base2 *pbase2 = new Derived;
```

The address of the new Derived object must be adjusted to address its Base2 subobject. The code to accomplish this is generated at compile time:

```
// transformation to support second base class
Derived *temp = new Derived;
Base2 *pbase2 = temp ? temp + sizeof( Base1 ) : 0;
```

Without this adjustment, any nonpolymorphic use of the pointer would fail, such as

```
// ok even if pbase2 assigned Derived object
pbase2->data_Base2;
```

When the programmer now wants to delete the object addressed by pbase2,

```
// must first invoke the correct virtual instance
// of the destructor, then apply operator delete
// pbase2 may require to be readjusted to address
// the beginning of the complete object
delete pbase2;
```

the pointer must be readjusted in order to again address the beginning of the Derived class object (presuming it still addresses the Derived class object). This offset addition, however, cannot directly be set up at compile time because the actual object that pbase2 addresses generally can be determined only at runtime.

The general rule is that the **this** pointer adjustment of a derived class virtual function invocation through a pointer (or reference) of a second or subsequent base class must be accomplished at runtime. That is, the size of the necessary offset and the code to add it to the **this** pointer must be tucked away somewhere by the compiler. The obvious first question is where?

Bjarne's original cfront solution was to augment the virtual table to hold the (possibly) necessary **this** pointer adjustment. Each virtual table slot, rather than simply being a pointer, became an aggregate containing both the possible offset and the address. The virtual function call changed from

```
( *pbase2->vptr[1])( pbase2 );
```

into

```
( *pbase2->vptr[1].faddr)
    ( pbase2 + pbase2->vptr[1].offset );
```

where faddr held the virtual function address and offset held the necessary **this** pointer adjustment.

The criticism of this solution is that it penalizes all virtual functions' invocations regardless of whether the offset adjustment is necessary, both in the cost of the extra access and addition of offset and in the increased size of each virtual table slot.

The more efficient solution is the use of a *thunk*. (When I first learned of the thunk, my professor jokingly told us that thunk is knuth spelled backwards and therefore he attributed the technique to Dr. Knuth.) First introduced in compiler technology, I believe, in support of ALGOL's unique pass-by-name semantics, the thunk is a small assembly stub that (a) adjusts the **this** pointer with the appropriate offset and then (b) jumps to the virtual function. For example, the thunk associated with the call of the Derived class destructor through a Base2 pointer might look as follows:

```
// Pseudo C++ code
pbase2_dtor_thunk:
    this += sizeof( base1 );
    Derived::~Derived( this );
```

(It is not that Bjarne was unaware of thunks. The problem is that a thunk is efficient only as an assembly code stub, not as a full-blown function call. Since cfront used C as its code generation language, it could not provide an efficient thunk implementation.)

The thunk implementation allows for the virtual table slot to remain a simple pointer, thereby removing any space overhead within the virtual table for the support of multiple inheritance. The address placed within each slot either directly addresses the virtual function or addresses an associated thunk, if an adjustment of the **this** pointer is necessary. This removes additional performance overhead on virtual functions that do not require **this** pointer adjustment. (This is believed to be the vast majority, although I have not seen any numbers.)

A second overhead of the **this** pointer adjustment is multiple entries for the same function depending on whether it is invoked through the derived (or leftmost base class) or through the second (or subsequent) base class. For example,

```
Base1 *pbase1 = new Derived;
Base2 *pbase2 = new Derived;

delete pbase1;
delete pbase2;
```

Although both delete invocations result in the execution of the same Derived class destructor, they require two unique virtual table entries:

1. `pbase1` does not require a **this** pointer adjustment (being left-most, it already points to the beginning of the Derived class object). Its virtual table slot requires the actual destructor address.

2. `pbase2` does require a **this** pointer adjustment. Its virtual table slot requires the address of the associated thunk.

Under multiple inheritance, a derived class contains $n - 1$ additional virtual tables, where n represents the number of its immediate base classes (thus single inheritance introduces zero additional tables). For the Derived class, then, two virtual tables are generated:

1. The primary instance shared with Base1, its leftmost base class

2. A secondary instance associated with Base2, the second base class

The Derived class object contains a vptr for each associated virtual table. (This is shown in Figure 4.2.) The vptrs are initialized within the constructor(s) through code generated by the compiler.

The traditional approach to supporting multiple virtual tables associated with a class is to generate each as an external object with a unique name. For example, the two tables associated with Derived are likely to be named

```
vtbl__Derived; // the primary table
vtbl__Base2__Derived; // the secondary table
```

Thus when a Base1 or Derived pointer is assigned the address of a Derived class object, the virtual table being accessed is the primary virtual table `vtbl__Derived`. When a Base2 pointer is assigned the address of a Derived class object, the virtual table being accessed is the second virtual table `vtbl__Base2__Derived`.

With the advent of runtime linkers in support of dynamic shared libraries, the linking of symbolic names can be extremely slow—up to 1 ms per name, for example, on a SparcStation 10. To better accommodate the performance of the runtime linker, the Sun compiler concatenates the multiple virtual tables into one. The pointers to the secondary virtual tables are generated by adding an offset to the name of the primary table. Under this strategy, each class has only one named virtual table. "For code used on a number of Sun projects [the speedup] was quite noticeable."[2]

Earlier in the chapter I wrote that there are three cases in which the presence of a second or subsequent base class affects the support of virtual

---

[2] From correspondence with Mike Ball, architect of the Sun C++ compiler.

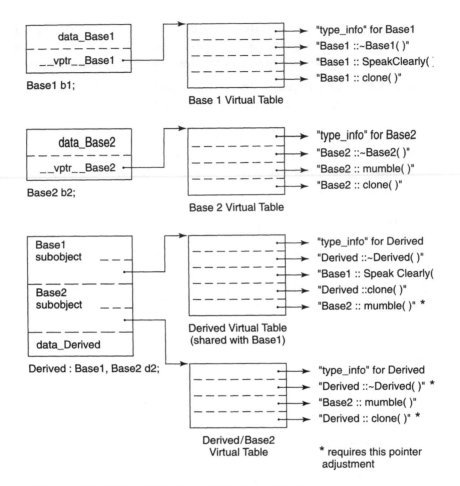

Figure 4.2   Virtual Table Layout: Multiple Inheritance

functions. In the first case, the derived class virtual function is invoked through a pointer of the second base class. For example,

```
Base2 *ptr = new Derived;

// invokes Derived::~Derived
// ptr must be adjusted backward by sizeof( Base1 )
delete ptr;
```

From Figure 4.2, you can see that at the point of the invocation, `ptr` addresses the Base2 subobject within the Derived class object. For this to execute correctly, `ptr` must be adjusted to address the beginning of the Derived class object.

The second case is a variant of the first and involves the invocation of an inherited virtual function of the second base class through a pointer of the derived class. In this case, the derived class pointer must be readjusted to address the second base subobject. For example,

```
Derived *pder = new Derived;

// invokes Base2::mumble()
// pder must be adjusted forward by sizeof( Base1 )
pder->mumble();
```

The third case fell out of a language extension that allows the return type of a virtual function to vary with regard to the base and publicly derived types of an inheritance hierarchy. This is illustrated by the Derived::clone() instance. The Derived instance of clone() returns a Derived class pointer but still overrides its two base class instances of clone(). The **this** pointer offset problem occurs when invoking clone() through a pointer of a second base class:

```
Base2 *pb1 = new Derived;

// invokes Derived* Derived::clone()
// return must be adjusted to address Base2 subobject
Base2 *pb2 = pb1->clone();
```

The Derived class instance of clone() is invoked and uses the thunk to readjust pb1 to address the beginning of the Derived class object. Now clone() returns a pointer to a new Derived class object, and the address must be adjusted to point to the Base2 subobject before being assigned to pb2.

The Sun compiler has implemented a strategy of "split functions" when the functions are deemed "small": Two functions are generated with the same algorithmic code. The second instance, however, adds the necessary offset to the pointer before returning it. Thus an invocation through either a Base1 or Derived pointer invokes the instance without the return adjustment, while an invocation through a Base2 pointer invokes the other instance.

When the functions are deemed "not small," the split function strategy gives way to one of multiple exit points within the function. Mike Ball estimates that this solution costs about three instructions per exit. Programmers not experienced with the OO paradigm might question the applicability of the split function, since it is limited to small functions. OO programming, however, promotes a style of localizing operations in many small virtual functions, often on the average of eight lines each.[3]

Function support for multiple entry points can eliminate the generation of many thunks. IBM, for example, is folding the thunk into the actual virtual function being invoked. The **this** pointer adjustment is executed at the top of the function; execution then falls through to the user portion of the code. Invocations not requiring the adjustment enter below that code.

Microsoft has patented a thunk elimination strategy based on what it calls "address points." The overriding function is set up to expect the address not of the derived class but of the class introducing the virtual function. This is the address point for the function (see [MICRO92] for a full discussion).

Virtual Functions under Virtual Inheritance

Consider the following virtual base class derivation of Point3d from Point2d:

```
class Point2d {
public:
   Point2d( float = 0.0, float = 0.0 );
   virtual ~Point2d();

   virtual void mumble();
   virtual float z();
   // ...
protected:
   float _x, _y;
};

class Point3d : public virtual Point2d{
public:
   Point3d( float = 0.0, float = 0.0, float = 0.0 );
   ~Point3d();

   float z();
protected:
   float _z;
};
```

Although Point3d has a single leftmost base class—Point2d—the beginning of Point3d and Point2d is no longer coincident (as they are under nonvir-

---

[3] An average length of eight lines for a virtual function is something I read somewhere—of course I've lost the citation. This conforms to my own experience, however.

tual single inheritance). This is shown in Figure 4.3. Since the Point2d and Point3d objects are no longer coincident, conversion between the two also requires a **this** pointer adjustment. Efforts to eliminate thunks under virtual inheritance in general have proved much more difficult.

Virtual base class support wanders off into the Byzantine when a virtual base class is derived from another virtual base class and support both virtual functions and nonstatic data members. Although I have a folder full of examples worked out and more than one algorithm for determining the proper offsets and adjustments, the material is simply too esoteric to warrant discussion in this text. My recommendation is not to declare nonstatic data members within a virtual base class. Doing that goes a long way in taming the complexity.

4.3 Function Efficiency

In the following set of tests, the cross-product of two three-dimensional points is calculated, in turn, as a nonmember friend function, a member function, an inline member function, and a virtual member function. The

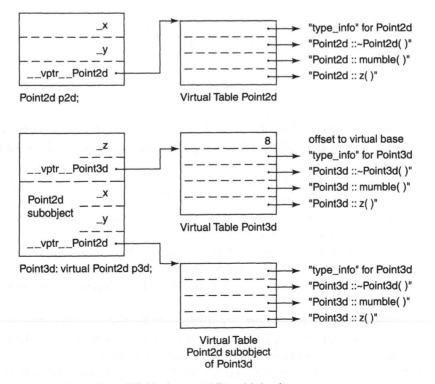

Figure 4.3 Virtual Table Layout: Virtual Inheritance

virtual member function instance is then executed under single, multiple, and virtual inheritances. Here is the cross-product implementation dressed up as a nonmember:

```
void
cross_product( const pt3d &pA, const pt3d &pB )
{
    pt3d pC;

    pC.x = pA.y * pB.z - pA.z * pB.y;
    pC.y = pA.z * pB.x - pA.x * pB.z;
    pC.z = pA.x * pB.y - pA.y * pB.x;
}
```

The main() function looks as follows (in this example invoking the cross-product as a nonmember function):

```
main() {
    pt3d pA( 1.725, 0.875, 0.478 );
    pt3d pB( 0.315, 0.317, 0.838 );

    for ( int iters = 0; iters < 10000000; iters++ )
            cross_product( pA, pB );

    return 0;
}
```

with the actual invocation of cross_product() varying as its representation alters across the different test programs. Table 4.1 shows the result of executing the test.

As the discussion in Section 4.2 shows, a nonmember, static member, and nonstatic member function are internally transformed into equivalent representations. So it's not surprising to see that there is no difference in performance between these three forms.

Nor is it surprising to see an approximately 25% performance speedup in the non-optimized inline version. The results of the optimized inline version, on the other hand, seems to border on the miraculous. What is going on?

The spectacular results are accounted for by the expressions—recognized as invariant—being hoisted out of the loop and therefore calculated only once. As this example illustrates, inline expansion not only saves the overhead associated with a function call but also provides additional opportunities for program optimization.

Table 4.1 Function Performance

	Optimized	Non-optimized
Inline Member	0.08	4.70
Nonmember Friend	4.43	6.13
Static Member	4.43	6.13
Nonstatic Member	4.43	6.13
Virtual Member		
CC	4.76	6.90
NCC	4.63	7.72
Virtual Member: Multiple Inheritance		
CC	4.90	7.06
NCC	4.96	8.00
Virtual Member: Virtual Inheritance		
CC	5.20	7.07
NCC	5.44	8.08

The virtual function instance was invoked through a reference rather than an object in order to make sure the invocation went through the virtual mechanism. The slowdown in performance varies from 4% to 11%. Some of the cost is reflected in the increased overhead of the Point3d constructor in setting the internal vptr 10 million times. Additional cost is accounted for by the fact that both CC and NCC (at least in NCC's cfront-compatible mode) use the delta-offset model to support virtual functions.

Recall that under this model, the offset required to adjust the **this** pointer to the proper address is stored within the virtual table. All invocations of the form

```
ptr->virt_func();
```

are transformed into a form like

```
// invocation of the virtual function
(*ptr->__vptr[ index ].addr)
   // passage of the adjusted this pointer
   ( ptr + ptr->__vptr[ index ].delta )
```

even though in most invocations, the stored value is 0 (only in the case of a second or subsequent base class or a virtual base class is the delta nonzero). Under this implementation, virtual invocation under both single and multiple inheritances share the same overhead. Under the thunk model, of course, the **this** pointer adjustment costs are localized to those calls requiring it.

The one puzzling result under these two implementations is the additional cost of the virtual function invocation under multiple inheritance. This is what one would expect by invoking a virtual function belonging to a second or subsequent base class with a compiler implementing the thunk model, but not with these two compilers. Because the **this** pointer adjustment is applied under both single and multiple inheritances, that overhead could not be accounting for the cost.

When I ran the tests under single inheritance, I was also puzzled to find that with each additional level of inheritance I added, the performance time of the virtual function executable increased significantly. At first, I couldn't imagine what was going on. Then, finally, after I stared at the code long enough, it dawned on me. The code within the main loop invoking the function is exactly the same regardless of the depth of the single inheritance hierarchy. Similarly, the manipulation of the coordinate values is exactly the same. The difference, which I had not earlier considered, is the presence of the local Point3d class object pC within cross_product(). In this implementation of cross_product(), the default Point3d constructor (no destructor is defined) is being applied a total of 10 million times. The increased cost of the executable with each additional level of single inheritance reflected the additional complexity of the constructor code being applied to pC. This also explained the additional overhead of the multiple inheritance call.

With the introduction of the virtual function, the class constructor is augmented to set the virtual table pointer within the constructor. Neither CC nor NCC optimize away the setting of the vptr in base class constructors in which there are no possible virtual function invocations, so each additional level of inheritance adds an additional setting of the vptr. In addition, in the CC and NCC versions the following test is inserted within the constructor for backward compatibility with pre-Release 2.0 versions of the language:

```
// invoked within each base & derived class constructor
if ( this || this = new( sizeof( *this )))
    // user code goes here
```

Prior to the introduction of class instances of operators **new** and **delete**, the only method of assuming memory management of the class was to assign to the **this** pointer within the constructor. The previous conditional test supports that. For cfront, backward compatibility for the semantics of "assignment to **this**" was promised until Release 4.0 (for various arcane reasons that are definitely *beneath* the scope of this text). Ironically, because NCC is distributed by SGI in "cfront compatibility mode," NCC also provides this backward compatibility. Except for backward compatibility, there is no longer any reason to include the conditional test within the constructor. Modern implementations separate invocation of operator **new** as an operation separate from the invocation of the constructor (Section 6.2), and the assignment to **this** semantics are no longer supported by the language.

Each additional base class or additional level of single inheritance under these implementations adds another (in this case totally unnecessary) test of the **this** pointer to the constructor. Execute the constructor 10 million times, and the performance slowdown becomes measurable. (This performance clearly reflects an implementation anomaly and not an aspect of the object model itself.)

In any case, I wanted to see if the additional expense of the constructor invocation was accounting for the additional performance time. I rewrote the function in two alternative styles that did away with the local object:

1. I added the object to hold the result as an additional argument to the function:

```
void
cross_product( pt3d &pC, const pt3d &pA, const pt3d &pB )
{
    pC.x = pA.y * pB.z - pA.z * pB.y;
    // the rest the same ...
}
```

2. I computed the result directly in the **this** object:

```
void
pt3d::
cross_product(const pt3d &pB )
{
    x = y * pB.z - z * pB.y;
    // the rest the same except that we use
    // the x, y, and z of this object ...

}
```

In both cases, this resulted in a uniform, average non-optimized execution time of 6.90 across the levels of single inheritance.

What's interesting is that the language does not provide a mechanism by which to indicate that an invocation of a default constructor is unnecessary and should be elided. That is, the declaration of the local pC class object does not in our use of it require a constructor to be applied, but we can eliminate its invocation only by eliminating our use of the local object.

4.4   Pointer-to-Member Functions

In Chapter 3, we saw that the value returned from taking the address of a nonstatic data member is the byte value of the member's position in the class layout (plus 1). One can think of it as an incomplete value. It needs to be bound to the address of a class object before an actual instance of the member can be accessed.

The value returned from taking the address of a nonstatic member function, if it is nonvirtual, is the actual address in memory where the text of the function is located. This value, however, is equally incomplete. It, too, needs to be bound to the address of a class object before an actual invocation of the member function is possible. The object's address serves as the **this** pointer argument required by all nonstatic member functions.

Recall that the syntax of declaring a pointer-to-member function is

```
double          // return type
( Point::*      // class the function is member
  pmf )         // name of pointer to member
();             // argument list
```

Thus one writes

```
double (Point::*coord)() = &Point::x;
```

to define and initialize a pointer to class member and writes

```
coord = &Point::y;
```

to assign a value to it. Invocation uses the pointer-to-member selection operators, either

```
( origin.*coord )();
```

or

```
( ptr->*coord )();
```

These are converted internally by the compiler to, respectively,

```
// Pseudo C++ Code
( *coord )( & origin );
```

and

```
// Pseudo C++ Code
( *coord )( ptr );
```

The pointer-to-member function declaration syntax and pointer-to-member selection operators serves literally as placeholders for the **this** pointer. (This is why static member functions, which are without a **this** pointer, are of type "pointer to function," not "pointer-to-member function.")

Use of a pointer to member would be no more expensive than a non-member pointer to function if it weren't for virtual functions and multiple inheritance (including, of course, virtual base classes), which complicate both the type and invocation of a pointer to member. In practice, for those classes without virtual functions or virtual or multiple base classes, the compiler can provide equivalent performance. In the next section, I look at how support for virtual functions complicates support for pointer-to-member functions.

Supporting Pointer-to-Virtual-Member Functions

Consider the following code fragment:

```
float (Point::*pmf)() = &Point::z;
Point *ptr = new Point3d;
```

pmf, a pointer to member, is initialized to address the virtual function point::z(). ptr is initialized to address an object of type Point3d. If we invoke z() directly through ptr:

```
ptr->z();
```

the instance invoked is Point3d::z(). What happens if we invoke z() indirectly through pmf:

```
( ptr->*pmf)();
```

Is `Point3d::z()` still invoked? That is, does the virtual mechanism work using pointer-to-member functions? The answer, of course, is yes. The question is how?

In the previous section, we saw that taking the address of a nonstatic member function yielded its address in memory. With regard to a virtual function, however, that address is unknown at compile time. What is known is the function's associated index into the virtual table. That is, taking the address of a virtual member function yields its index into its class's associated virtual table.

For example, if we have the following simplified declaration of Point:

```
class Point
{
public:
    virtual ~Point();
    float x();
    float y();
    virtual float z();
    // ...
};
```

then taking the address of the destructor

```
&Point::~Point; //Pseudo C++
```

yields 1. Taking the address of either `x()` or `y()`

```
&Point::x;
&Point::y;
```

yields their actual memory locations, since they are not virtual. Taking the address of `z()`

```
&Point::z;
```

yields 2. The invocation of `z()` through `pmf`, then, becomes translated internally into a compile-time expression of the following general form:

```
( * ptr->vptr[ (int)pmf ])( ptr );
```

Evaluation of a pointer-to-member function is complicated by the dual values it can hold and by the very different invocation strategies those values require. The internal definition of `pmf`, that is,

```
float (pointer::*pmf)();
```

must permit the function to address both the nonvirtual x() and the virtual z() member function. They both have the same function prototype:

```
// both can be assigned to pmf
float point::x(){ return _x; }
float point::z(){ return 0; }
```

although one yields an address in memory (a large number) and the other an index into the virtual table (a small number). Internally, the compiler must define pmf such that (a) it can hold both values and (b) more important, the type of the value can be distinguished. Any ideas?

In the pre-Release 2.0 cfront implementation, both values were contained in an ordinary pointer. How did cfront distinguish between an actual memory address and an index into the virtual table? It used the following trick:

```
((( int ) pmf ) & ~127 )
    ? // non-virtual invocation
    ( *pmf )( ptr )

    : // virtual invocation
    ( * ptr->vptr[ (int) pmf ]( ptr );
```

As Stroustrup wrote [LIPP88]:

> Of course, this implementation assumes a limit of 128 virtual functions to an inheritance graph. This is not desirable, but in practice it has proved viable. The introduction of multiple inheritance, however, requires a more general implementation scheme and provides an opportunity to remove the limit on the number of virtual functions.

Pointer-to-Member Functions under MI

For pointers to members to support both multiple and virtual inheritances, Stroustrup designed the following aggregate structure (see [LIPP88] for the original presentation):

```
// fully general structure to support
// pointer to member functions under MI
```

```
struct __mptr {
   int delta;
   int index;
   union {
       ptrtofunc  faddr;
       int        v_offset;
   };
};
```

What do these members represent? The index and faddr members, respectively, hold either the virtual table index or the nonvirtual member function address. (By convention, index is set to –1 if it does not index into the virtual table.) Under this model, an invocation such as

```
( ptr->*pmf )()
```

becomes

```
( pmf.index < 0 )
   ? // non-virtual invocation
   ( *pmf.faddr )( ptr )

   : // virtual invocation
   ( * ptr->vptr[ pmf.index ]( ptr );
```

One criticism of this approach is that every invocation is charged with the cost of checking whether the call is virtual or nonvirtual. Microsoft removed this check (and therefore the presence of the index member) by introducing what it terms a *vcall thunk*. Under this strategy, faddr is assigned either the actual member function address—if the function is nonvirtual—or the address of the vcall thunk. Invocation of both virtual and nonvirtual instances are transparent; the vcall thunk extracts and invokes the appropriate slot of the associated virtual table.

A second side effect of this aggregate representation is the need to generate a temporary object when passing a literal pointer to member. For example, if we have the following:

```
extern Point3d foo( const Point3d&, Point3d (Point3d::*)() );
void bar( const Point3d& p ) {
   Point3d pt = foo( p, &Point3d::normal );
   // ...
}
```

the value of the expression

```
&Point3d::normal
```

is something like

```
{ 0, -1, 10727417 }
```

and requires the generation of a temporary object initialized with the explicit values

```
// Pseudo C++ code
__mptr temp = { 0, -1, 10727417 };

foo( p, temp );
```

The `delta` member represents the **this** pointer offset, while the `v_offset` member holds the location of the vptr of a virtual (or second or subsequent) base class. (If the vptr is placed at the beginning of the class object, this field becomes unnecessary. The trade off is in decreased C object compatibility. See Section 3.4.) Both of these members are necessary only in the presence of either multiple or virtual inheritance, and so many compilers provide multiple internal pointer-to-member representations based on the characteristics of the class. Microsoft, for example, provides three flavors:

1. A single inheritance instance (which simply holds either the vcall thunk or function address)

2. A multiple inheritance instance (which holds the `faddr` and `delta` members)

3. A virtual inheritance instance (which holds four members!)

Pointer-to-Member Efficiency

In the following set of tests, the cross-product function is invoked indirectly in turn through a pointer to a nonmember function, a pointer to a class member function, a pointer to a virtual member function, and then as a set of calls to nonvirtual and virtual member functions of multiple inheritance and virtual inheritance hierarchies. In the first test, a pointer to a nonmember cross-product implementation is executed by using the following `main()` function:

```
main() {
    pt3d pA( 1.725, 0.875, 0.478 );
    pt3d pB( 0.315, 0.317, 0.838 );
    pt3d* ( *pf )( const pt3d&, const pt3d& ) =
        cross_product;

    for ( int iters = 0; iters < 10000000; iters++ )
        ( *pf)( pA, pB );

    return 0;
}
```

where the declaration and invocation of the pointer-to-class member looks as follows:

```
pt3d* (pt3d::*pmf)(const pt3d& ) const =
        &pt3d::cross_product;

for ( int iters = 0; iters < 10000000; iters++ )
            (pA.*pmf)( pB );
```

The support of pointer-to-class member functions under both CC and NCC takes the following internal form. The call

```
(*pA.pmf)( pB );
```

becomes transformed into the general conditional test

```
pmf.index < 0
    ? ( *pmf.faddr )( &pA + pmf.delta, pB
    : ( *pA.__vptr__pt3d[ pmf.index].faddr )( &pA +
        pA.__vptr_pt3d[pmf.index].delta, pB)
```

Recall that a pointer-to-member is a structure holding three members: index, faddr, and delta. index either holds an index into the virtual function table or is set to -1 to indicate the member function is nonvirtual. faddr holds the nonvirtual member function's address. delta holds a possible **this** pointer adjustment. Table 4.2 shows the result of executing the test.

Table 4.2 Pointer to Function Performance

	Optimized	Non-optimized
Pointer-to-Nonmember Function (void (*p)(...))		
	4.30	6.12
Pointer-to-Member Function (PToM): Non-Virtual		
CC	4.30	6.38
NCC	4.89	7.65
PToM: Multiple Inheritance: Nonvirtual		
CC	4.30	6.32
NCC	5.25	8.00
PToM: Virtual Inheritance: Nonvirtual		
CC	4.70	6.84
NCC	5.31	8.07
Pointer-to-Member Function (PToM): Virtual		
CC	4.70	7.39
NCC	5.64	8.40
PToM: Multiple Inheritance: Virtual		
(Note: CC generated bad code that Segment Faulted)		
NCC	5.90	8.72
PToM: Virtual Inheritance: Virtual		
(Note: CC generated bad code that Segment Faulted)		
NCC	5.84	8.80

4.5 Inline Functions

Here is a possible implementation of the addition operator for our Point class:

```
class Point {
    friend Point
        operator+( const Point&, const Point& );
    ...
};
```

```
Point
operator+( const Point &lhs, const Point &rhs )
{
    point new_pt;

    new_pt._x = lhs._x + rhs._x;
    new_pt._y = lhs._y + rhs._y;

    return new_pt;
}
```

In theory, a cleaner implementation would make use of the inline set and get public access functions:

```
// void Point::x( float new_x ) { _x = new_x; }
// float Point::x() { return _x; }

new_pt.x( lhs.x() + rhs.x() );
```

By restricting direct access to the _x data member to these two functions, we minimize the impact of any later change in the representation of the data member, for example, moving it up or down the inheritance hierarchy. By declaring these access functions inline, we maintain the performance efficiency of direct member access, while achieving the encapsulation of a function call. Moreover, the addition operator need no longer be declared a friend of Point.

In practice, however, we cannot force the inlining of any particular function, although a cfront customer once issued a high-priority modification request asking for the addition of a **must_inline** keyword. The **inline** keyword (or the definition of a member function (or friend) within a class declaration) is only a request. For the request to be honored, the compiler must believe it can "reasonably" expand the function in an arbitrary expression.

When I say the compiler believes it can "reasonably" expand an inline function, I mean that at some level the execution cost of the function is by some measure less than the overhead of the function call and return mechanism. cfront determines this by a complexity measure heuristic, usually by counting the number of assignments, the number of function calls, the number of virtual function calls, and so on. Each category of expression is weighted, and the complexity of the inline function is determined as a sum of its operations. Obviously, the values assigned to the complexity measure are open to debate.

In general, there are two phases to the handling of an inline function:

1. The analysis of the function definition to determine the "intrinsic inline-ability" of the function (intrinsic in this context means unique to an implementation).

If the function is judged non-inlineable, due either to its complexity or its construction, it is turned into a static function and a definition is generated within the module being compiled. In an environment supporting separately compiled modules, there is little alternative for the compiler. Ideally, a linker cleans up the multiple instances generated. In general, however, current linkers doing this do not clean up any debugging information also generated with the call. This can be done via the UNIX **strip** command.

2. The actual inline expansion of the function at a point of call. This involves argument evaluation and management of temporaries.

It is at this point of expansion that an implementation determines whether an individual call is non-inlineable. In cfront, for example, a second or subsequent invocation of the same inline function within a single expression, such as our theoretically improved use of the Point class access functions

```
new_pt.x( lhs.x() + rhs.x() );
```

is not expanded. That is, under cfront, this expression becomes

```
// Pseudo C++ code suggesting inline expansion
new_pt._x = lhs._x + x__5PointFV( &rhs );
```

which is not at all an improvement! All we can do at this point is rewrite the expression to work around a timid inline implementation:

```
// yuck:   fix the inline support  :-(
new_pt.x( lhs._x + rhs._x );
```

The comment, of course, is necessary to let future readers of our code know that we considered using the public inline interface and had to back off!

Are other compilers as restricted as cfront in handling inline expansion? No. However, compiler vendors en mass (that is, both on the UNIX and PC side) unfortunately seem to consider it unnecessary to discuss in any detail the extent of or constraints on their inline support. In general, you have to poke around the assembler to see what has or hasn't been inlined.

Formal Arguments

What actually happens during an inline expansion? Each formal argument is replaced with its corresponding actual argument. If the actual argument exhibits a side effect, it cannot simply be plugged into each occurrence of the formal argument—that would result in multiple evaluations of the actual argument. In general, handling actual arguments that have side effects requires the introduction of a temporary object. If, on the other hand, the actual argument is a constant expression, we'd like it to be evaluated prior to its substitution; subsequent constant folding may also be performed. If it is neither a constant expression nor an expression with side effects, a straight substitution of each actual argument with the associated formal argument is carried out.

For example, say we have the following simple inline function:

```
inline int
min( int i, int j )
{
    return i < j ? i : j;
}
```

and the following three invocations of the inline function:

```
inline int
foobar()
{
    int minval;
    int val1 = 1024;
    int val2 = 2048;

/*(1)*/minval = min( val1, val2 );
/*(2)*/minval = min( 1024, 2048 );
/*(3)*/minval = min( foo(), bar()+1 );

    return minval;
}
```

The inline expansion of the line marked (1) is a straightforward substitution:

```
//(1)      simple argument substitution
minval = val1 < val2 ? val1 : val2;
```

while the inline expansion of the line marked (2) involves constant folding:

```
// (2)        constant folding following substitution
minval = 1024;
```

Finally, the inline expansion of the line marked (3) involves argument side effects and the introduction of a temporary object in order to avoid multiple evaluations:

```
// (3)        side-effects and introduction of temporary
int t1;
int t2;

minval =
    ( t1 = foo() ), ( t2 = bar() + 1 ),
    t1 < t2 ? t1 : t2;
```

Local Variables

What if we change the definition slightly, adding a local variable to the inline definition:

```
inline int
min( int i, int j )
{
    int minval = i < j ? i : j;
    return minval;
}
```

What support or special handling does the local variable require? For example, if we have the following call of min() :

```
{
    int local_var;
    int minval;

    // ...
    minval = min( val1, val2 );
}
```

an expansion that maintained the local variable might look something like the following (in theory, in this example the local inline variable can be optimized out and the value directly computed on minval):

```
{
    int local_var;
    int minval;
```

```
// mangled inline local variable
int __min_lv_minval;

minval =
    ( __min_lv_minval =
        val1 < val2 ? val1 : val2 ),
      __min_lv_minval;
{
```

In general, each local variable within the inline function must be introduced into the enclosing block of the call as a uniquely named variable. If the inline function is expanded multiple times within one expression, each expansion is likely to require its own set of the local variables. If the inline function is expanded multiple times in discrete statements, however, a single set of the local variables can probably be reused across the multiple expansions.

The combination of local variables within an inline function together with arguments to the call with side effects can result in a surprising number of internally generated temporaries within the site of the expansion, particularly if it is expanded multiple times within a single expression. For example, the following call

```
minval = min( val1, val2 ) + min( foo(), foo()+1 );
```

might be expanded as follows:

```
// generated temps for local variable
int __min_lv_minval__00;
int __min_lv_minval__01;

// generated temps to hold side-effects
int t1;
int t2;

minval =
    (( __min_lv_minval__00 =
        val1 < val2 ? val1 : val2 ),
      __min_lv_minval__00 )
    +
    (( __min_lv_minval__01 = ( t1 = foo() ),
       ( t2 = foo() + 1 ),
       t1 < t2 ? t1 : t2 ),
      __min_lv_minval__01 );
```

Inline functions provide a necessary support for information hiding by providing efficient access to nonpublic data encapsulated within a class. They

are also a safe alternative to the **#define** preprocessor macro expansion re-
lied on so heavily in C. (This is particularly true if the arguments to the
macro contain side effects.) However, an inline expansion, if invoked
enough times within a program, can generate a great deal more text than
may at first seem obvious from its definition and so result in unsuspected
"code bloat."

As I've demonstrated, arguments with side effects, multiple calls within
a single expression, and multiple local variables within the inline itself can
all create temporaries that the compiler may or may not be able to remove.
Also, the expansion of inlines within inlines can cause a seemingly trivial
inline to not be expanded due to its "concatenated complexity." This may
occur in constructors for complex class hierarchies or in a chain of seemingly innocent inline calls within an object hierarchy, each of which executes
a small set of operations and then dispatches a request to another object.
Inline functions provide a powerful tool in the production of safe but efficient programs. They do, however, require more attention than their equivalent non-inline instances.

Chapter 5

Semantics of Construction, Destruction, and Copy

Consider the following abstract base class declaration:

```
class Abstract_base {
public:
   virtual ~Abstract_base() = 0;
   virtual void interface() const = 0;
   virtual const char*
      mumble () const { return _mumble; }
protected:
   char *_mumble;
};
```

Do you see any problems? Although the class is designed to serve as an abstract base class (the presence of a pure virtual function disallows independent instances of Abstract_base to be created), the class still requires an explicit constructor in order to initialize its one data member, _mumble. Without that initialization, a local object of a class derived from Abstract_base will have its instance of _mumble uninitialized. For example:

```
class Concrete_derived : public Abstract_base {
public:
   Concrete_derived();
   // ...
};
```

```
void foo()
{
    // Abstract_base::_mumble uninitialized
    Concrete_derived trouble;
    // ...
}
```

One might argue that the designer of Abstract_base intended for each class derived from it to provide a first value for _mumble. However, if that's the case, the only way to require that of the derived class is to provide a protected Abstract_base constructor that takes one argument:

```
Abstract_base::
Abstract_base( char *mumble_value = 0 )
    : _mumble( mumble_value )
    {}
```

In general, the data members of a class should be initialized and assigned to only within the constructor and other member functions of that class. To do otherwise breaks encapsulation, thereby making maintenance and modification of the class more difficult.

Alternatively, one might argue that the design error is not the absence of an explicit constructor, but rather the declaration of a data member within an abstract base class. This is a stronger argument (separating interface and implementation), but it does not hold universally. Lifting up data members shared among several derived types can be a legitimate design choice.

Presence of a Pure Virtual Destructor

Programmers new to C++ are often surprised to learn that one may both define *and* invoke a pure virtual function, provided it is invoked statically and not through the virtual mechanism. For example, one can legally code the following:

```
// ok:  definition of pure virtual function
//      but may only be invoked statically ...

inline void
Abstract_base::interface()
{
    // ...
}
```

```
inline void
Concrete_derived::interface()
{
    // ok: static invocation
    Abstract_base::interface();

    // ...
}
```

Whether one does so is a decision left to the class designer in all but one instance. The exception is a pure virtual destructor: It must be defined by the class designer. Why? Every derived class destructor is internally augmented to statically invoke each of its virtual base and immediate base class destructors. The absence of a definition of any of the base class destructors in general results in a link-time error.

One could argue, shouldn't the invocation of a pure virtual destructor be suppressed by the compiler during the augmentation of the destructor of the derived class? No. The class designer may actually have defined an instance of the pure virtual destructor (just as `Abstract_base::interface()` is defined in the previous example). The design itself may depend on the language's guarantee that each destructor within the hierarchy of a class object is invoked. The compiler cannot suppress the call.

But one then could argue, shouldn't the compiler know enough to synthesize the definition of the pure virtual destructor if the designer of the class either forgot or did not know it needed to be defined? No. The compiler by itself can't know that because of the separate compilation model of an executable. An environment may provide a facility to discover the absence at link time and to reinvoke the compiler with a directive to synthesize an instance, but I am not aware of any current implementation that does so.

A better design alternative is to not declare a virtual destructor as pure.

Presence of a Virtual Specification

`Abstract_base::mumble()` is a bad choice for a virtual function because its algorithm is not type dependent and is therefore highly unlikely to be overridden by a subsequent derived class. Moreover, because its nonvirtual implementation is inline, the performance penalty may be significant if it is frequently invoked.

However, couldn't a compiler, through analysis, determine that only a single instance of the function exists within the class hierarchy. In so doing, could it not transform the call into a static invocation, thereby allowing for the inline expansion of the call? But what happens if the hierarchy is subsequently added to and the new class introduces a new instance of the function? This new class invalidates the optimization. The function must now be recompiled (or perhaps a second, polymorphic instance generated, with the compiler determining through flow analysis which instance needs to be invoked). The function, however, may exist as a binary within a library. Unearthing this dependency is likely to require some form of persistent program database or library manager.

In general, it is still a bad design choice to declare all functions virtual and to depend on the compiler to optimize away unnecessary virtual invocations.

Presence of const within a Virtual Specification

Determining the **const**-ness of a virtual function may seem rather trivial, but in practice it is not easy to do within an abstract base class. Doing so means predicting the usage of a potentially infinite number of subclass implementations. Not declaring a function **const** means the function cannot be called by a **const** reference or **const** pointer argument—at least not without resorting to a casting away of the **const**. Considerably more problematic is declaring a function **const** and then discovering that, in practice, a derived instance really does need to modify a data member. I don't know of a generally agreed upon approach, but I can bear witness to the problem. In my code, I tend toward leaving off the **const**.

A Reconsidered Class Declaration

The previous discussion suggests that the following redeclaration of Abstract_base would seem the more appropriate design:

```
class Abstract_base {
public:
   virtual ~Abstract_base();
   virtual void interface() = 0;
   const char* mumble () const { return _mumble; }

protected:
   Abstract_base( char *pc = 0 );

   char *_mumble;
};
```

5.1 Object Construction without Inheritance

Consider the following generic program fragment:

```
(1)    Point global;
(2)
(3)    Point foobar()
(4)    {
(5)        Point local;
(6)        Point *heap = new Point;
(7)        *heap = local;
(8)        // ... stuff ...
(9)        delete heap;
(10)       return local;
(11)   }
```

Lines 1, 5, and 6 represent the three varieties of object creation: global, local, and heap memory allocation. Line 7 represents the assignment of one class object with another, while line 10 represents the initialization of the return value with the local Point object. Line 9 explicitly deletes the heap object.

The lifetime of an object is a runtime attribute of an object. The local object's lifetime extends from its definition at line 5 through line 10. The global object's lifetime extends for the entire program execution. The lifetime of an object allocated on the heap extends from the point of its allocation using operator **new** through application of operator **delete**.

Here is a first declaration of Point, written as it might be in C. The Standard speaks of this Point declaration as *Plain Ol' Data*.

```
typedef struct
{
    float x, y, z;
} Point;
```

What happens when this declaration is compiled under C++? Conceptually, a trivial default constructor, trivial destructor, trivial copy constructor, and trivial copy assignment operator are internally declared for Point. In practice, all that happens is that the compiler has analyzed the declaration and tagged it to be Plain Ol' Data.

When the compiler encounters the definition

```
(1)    Point global;
```

then conceptually, the definition of both Point's trivial constructor and destructor are generated and invoked (the constructor at program startup and the destructor usually within the system-generated call to exit() upon completion of main()). In practice, however, these trivial members are neither defined nor invoked, and the program behaves exactly as it would in C.

Well, with one minor exception. In C, global is treated as a *tentative* definition because it is without explicit initialization. A tentative definition can occur multiple times within the program. Those multiple instances are collapsed by the link editor, and a single instance is placed within the portion of the program data segment reserved for uninitialized global objects (for historical reasons, it's called the BSS, an abbreviation of Block Started by Symbol, an IBM 704 assembler pseudo-op).

In C++, tentative definitions are not supported because of the implicit application of class constructors. (Admittedly the language could have distinguished between class objects and Plain Ol' Data, but doing so seemed an unnecessary complication.) global, therefore, is treated within C++ as a full definition (precluding a second or subsequent definition). One difference between C and C++, then, is the relative unimportance of the BSS data segment in C++. All global objects within C++ are treated as initialized.

The local Point object within foobar() on line 5 is similarly neither constructed nor destructed. Of course, leaving the local Point object uninitialized is a potential program bug if a first use depends on its being set, such as on line 7. The initialization of heap on Line 6

```
(6)        Point *heap = new Point;
```

is transformed into a call of the library instance of operator **new**

```
        Point *heap = __new( sizeof( Point ));
```

Again, there is no default constructor applied to the Point object returned by the call to operator **new**. The assignment to this object on the next line would solve this problem if local were properly initialized:

```
(7)        *heap = local;
```

This assignment should generate a compiler warning of the general form

```
warning, line 7: local is used before being initialized.
```

Conceptually, this assignment triggers the definition of the trivial copy assignment operator, which is then invoked to carry out the assignment.

Again, in practice, since the object is Plain Ol' Data, the assignment remains a bitwise copy exactly as it is in C. The deletion of heap on Line 9

```
(9)        delete heap;
```

is transformed into a call of the library instance of operator **delete**

```
    __delete( heap );
```

Again, conceptually, this triggers the generation of the trivial destructor for Point. But, as we've seen, the destructor, in practice, is neither generated nor invoked. Finally, the return of local by value conceptually triggers the definition of the trivial copy constructor, which is then invoked, and so on. In practice, the return remains a simple bitwise operation of Plain Ol' Data.

Abstract Data Type

The second declaration of Point provides full encapsulation of private data behind a public interface but does not provide any virtual function interface:

```
class Point {
public:
    Point( float x = 0.0, float y = 0.0, float z = 0.0 )
        : _x( x ), _y( y ), _z( z ) {}

    // no copy constructor, copy operator
    // or destructor defined ...

    // ...
private:
    float _x, _y, _z;
};
```

The size of an encapsulated Point class object remains unchanged: the three contiguous coordinate float members. Neither the private nor public access labels nor the member function declarations take up any space within the object.

We do not define either a copy constructor or copy operator for our Point class because the default bitwise semantics are sufficient. Nor do we provide a destructor; the default program management of memory is sufficient.

The definition of a global instance

```
Point global; // apply Point::Point( 0.0, 0.0, 0.0 );
```

now has the default constructor applied to it. Since global is defined at global scope, its initialization needs to be deferred until program startup (see Section 6.1 for a full discussion).

In the special case of initializing a class to *all* constant values, an explicit initialization list is slightly more efficient than the equivalent inline expansion of a constructor, even at local scope (although at local scope, this may seem slightly nonintuitive. You'll see some numbers on this in Section 5.4). For example, consider the following code fragment:

```
struct Point { float _x, _y, _z; };
void mumble(){
    Point local1 = { 1.0, 1.0, 1.0 };
    Point local2;

    // equivalent to an inline expansion
    // the explicit initialization is slightly faster
    local2._x = 1.0;
    local2._y = 1.0;
    local2._z = 1.0;
}
```

local1's initialization is slightly more efficient than that of local2's. This is because the values within the initialization list can be placed within local1's memory during placement of the function's activation record upon the program stack.

There are three drawbacks of an explicit initialization list:

1. It can be used only if all the class members are public.

2. It can specify only constant expressions (those able to be evaluated at compile time).

3. Because it is not applied automatically by the compiler, the likelihood of failure to initialize an object is significantly heightened.

As a result, can the use of an explicit initialization list provide a performance increase significant enough to compensate for its software engineering drawbacks? In general, no. In practice, however, it can make a

difference in certain special cases. For example, perhaps you are hand-build-
ing some large data structure, such as a color palette, or you are dumping
into program text large amounts of constant values, such as the control vertices and knot values of a complex geometric model created in a package
such as Alias or SoftImage. In these cases, an explicit initialization list performs better than an inline constructor, particularly for global objects.

At the compiler level, a possible optimization would be recognition of
inline constructors that simply provide a member-by-member assignment of
constant expressions. The compiler might then extract those values. It would
treat them the same as those supplied in an explicit initialization list, rather
than expanding the constructor as a sequence of assignment statements.

The definition of the local Point object

```
{
    Point local;
    // ...
}
```

is now followed by the inline expansion of the default Point constructor:

```
{
    // inline expansion of default constructor
    Point local;
    local._x = 0.0; local._y = 0.0; local._z = 0.0;
    // ...
}
```

The allocation of the Point object on the heap on line 6

```
(6)       Point *heap = new Point;
```

now includes a conditional invocation of the default Point constructor

```
// Pseudo C++ Code
Point *heap = __new( sizeof( Point ));
if ( heap != 0 )
   heap->Point::Point();
```

which is then inline expanded. The assignment of the local object to the object pointed to by heap

```
(7)       *heap = local;
```

remains a simple bitwise copy, as does the return of the local object by value:

```
(10)        return local;
```

The deletion of the object addressed by heap

```
(9)         delete heap;
```

does not result in a destructor call, since we did not explicitly provide an instance.

Conceptually, our Point class has an associated default copy constructor, copy operator, and destructor. These, however, are trivial and are not in practice actually generated by the compiler.

Preparing for Inheritance

Our third declaration of Point prepares for inheritance and the dynamic resolution of certain operations, in this case limited to access of the coordinate member, z:

```
class Point
public:
   Point( float x = 0.0, float y = 0.0 )
        : _x( x ), _y( y ) {}

   // no destructor, copy constructor, or
   // copy operator defined ...

   virtual float z();
   // ...
protected:
   float _x, _y;
};
```

We again do not define a copy constructor, copy operator, or destructor. All our members are stored by value and are therefore well behaved on a program level under the default semantics. (Some people would argue that the introduction of a virtual function should always be accompanied by the declaration of a virtual destructor. But doing that would buy us nothing in this case.)

The introduction of the virtual function triggers the addition of a virtual table pointer within each Point object. This provides us with the flexibility of a virtual interface, but at the cost of an additional word of storage per object. How significant is this? Clearly that depends on the application and general domain. In the 3D modeling domain, if you were to represent a complex geometric shape that has 60 NURB surfaces with 512 control vertices per surface, the 4-byte overhead per Point object would approach 200,000 bytes. This may or may not be significant. Whether it was would have to be weighed against the practical benefits of polymorphism in the design. What you want to avoid is becoming aware of the issue only after the implementation is complete.

In addition to the vptr added within each class object, the introduction of the virtual function causes the following compiler-driven augmentations to our Point class:

- The constructor we've defined has code added to it to initialize the virtual table pointer. This code has to be added after the invocation of any base class constructors but before execution of any user-supplied code. For example, here is a possible expansion of our Point constructor:

```
// Pseudo C++ Code: internal augmentation
Point*
Point::Point( Point *this,
              float x, float y )
{
    // set the object's virtual table pointer
    this->__vptr__Point = __vtbl__Point;

    // expand member initialization list
    this->_x = x;
    this->_y = y;

    // return this object ...
    return this;
}
```

- Both a copy constructor and a copy operator need to be synthesized, as their operations are now nontrivial. (The implicit de-

structor remains trivial and so is not synthesized.) A bitwise
operation might otherwise result in an invalid setting of the vptr
if a Point object is initialized or assigned with a derived class
object.

```
// Pseudo C++ Code:
// internal synthesis of copy constructor
inline Point*
Point::Point( Point *this, const Point &rhs )
{
    // set the object's virtual table pointer
    this->__vptr__Point = __vtbl__Point;

    // `bitblast' contiguous portion of rhs'
    // coordinates into this object or provide
    // a member by member assignment ...

    return this;
}
```

The compiler, in an optimization, may copy contiguous chunks of one
object into another rather than implement a strict memberwise assignment.
The Standard requires implementations to defer the actual synthesis of
these nontrivial members until an actual use is encountered.

As a convenience, I've reproduced foobar() here:

```
(1)    Point global;
(2)
(3)    Point foobar()
(4)    {
(5)        Point local;
(6)        Point *heap = new Point;
(7)        *heap = local;
(8)        // ... stuff ...
(9)        delete heap;
(10)       return local;
(11)   }
```

The initialization of global on line 1, the initialization of heap on line 6, and
the deletion of heap on line 9 remain exactly the same as for the earlier representation of Point. The memberwise assignment, however, of line 7

```
*heap = local;
```

is likely to trigger the actual synthesis of the copy assignment operator and an inline expansion of its invocation, substituting heap for the **this** pointer and local for the rhs argument.

The most dramatic impact on our program is the return of local by value on line 10. In the presence of the copy constructor, foobar() is likely to be transformed as follows (this is discussed in greater detail in Section 2.3):

```
// Pseudo C++ code: transformation of foobar()
// to support copy construction

void foobar( Point &__result )
{
    Point local;
    local.Point::Point( 0.0, 0.0 );

    // heap remains the same ...

    // application of copy constructor
    __result.Point::Point( local );

    // destruction of local object would go here
    // had Point defined a destructor:
    // local.Point::~Point();

    return;
}
```

And if the named return value (NRV) optimization is supported, the function is further transformed as follows:

```
// Pseudo C++ code: transformation of foobar()
// to support named return value optimization

void foobar( Point &__result )
{
    __result.Point::Point( 0.0, 0.0 );

    // heap remains the same ...

    return;
}
```

In general, if your design includes a number of functions requiring the definition and return of a local class object by value, such as arithmetic operations of the form

```
T operator+( const T&, const T& )
{
    T result;
    // ... actual work ...
    return result;
}
```

then it makes good sense to provide a copy constructor even if the default memberwise semantics are sufficient. Its presence triggers the application of the NRV optimization. Moreover, as I showed in the previous example, its application removes the need for invoking the copy constructor, since the results are being directly computed within the object to be returned.

5.2 Object Construction under Inheritance

When we define an object, such as

```
T object;
```

exactly what happens? If there is a constructor associated with T (either user supplied or synthesized by the compiler), it is invoked. That's obvious. What is sometimes less obvious is what the invocation of a constructor actually entails.

Constructors can contain a great deal of hidden program code because the compiler augments every constructor to a greater or lesser extent depending on the complexity of T's class hierarchy. The general sequence of compiler augmentations is as follows:

1. The data members initialized in the member initialization list have to be entered within the body of the constructor in the order of member declaration.

2. If a member class object is not present in the member initialization list but has an associated default constructor, that default constructor must be invoked.

3. Prior to that, if there is a virtual table pointer (or pointers) contained within the class object, it (they) must be initialized with the address of the appropriate virtual table(s).

4. Prior to that, all immediate base class constructors must be invoked in the order of base class declaration (the order within the member initialization list is not relevant).

- If the base class is listed within the member initialization list, the explicit arguments, if any, must be passed.

- If the base class is not listed within the member initialization list, the default constructor (or default memberwise copy constructor) must be invoked, if present.

- If the base class is a second or subsequent base class, the **this** pointer must be adjusted.

5. Prior to that, all virtual base class constructors must be invoked in a left-to-right, depth-first search of the inheritance hierarchy defined by the derived class.

- If the class is listed within the member initialization list, the explicit arguments, if any, must be passed. Otherwise, if there is a default constructor associated with the class, it must be invoked.

- In addition, the offset of each virtual base class subobject within the class must somehow be made accessible at runtime.

- These constructors, however, may be invoked if, and only if, the class object represents the "most-derived class." Some mechanism supporting this must be put into place.

In this section, I consider the augmentations necessary to constructors in order to support the language-guaranteed semantics of the class. I again illustrate the discussion with the help of a Point class. (I added a copy constructor, copy operator, and virtual destructor in order to illustrate the behavior of subsequent containing and derived classes in the presence of these functions.)

```
class Point {
public:
    Point( float x = 0.0, float y = 0.0 );
    Point( const Point& );
    Point& operator=( const Point& );

    virtual              ~Point();
    virtual float        z(){ return 0.0; }
    // ...
protected:
    float _x, _y;
};
```

Before I introduce and step through an inheritance hierarchy rooted in Point, I'll quickly look at the declaration and augmentation of a class Line, which is composed of a begin and end point:

```
class Line {
    Point _begin, _end;
public:
    Line( float=0.0, float=0.0, float=0.0, float=0.0 );
    Line( const Point&, const Point& );

    draw();
    // ...
};
```

Each explicit constructor is augmented to invoke the constructors of its two member class objects. For example, the user constructor

```
Line::Line( const Point &begin, const Point &end )
        : _end( end ), _begin( begin )
    {}
```

is internally augmented and transformed into

```
// Pseudo C++ Code: Line constructor augmentation
Line*
Line::Line( Line *this,
            const Point &begin, const Point &end )
{
    this->_begin.Point::Point( begin );
    this->_end.Point::Point( end );
    return this;
}
```

Since the Point class declares a copy constructor, a copy operator, and a destructor (virtual in this case), the implicit copy constructor, copy operator, and destructor for Line are nontrivial.

When the programmer writes

```
Line a;
```

the implicit Line destructor is synthesized. (If Line were derived from Point, the synthesized destructor would be virtual. However, because Line only contains Point objects, the synthesized Line destructor is nonvirtual).

Within it, the destructors for its two member class objects are invoked in the reverse order of their construction:

```
// Pseudo C++ Code: Line destructor synthesis
inline void
Line::~Line( Line *this )
{
    this->_end.Point::~Point();
    this->_begin.Point::~Point();
}
```

Of course, if the Point destructor is inline, each invocation is expanded at the point of call. Notice that although the Point destructor is virtual, its invocation within the containing class destructor is resolved statically.

Similarly, when the programmer writes

```
Line b = a;
```

the implicit Line copy constructor is synthesized as an inline public member.

Finally, when the programmer writes

```
a = b;
```

the implicit copy assignment operator is synthesized as an inline public member.

While poking around cfront recently, I noticed that when generating the copy operator, it does not condition the copy by a guard of the form

```
if ( this == &rhs ) return *this;
```

As a result, it applies redundant copying for expressions such as

```
Line *p1 = &a;
Line *p2 = &a;
*p1 = *p2;
```

This is not unique to cfront, I discovered; Borland also leaves off a guard, and I suspect this is true of most compilers. In the case of a compiler-synthesized copy operator, the duplication is safe but redundant, since no deallocation of resources is involved. Failure to check for an assignment to self in a user-supplied copy operator is a common pitfall of the beginner programmer; for example,

```
// User supplied copy assignment operator
// forgets to provide a guard against self-copy

String&
String::operator=( const String &rhs ) {
   // need guard here before deallocate resources
   delete [] str;
   str = new char[ strlen( rhs.str ) + 1 ];
   ...
}
```

Under the category of good intentions not acted upon, I had many times thought of adding a warning message to cfront for the case when, within a copy operator, the operator lacked a guard against self-copy but contained a **delete** operator upon one of its members. I still think a message warning of this would be useful to the programmer.

Virtual Inheritance

Consider the following virtual derivation from our Point class:

```
class Point3d : public virtual Point {
public:
   Point3d( float x = 0.0, float y = 0.0, float z = 0.0 )
         : Point( x, y ), _z( z ) {}
   Point3d( const Point3d& rhs )
         : Point( rhs ), _z( rhs._z ) {}
   ~Point3d();
   Point3d& operator=( const Point3d& );

   virtual float z(){ return _z; }
   // ...
protected:
   float _z;
};
```

The conventional constructor augmentation does not work due to the shared nature of the virtual base class:

```
// Pseudo C++ Code:
// Invalid Constructor Augmentation
Point3d*
Point3d::Point3d( Point3d *this,
         float x, float y, float z )
{
```

```
    this->Point::Point( x, y );
    this->__vptr__Point3d = __vtbl__Point3d;
    this->__vptr__Point3d__Point =
        __vtbl__Point3d__Point;
    this->_z = rhs._z;
    return this;
}
```

Do you see what's wrong with this augmentation of the Point3d constructor?

Consider the following three class derivations:

```
class Vertex    : virtual public Point { ... };
class Vertex3d : public Point3d, public Vertex { ... };
class PVertex   : public Vertex3d { ... };
```

The constructor for Vertex must also invoke the Point class constructor. However, when Point3d and Vertex are subobjects of Vertex3d, their invocations of the Point constructor must not occur; rather, Vertex3d, as the most-derived class, becomes responsible for initializing Point. In the subsequent PVertex derivation, it, not Vertex3d, is responsible for the initialization of the shared Point subobject.

The traditional strategy for supporting this sort of "now you initialize the virtual base class, now you don't" is to introduce an additional argument in the constructor(s) indicating whether the virtual base class constructor(s) should be invoked. The body of the constructor conditionally tests this argument and either does or does not invoke the associated virtual base class constructors. Here is this strategy of Point3d constructor augmentation:

```
// Pseudo C++ Code:
// Constructor Augmentation with Virtual Base class
Point3d*
Point3d::Point3d( Point3d *this, bool __most_derived,
        float x, float y, float z )
{
    if ( __most_derived != false )
        this->Point::Point( x, y);

    this->__vptr__Point3d = __vtbl__Point3d;
    this->__vptr__Point3d__Point =
        __vtbl__Point3d__Point;

    this->_z = rhs._z;
    return this;
}
```

Within a subsequently derived class, such as Vertex3d, the invocation of the Point3d and Vertex constructors always sets the __most_derived argument to false, thus suppressing the Point constructor invocation within both constructors.

```
// Pseudo C++ Code:
// Constructor Augmentation with Virtual Base class
Vertex3d*
Vertex3d::Vertex3d( Vertex3d *this, bool __most_derived,
        float x, float y, float z )
{
    if ( __most_derived != false )
           this->Point::Point( x, y);

    // invoke immediate base classes,
    // setting __most_derived to false

    this->Point3d::Point3d( false, x, y, z );
    this->Vertex::Vertex( false, x, y );

    // set vptrs
    // insert user code

    return this;
}
```

This strategy gets the semantics right. For example, when we define

```
Point3d origin;
```

the Point3d constructor correctly invokes its Point virtual base class subobject. When we define

```
Vertex3d cv;
```

the Vertex3d constructor correctly invokes the Point constructor. The Point3d and Vertex constructors do everything but that invocation. So, if the behavior is right, then what's wrong?

A number of us have noticed that the conditions under which the virtual base class constructors are invoked is well defined. They are invoked when a complete class object is being defined, such as origin; they are not invoked when the object serves as a subobject of an object of a subsequently derived class.

Leveraging this knowledge, we can generate better-performing constructors at the expense of generating more program text. Some newer implementations split each constructor into a complete object and a subobject instance. The complete object version unconditionally invokes the virtual base constructors, sets all vptrs, and so on. The subobject version does not invoke the virtual base class constructors, may possibly not set the vptrs, and so on. (I look at the issue of setting the vptr in the next section.) This splitting of the constructor should result in considerable program speed up. Unfortunately, I do not have access to a compiler that actually does this and so have no numbers to confirm this. (During the Foundation project, however, Rob Murray, out of frustration I suspect, hand-optimized cfront's C output to elide unnecessary conditional tests and the setting of the vptr. He reported a measurable speed up.)

The Semantics of the vptr Initialization

When we define a PVertex object, the order of constructor calls is

```
Point( x, y );
Point3d( x, y, z );
Vertex( x, y, z );
Vertex3d( x, y, z );
PVertex( x, y, z );
```

Assume each class within its hierarchy defines an instance of a virtual function size() that returns the size in bytes of the class. For example, if we were to write

```
PVertex pv;
Point3d p3d;

Point *pt = &pv;
```

the call

```
pt->size();
```

would return the size of the PVertex class and

```
pt = &p3d
pt->size();
```

would return the size of the Point3d class.

Further assume that each constructor within the class hierarchy contains an invocation of size(). For example,

```
Point3d::Point3d( float x, float y, float z )
    : _x( x ), _y( y ), _z( z )
{
    if ( spyOn )
        cerr << "within Point3d::Point3d()"
             << " size: " << size() << endl;
}
```

When we define our PVertex object, what should the outcome of the five constructor calls look like? Should each invocation of size() resolve to PVertex::size() (that's what we're constructing, after all)? Or should each invocation resolve to the associated size() instance of the class whose constructor is currently executing?

The language rule is that inside the Point3d constructor, the invocation of size() must resolve to the Point3d instance, not the PVertex instance. More generally, within the constructors (and destructor) of a class (in this case, our Point3d class), the invocation of a virtual function by the object under construction (in this case, our PVertex object) is limited to the virtual functions active within the class (that is, our Point3d class). This is necessary because of the class order of constructor invocation: Classes are built from the bottom up and then the inside out. As a result, the derived instance is not yet constructed while the base class constructor executes. The PVertex object is not a complete PVertex object until the completion of its constructor. While the Point3d constructor executes, only its Point3d subobject is yet constructed.

This means that as each of the PVertex base class constructors are invoked, the compilation system must guarantee that the appropriate instance of size() is invoked. How might that be done?

Were invocations limited to direct calls from within the constructor (or destructor), the solution would be reasonably straightforward: Simply resolve each call statically, never invoking the virtual mechanism. Within the Point3d constructor, for example, explicitly invoke Point3d::size().

What happens, however, if within size() a subsequent virtual function call occurs? In this case, that call too must resolve to the Point3d instance. In other cases, however, the call is genuinely virtual and must go through the virtual mechanism. That is, somehow we must "sensitize" the virtual mechanism itself to be aware of whether the call is originating from within a constructor.

One way we could do that, I suppose, is to set a flag from within the constructor (or destructor) saying essentially, "Hey, no, this time resolve the call statically." We could then generate conditional invocations based on the state of the flag.

This would work, although it feels both inelegant and inefficient—a good example of a hack. We could even cover ourselves with a program source comment such as

```
// yuck!!! fix the language semantics!
```

This solution feels more like a response to the failure of our first design strategy than a solution to the underlying problem, that is, the need to constrain the set of candidate virtual functions to be considered during execution of a constructor.

Consider for a moment what actually determines the virtual function set active for a class: the virtual table. How is that virtual table accessed and thus the active set of virtual functions determined? By the address to which the vptr is set. So to control the set of active functions for a class, the compilation system need simply control the initialization and setting of the vptr. (It is the compiler's responsibility to set the vptr, of course, not something the programmer need or should worry about.)

How should the vptr initialization be handled? Essentially, this depends on when the vptr should be initialized within the constructor. There are three choices:

1. First, before anything else happens

2. After invocation of the base class constructors but before execution of user-provided code or the expansion of members initialized within the member initialization list

3. Last, after everything else has happened

The answer is after the invocation of the base class constructors. The other two choices do nothing. If you don't believe that, work through the invocation of `size()` under strategy 1 or 3. Strategy 2 solves the problem of constraining the set of candidate virtual functions within the class. If each constructor waits to set its object's vptr until after its base class constructors have executed, then the correct instance of the virtual function is invoked each time.

By having each base class constructor set its object's vptr to the virtual table associated with its class, the object under construction literally becomes an object of that class for the duration of the constructor. That is, a PVertex object in turn becomes a Point object, a Point3d object, a Vertex object, a Vertex3d object, and then a PVertex object. Within each base class constructor, the object is indistinguishable from a complete object of the constructor's class. For objects, ontogeny recapitulates phylogeny. The general algorithm of constructor execution is as follows:

1. Within the derived class constructor, all virtual base class and then immediate base class constructors are invoked.

2. That done, the object's vptr(s) are initialized to address the associated virtual table(s).

3. The member initialization list, if present, is expanded within the body of the constructor. This must be done after the vptr is set in case a virtual member function is called.

4. The explicit user-supplied code is executed.

For example, given the following user-defined PVertex constructor:

```
PVertex::PVertex( float x, float y, float z )
    : _next( 0 ), Vertex3d( x, y, z ),
      Point( x, y )
{
    if ( spyOn )
        cerr << "within PVertex::PVertex()"
             << " size: " << size() << endl;
}
```

a likely internal expansion would look something like this:

```
// Pseudo C++ Code
// expansion of PVertex constructor
PVertex*
PVertex::PVertex( Pvertex* this,
          bool __most_derived,
          float x, float y, float z )
{
    // conditionally invoke the virtual base constructor
    if ( __most_derived != false )
        this->Point::Point( x, y );
```

```
    // unconditional invocation of immediate base
    this->Vertex3d::Vertex3d( x, y, z );

    // initialize associated vptrs

    this->__vptr__PVertex = __vtbl__PVertex;
    this->__vptr__Point__PVertex =
            __vtbl__Point__PVertex;

    // explicit user code
    if ( spyOn )
        cerr << "within PVertex::PVertex()"
            << " size: "
            // invocation through virtual mechanism
            << (*this->__vptr__PVertex[ 3 ].faddr)(this)
            << endl;

    // return constructed object
    return this;
}
```

This resolves our stated problem of constraining the virtual mechanism perfectly. But, is it a perfect solution? Suppose our Point constructor is defined as

```
Point::Point( float x, float y )
    : _x( x ), _y( y ){}
```

and our Point3d is defined as

```
Point3d::Point3d( float x, float y, float z )
    : Point( x, y ), _z( z ){}
```

Further suppose our Vertex and Vertex3d constructors are defined in a similar manner. Do you see how our solution is less than perfect even though we've solved our problem perfectly?

There are two conditions under which the vptr must be set:

1. When a complete object is being constructed. If we declare a Point object, the Point constructor must set its vptr.

2. When, within the construction of a subobject, a virtual function call is made either directly or indirectly

If we declare a PVertex object, then because of our latest definitions of its base class constructors, its vptr is needlessly being set within each base class constructor. The solution is to split the constructor into a complete object instance and a subobject instance. In the subobject instance, the setting of the vptr is elided if possible.

Given what we know, you should be able to answer the following question: Is it safe to invoke a virtual function of the class within its constructor's member initialization list? Physically, it is always safe when the function is applied to the initialization of a data member of the class. This is because, as we've seen, the vptr is guaranteed to have been set by the compiler prior to the expansion of the member initialization list. It may not be semantically safe, however, because the function itself may depend on members that are not yet initialized. It is not an idiom I recommend. However, from the point of view of the integrity of the vptr, it is a safe operation.

What about when providing an argument for a base class constructor? Is it still physically safe to invoke a virtual function of the class within its constructor's member initialization list? No. The vptr is either not set or set to the wrong class. Further, any of the data members of the class that are accessed within the function are guaranteed to not yet be initialized.

5.3   Object Copy Semantics

When designing a class, we have three choices regarding the assignment of one class object with another:

1. Do nothing, thereby allowing for the default behavior.

2. Provide an explicit copy assignment operator.

3. Explicitly disallow the assignment of one class object with another.

Disallowing the copying of one class object with another is accomplished by declaring the copy assignment operator private and not providing a definition. (By making it private, we disallow assignment everywhere except within member functions and friends of the class. By our not providing a definition, then if a member function or friend were to attempt to effect a copy, the program would fail to link. Admittedly, having to depend on properties of the linker—that is, on properties outside of the language itself—is not fully satisfactory.)

In this section, I examine the semantics of the copy assignment operator and how they are generally modeled. Again, I illustrate the discussion with the help of a Point class:

```
class Point {
public:
    Point( float x = 0.0, y = 0.0 );
    //...( no virtual functions
protected:
    float _x, _y;
};
```

There is no reason to prohibit the copying of one Point object with another in this implementation. So the question is whether the default behavior is sufficient. If all we want to support is the simple assignment of one Point object to another, then the default behavior is both sufficient and efficient and there is no reason to provide an explicit instance of the copy assignment operator.

A copy assignment operator is necessary only if the default behavior results in semantics that are either unsafe or incorrect. (For a complete discussion of memberwise copy and its potential pitfalls, see [LIPP91c].) Is the default memberwise copy behavior unsafe or incorrect for our Point objects? No, the coordinates are contained by value, so there are no aliasing or memory leaks that can occur. Moreover, by our providing a copy assignment operator, the program may actually run slower.

If we don't provide a copy assignment operator for our Point class and thus rely on the default memberwise copy, does the compiler actually generate an instance? The answer is the same as for a copy constructor: in practice, no. Provided bitwise copy semantics hold for the class, the implicit copy assignment operator is considered trivial and is not synthesized.

A class does not exhibit bitwise copy semantics for the default copy assignment operator in the following cases (this is covered in detail in Section 2.2):

1. When the class contains a member object of a class for which a copy assignment operator exists

2. When the class is derived from a base class for which a copy assignment operator exists

3. When the class declares one or more virtual functions (we must not copy the vptr address of the right-hand class object, since it might be a derived class object)

4. When the class inherits from a virtual base class (this is independent of whether a copy operator exists for the base class)

The Standard speaks of copy assignment operators' not exhibiting bitwise copy semantics as nontrivial. In practice, only nontrivial instances are synthesized.

For our Point class, then, the assignment

```
Point a, b;
...
a = b;
```

is accomplished as a bitwise copy of Point b into Point a; no copy assignment operator is invoked. Semantically and with regard to performance, this is exactly what we want. Note that we still may want to provide a copy constructor in order to turn on the named return value (NRV) optimization. The presence of the copy constructor should not bully us into providing a copy assignment operator if one is not needed.

That said, I am now going to introduce a copy assignment operator in order to illustrate the behavior of that operator under inheritance:

```
inline
Point&
Point::operator=( const Point &p )
{
    _x = p._x;
    _y = p._y;
}
```

Now let's derive our Point3d class (note the virtual inheritance):

```
class Point3d : virtual public Point {
public:
    Point3d( float x = 0.0, y = 0.0, float z = 0.0 );
    ...
protected:
    float _z;
};
```

If we do not define a copy assignment operator for Point3d, the compiler needs to synthesize one based on items 2 and 4 above. The synthesized instance might look as follows:

```
// Pseudo C++ Code: synthesized copy assignment operator
inline Point3d&
Point3d::operator=( Point3d *const this, const Point3d &p )
{
    // invoke the base class instance
    this->Point::operator=( p );

    // memberwise copy the derived class members
    _z = p._z;
    return *this;
}
```

One of the nonorthogonal aspects of the copy assignment operator with regard to that of the copy constructor is the absence of a *member assignment list*—that is, a list parallel to that of the member initialization list. Thus we cannot write

```
// Pseudo C++ Code: not supported feature
inline Point3d&
Point3d::operator=( const Point3d &p )
        : Point( p3d ), z( p3d._z )
{}
```

but must write one of two alternative ways of invoking the Base copy assignment operator, either

```
Point::operator=( p3d );
```

or

```
( *(Point*)this ) = p3d;
```

The absence of this copy assignment list may seem a minor point, but without it, the compiler generally cannot suppress the intermediate base class copy operators from being invoked. For example, here is the Vertex copy operator, where Vertex is also virtually derived from Point:

```
// class Vertex : virtual public Point
```

```
inline Vertex&
Vertex::operator=( const Vertex &v )
{
    this->Point::operator=( v );
    _next = v._next;
    return *this;
}
```

Now let's derive Vertex3d from Point3d and Vertex. Here is the Vertex3d copy assignment operator:

```
inline Vertex3d&
Vertex3d::operator=( const Vertex3d &v )
{
    this->Point::operator=( v );
    this->Point3d::operator=( v );
    this->Vertex::operator=( v );
    . . .
}
```

How is the compiler going to suppress the user-programmed instances of the Point copy assignment operator within the Point3d and Vertex copy assignment operators? The compiler can't duplicate the traditional constructor solution of inserting additional arguments. This is because unlike constructors and the destructor, taking the address of the copy assignment operator is legal. Thus this is perfectly legitimate code, for example, although it perfectly confounds attempts to be smart about the copy assignment operator:

```
typedef Point3d& (Point3d::*pmfPoint3d)(const Point3d&);

pmfPoint3d pmf = &Point3d::operator=;
( x.*pmf)( x );
```

We can't reasonably support this, however, and still insert an arbitrary number of arguments to the copy assignment operator based on the peculiar characteristics of its inheritance hierarchy. (This has also proved problematic in the support for the allocation of arrays of class objects containing virtual base classes. See Section 6.2 for a discussion.)

Alternatively, the compiler might generate split functions for the copy assignment operator to support the class as the most derived and as an intermediate base class. The split function solution is reasonably well defined if the copy assignment operator is generated by the compiler; it is not well defined if programmed by the designer of the class. For example, how does one split something like the following, particularly if `init_bases()` is virtual:

```
inline Vertex3d&
Vertex3d::operator=( const Vertex3d &v )
{
    init_bases( v );

    . . .
}
```

Actually, the copy assignment operator is ill behaved under virtual inheritance and needs to be carefully designed and documented. In practice, many compilers don't even try to get the semantics right. They invoke each virtual base instance within each intermediate copy assignment operator, thus causing multiple instances of the virtual base class copy assignment operator to be invoked. Cfront does this as well as the Edison Design Group's front-end, Borland's 4.5 C++ compiler, and Symantec's latest C++ Compiler under Windows. My guess is your compiler does it as well. What does the Standard have to say about this?

> It is unspecified whether subobjects representing virtual base classes are assigned more than once by the implicitly defined copy assignment operator (Section 12.8).

A language-based solution would be to provide a "member copy list" extension to the copy assignment operator. Short of this, any solution is program-based and therefore somewhat complicated and error prone. Admittedly, it is a weakness in the language and something one should always examine carefully in code reviews of designs that use virtual base classes.

One way to ensure the most-derived class effects the virtual base class subobject copy is to place an explicit call of that operator last in the derived class instance of the copy assignment operator:

```
inline Vertex3d&
Vertex3d::operator=( const Vertex3d &v )
{
    this->Point3d::operator=( v );
    this->Vertex::operator=( v );
```

```
       // must place this last if your compiler does
       // not suppress intermediate class invocations
       this->Point::operator=( v );

       ...
}
```

This doesn't elide the multiple copies of the subobject, but it does guarantee the correct final semantics. Alternative solutions require factoring out the virtual subobject copying into a separate function and conditionally invoking it depending on the call path.

I recommend not permitting the copy operation of a virtual base class whenever possible. An even stronger recommendation: Do not declare data within any class that serves as a virtual base class.

5.4 Object Efficiency

In the following set of performance tests, the cost of object construction and copy is measured as the Point3d class declaration increases in complexity as Plain Ol' Data, then as an abstract data type (ADT), and then as single, multiple, and virtual inheritances are incorporated in turn. The following function is used as the primary measure:

```
Point3d lots_of_copies( Point3d a,  Point3d b )
{
       Point3d pC = a;

       pC = b;   // 1
       b  = a;   // 2

       return pC;
}
```

It contains four memberwise initializations: the two formal arguments, the return value, and the local object pC. It also contains two memberwise copies, those of pC and b on the lines labeled //1 and //2, respectively. The main() function looks as follows:

```
main() {
       Point3d pA( 1.725, 0.875, 0.478 );
       Point3d pB( 0.315, 0.317, 0.838 );
       Point3d pC;
```

```
      for ( int iters = 0; iters < 10000000; iters++ )
          pC = lots_of_copies( pA, pB );

      return 0;
}
```

In the first two programs, the representation is that of a **struct** and a **class** with public data:

```
struct Point3d { float x, y, z; };
class  Point3d { public: float x, y, z; };
```

and the initialization of both pA and pB is through the use of an explicit initialization list:

```
Point3d pA = { 1.725, 0.875, 0.478 };
Point3d pB = { 0.315, 0.317, 0.838 };
```

Both of these representations exhibit bitwise copy semantics, so one expects them to execute equivalent best times for this set of program tests. The results are as follows

```
Memberwise Initialization and Copy:
        Public Data Members
        Bitwise Copy Semantics
```

	Optimized	Non-optimized
CC	5.05	6.39
NCC	5.84	7.22

The better CC performance is due to an additional six assembler instructions generated in the NCC loop. This "overhead" does not reflect any specific C++ semantics or a poorer handling of the code by the NCC front-end—the intermediate C output of both compilers is largely equivalent. It is simply a quirk of the back-end code generator.

In the next test, the only change is the encapsulation of the data members and the use of inline access functions and an inline constructor to initialize each object. The class still exhibits bitwise copy semantics, so common sense would tell you that the runtime performance should be the same. Actually, it is slightly off:

```
Memberwise Initialization and Copy:
Private Data Members:
  Inline Access and Inline Construction
     Bitwise Copy Semantics
```

	Optimized	Non-optimized
CC	5.18	6.52
NCC	6.00	7.33

I had thought that the difference in performance had to do not with the execution of lots_of_copies() but with the initialization of the class objects within main(). So I modified the struct initialization as follows to duplicate the inline expansion of the inline class constructor:

```
main() {
     Point3d pA;
     pA.x = 1.725;   pA.y =0.875; pA.z = 0.478;

     Point3d pB;
     pB.x = 0.315; pB.y = 0.317;   pB.z = 0.838;

     // ... rest the same
```

and found that times increased for both executions. They now mirrored those for the encapsulated class representation:

```
Memberwise Initialization and Copy:
Public Data Members:
   Individual Member Initialization
   Bitwise Copy Semantics
```

	Optimized	Non-optimized
CC	5.18	6.52
NCC	5.99	7.33

The initialization of a coordinate member through the inline expansion of the constructor results in a two-instruction assembler sequence: one to load the constant value within a register and the other to do the actual storage of the value:

```
# 20  pt3d pA( 1.725, 0.875, 0.478 );
li.s  $f4, 1.7250000238418579e+00
s.s   $f4, 76($sp)
# etc.
```

The initialization of a coordinate member through the explicit initialization list results in a one-expression store because the constant value is "preloaded":

```
$$7:
    .float 1.7250000238418579e+00
    # etc.
```

The other difference between the encapsulated and nonencapsulated Point3d declaration is in the semantics of

```
Point3d pC;
```

Under the ADT representation, pC is automatically initialized with the inline expansion of its default constructor even though, in this instance, it would be safe to leave it uninitialized. On the one hand, although these differences are small indeed, they serve up an interesting caveat to assertions that encapsulation with inline support is the exact equivalent of direct data manipulation common in C programs. On the other hand, these differences generally are not significant and provide no reason for dismissing the software engineering benefits of data encapsulation. They are something to keep in mind for special-case critical code areas.

In the next test, I separated the Point3d representation into a concrete three-level single inheritance hierarchy of the form

```
class Point1d {}; // _x
class Point2d : public Point1d {}; // _y
class Point3d : public Point2d {}; // _z
```

without introducing any virtual functions. Since the Point3d class still exhibits bitwise copy semantics, the addition of single inheritance should not affect the cost of memberwise object initialization or copy. This is borne out by the results:

```
        Memberwise Initialization and Copy:
        Single Inheritance:
            Protected Members: Inline Access
            Bitwise Copy Semantics
```

	Optimized	Non-optimized
CC	5.18	6.52
NCC	6.26	7.33

The following multiple inheritance relationship is admittedly contrived. Still, in terms of its member distribution, it does the job, at least in terms of providing us with a test :-) .

```
class Point1d {}; // _x
class Point2d {}; // _y
class Point3d
    : public Point1d, public Point2d {}; // _z
```

Since the Point3d class continues to exhibit bitwise copy semantics, the addition of multiple inheritance should not add to the cost of either memberwise object initialization or copy. This proved to be the case except for the optimized CC version, which surprisingly ran slightly better:

```
Memberwise Initialization and Copy:
Multiple Inheritance:
    Protected Members: Inline Access
    Bitwise Copy Semantics
```

	Optimized	Non-optimized
CC	5.06	6.52
NCC	6.26	7.33

In all the tests so far, the differences in all these versions interestingly enough revolves around the cost of initializing the three local objects rather than the expense of the memberwise initialization and copy. These operations were carried out uniformly, since all these representations so far support bitwise copy semantics. The introduction of virtual inheritance, however, changes all that. The following one-level virtual inheritance hierarchy:

```
class Point1d { ... };
class Point2d : public virtual Point1d { ... };
class Point3d : public Point2d { ... };
```

effectively disallows bitwise copy semantics for the class (the first level of virtual inheritance effectively disallows it; the second level merely compounds it). Synthesized inline instances of the copy constructor and copy assignment operator are generated and are now applied. This result is a significant increase in performance cost:

```
Memberwise Initialization and Copy:
Virtual Inheritance: One Level
   Synthesized Inline Copy Constructor
   Synthesized Inline Copy Operator
```

	Optimized	Non-optimized
CC	15.59	26.45
NCC	17.29	23.93

To understand this number better, I then stepped back through the previous representations, beginning with the encapsulated class declaration and added a virtual function. Recall that this disallows bitwise copy semantics. Synthesized inline instances of the copy constructor and copy assignment operator are now generated and applied. The performance increase was not nearly as pronounced but still is about 40—50% greater than bitwise copy support. If the functions were user-supplied non-inline instances, the cost would be still greater:

```
Memberwise Initialization and Copy:
Abstract Data Type: Virtual Function
   Synthesized Inline Copy Constructor
   Synthesized Inline Copy Operator
```

	Optimized	Non-optimized
CC	8.34	9.94
NCC	7.67	13.05

Following are the times for the other representations with bitwise copy semantics replaced with an inline synthesized memberwise copy constructor and copy assignment operator. These times reflect an increased default cost of object construction and copy as the complexity of the inheritance hierarchy increases.

```
Memberwise Initialization and Copy:
   Synthesized Inline Copy Constructor
   Synthesized Inline Copy Operator
```

	Optimized	Non-optimized
Single Inheritance		
CC	12.69	17.47
NCC	10.35	17.74

Multiple Inheritance

CC	14.91	21.51
NCC	12.39	20.39

Virtual Inheritance: Two Levels

CC	19.90	29.73
NCC	19.31	26.80

5.5   Semantics of Destruction

If a destructor is not defined by a class, the compiler synthesizes one only if the class contains either a member or base class with a destructor. Otherwise, the destructor is considered to be trivial and is therefore neither synthesized nor invoked in practice. Our Point class, for example, by default does not have a destructor synthesized for it, even though it contains a virtual function:

```
class Point {
public:
   Point( float x = 0.0, float y = 0.0 );
   Point( const Point& );

   virtual float z();

   // ...
private:
   float _x, _y;
};
```

Similarly, were we to compose a Line class of two Point objects,

```
class Line {
public:
   Line( const Point&, const Point& );
   // ...

   virtual draw();
   // ...
protected:
   Point _begin, _end;
};
```

Line would not have a destructor synthesized for it because Point is with-out a destructor.

Also, when we derive Point3d from Point—even if the derivation is vir-tual—if we do not declare a destructor, the compiler in practice has no need to synthesize one.

With both the Point and Point3d classes, a destructor is unnecessary, so providing one is inefficient. You should resist what I call the primal urge to-ward symmetry: You've defined a constructor, so it just feels right to pro-vide a destructor as well. In practice, you should provide a destructor because it is needed, not because it "feels" right, or, well, because you're not sure if you need one.

To determine if a class needs a program level destructor (or constructor, for that matter), consider the case where the lifetime of a class object termi-nates (or begins). What, if anything, needs to be done to guarantee that ob-ject's integrity? This is preferably what you need to program (or else the user of your class has to). This is what should go into the destructor (or con-structor). For example, given

```
{
    Point pt;
    Point *p = new Point3d;
    foo( &pt, p );
    ...
    delete p;
}
```

we see that both pt and p must be initialized to some coordinate values be-fore being used as arguments to foo(). A constructor is necessary because otherwise the user is required to explicitly provide the coordinate values. Generally, the user cannot examine the state of a local or heap variable to determine whether it has been initialized. It's incorrect to consider the con-structors as program overhead because their work otherwise still is re-quired. Without them, use of the abstraction is more error prone.

What about when we explicitly delete p? Is any programming neces-sary? Would you write, prior to applying the **delete** operator,

```
p->x( 0 ); p->y( 0 );
```

No, of course not. There is no reason to reset the coordinate values prior to deleting the object. Nor are there any resources to reclaim. There is no user level programming required prior to the termination of the lifetimes of both pt and p; therefore, there is no need for a destructor.

Consider our Vertex class, however. It maintains a list of adjacent vertices, and having the list of adjacent vertices traversed and deleted in turn on the termination of a vertex object (may) makes sense. If this (or some other semantics) is desired, this is the program-level work of the Vertex destructor.

When we derive Vertex3d from both Point3d and Vertex, if we don't provide an explicit Vertex3d destructor, then we still require the Vertex destructor to be invoked upon termination of a Vertex3d object. Thus the compiler needs to synthesize a Vertex3d destructor whose only work will be to invoke the Vertex destructor. If we provide a Vertex3d destructor, the compiler augments it to invoke the Vertex destructor after the user-supplied code is executed. A user-defined destructor is augmented in much the same way as are the constructors, except in reverse order:

1. If the object contains a vptr, it is reset to the virtual table associated with the class.

2. The body of the destructor is then executed; that is, the vptr is reset prior to evaluating the user-supplied code.

3. If the class has member class objects with destructors, these are invoked in the reverse order of their declaration.

4. If there are any immediate nonvirtual base classes with destructors, these are invoked in the reverse order of their declaration.

5. If there are any virtual base classes with destructors and this class represents the most-derived class, these are invoked in the reverse order of their original construction.

As with constructors, current thinking on the best implementation strategy for the destructor is to maintain two destructor instances:

1. A complete object instance that always sets the vptr(s) and invokes the virtual base class destructors

2. A base class subobject instance that never invokes the virtual base class destructors and sets the vptr(s) only if a virtual function may be invoked from within the body of the destructor

An object's lifetime ends with the beginning of its destructor's execution. As each base class destructor is evoked in turn, the derived object in effect becomes a complete object of that type. A PVertex object, for example, becomes in turn a Vertex3d object, a Vertex object, a Point3d object, and then a Point object before its actual storage is reclaimed. Where member functions are invoked within the destructor, this object metamorphosis is effected through the resetting of the vptr within each destructor before user code is executed. The actual semantics of applying destructors within the program are examined in Chapter 6.

Chapter 6

Runtime Semantics

Imagine we have the apparently simple expression

```
if ( yy == xx.getValue() ) ...
```

where xx and yy are defined as

```
X xx;
Y yy;
```

class Y is defined as

```
class Y {
public:
    Y();
    ~Y();
    operator==( const Y& ) const;
    // ...
};
```

and class X is defined as

```
class X {
public:
    X();
    ~X();
    operator Y() const;
    X getValue();
    // ...
};
```

Simple stuff, right? Okay, let's look at how the expression is handled.

First, we determine the actual instance of the equality operator that is being referenced. In this case, this resolves to the overloaded Y member instance. This is the first transformation of our expression:

```
// resolution of intended operator
if ( yy.operator==( xx.getValue() ))
```

Y's equality operator requires an argument of type Y. getValue(), however, returns an object of type X. Either there is a way to transform an object of class X into a Y object or the expression is in error. In this case, X provides a conversion operator that turns an X object into a Y object. This needs to be applied to the return value of getValue(). Here is the second transformation of our expression:

```
// conversion of getValue()'s return value
if ( yy.operator==( xx.getValue().operator Y() ))
```

All that's happened so far is that the compiler has augmented our program text with the implicit class semantics of our expression. However, we could have explicitly written the expression in this form if we wanted. (No, I am not recommending this. However, it does make the compilation a tad swifter!)

Although the program text is semantically correct, it is not yet instructionally correct. Next we must generate temporaries to hold the return values of our function calls:

- Generate a temporary of class X to hold the return value of getValue():

  ```
  X temp1 = xx.getValue();
  ```

- Generate a temporary of class Y to hold the return value of operator Y():

  ```
  Y temp2 = temp1.operator Y();
  ```

- Generate a temporary of type int to hold the return value of the equality operator:

  ```
  int temp3 = yy.operator==( temp2 );
  ```

Finally, the language requires that we apply the appropriate destructor to each class object temporary. This results in a code transformation of our expression of the following general form:

```
// Pseudo C++ code
// transformation of conditional expression:
// if ( yy == xx.getValue() ) ...
{
    X temp1 = xx.getValue();
    Y temp2 = temp1.operator Y();
    int temp3 = yy.operator==( temp2 );

    if ( temp3 ) ...

    temp2.Y::~Y();
    temp1.X::~X();
}
```

Wow, that's quite a lot of stuff. This is one of the hard things about C++: the difficulty of knowing the complexity of an expression simply by inspecting the source code. In this chapter, I look at some of the transformations that occur at runtime. I return to the issue of temporary generation in detail in Section 6.3.

6.1   Object Construction and Destruction

In general, constructor and destructor insertion is as you would expect:

```
// Pseudo C++ Code
{
    Point point;
    // point.Point::Point() generally inserted here
    ...
    // point.Point::~Point() generally inserted here
}
```

It gets slightly more confusing when there are multiple exits from a block or function. The destructor must be placed at each exit point at which the object is "alive"; for example,

```
{
    Point point;
    // constructor goes here ...
```

```
switch( int( point.x() )) {
   case -1:
      // mumble;
      // destructor goes here
      return;
   case 0:
      // mumble;
      // destructor goes here
      return;
   case 1:
      // mumble;
      // destructor goes here
      return;
   default:
      // mumble;
      // destructor goes here
      return;
}

// destructor goes here
}
```

In this example, the destructor for point must be generated prior to the **return** statement at the four exit points within the **switch** statement. It is also likely to be generated just prior to the block's closing brace, although an analysis of the block reveals the program could never fall past the **switch** statement to reach it.

Similarly, the presence of a **goto** statement may require multiple destructor invocations. For example, in this code fragment

```
{
   if ( cache )
      // check cache; if match, return 1

   Point xx;
   // constructor goes here

   while ( cvs.iter( xx ))
      if ( xx == value )
         goto found;

   // destructor goes here
   return 0;

found:
   // cache item
```

```
    // destructor goes here
    return 1;
}
```

Destructor invocations must be placed prior to the last two **return** statements. The destructor does not need to be invoked prior to the initial **return** because, of course, the object has not yet been defined.

In general, place an object as close as possible to the code segment actually using it. Doing this can save you unnecessary object creation and destruction, as would be the case, for example, if we had defined our Point object prior to checking our cache. This may seem self-evident, but many Pascal and C programmers using C++ still place all their objects at the beginning of a function or local block.

Global Objects

If we have the following program fragment:

```
Matrix identity;

main()
{
    // identity must be initialized by this point!
    Matrix m1 = identity;
    ...
    return 0;
}
```

the language guarantees that identity is constructed prior to the first user statement of main() and destructed following the last statement of main(). A global object such as identity with an associated constructor and destructor is said to require both static initialization and deallocation.

All globally visible objects in C++ are placed within the program data segment. If an explicit initial value is specified, the object is initialized with that value; otherwise, the memory associated with the object is initialized to 0. Thus in this code fragment:

```
int v1 = 1024;
int v2;
```

both v1 and v2 are allocated within the program's data segment—v1 with an initial value of 1024 and v2 with 0. (This differs from C where v2 is considered a tentative definition.) In C, a global object can be initialized only by a constant expression, that is, one that can be evaluated at compile time. A constructor, of course, is not a constant expression. Although the class object can be placed within the data segment during compilation with its memory zeroed out, its constructor cannot be applied until program startup. The need to evaluate an initialization expression for an object stored within the program's data segment is what is meant by an object's requiring static initialization.

When cfront was the only C++ implementation and portability across machines was more important than efficiency, a portable but costly method of static initialization (and deallocation) was provided, affectionately called *munch*. cfront was constrained in that its solution had to work on every UNIX platform—from a Cray through the VAX and Sun to the UNIX PC briefly put out by AT&T. It could make no assumptions either about the associated link editor or object-file format under which it might be running. Because of this constraint, the following munch strategy emerged:

1. Within each file that requires static initialization, generate an __sti() function containing the necessary constructor invocations or inline expansions. identity, for example, would cause the following __sti() function to be generated within the file *matrix.c*:

   ```
   __sti__matrix_c__identity() {
       // Pseudo C++ Code
       identity.Matrix::Matrix();
   }
   ```

   where __matrix_c is an encoding of the file name and __identity represents the first nonstatic object defined within the file. Appending these two names to __sti provided a unique identifier within the executable. (Andy Koenig and Bjarne worked out this "fake static" encoding scheme in response to name-clash agonies reported by Jim Coplien.)

2. Similarly, within each file that requires a static deallocation, generate an __std() function containing the necessary destructor invocations or inline expansions. In our example, an __std() function is generated to invoke the Matrix destructor on identity.

3. Provide a set of runtime library munch functions: a _main() function to invoke all the __sti() functions within the executable and an exit() function to analogously invoke all the __std() functions.

cfront inserted a _main() call as the new first statement within main(). The exit() function rather than the C library exit() function was linked in by cfront's **CC** command by placing the C++ standard library first on the command line. (In general this worked, but one still had to cross one's fingers and murmur an incantation when porting cfront to each new platform. For example, the HP workstation compilation system initially refused to pull in the munch exit() routine for reasons I've thankfully forgotten but which were quite desperate at the time. The desperation came from having a user discover that his or her static destructors were not getting called.)

The last issue to resolve was how to collect the associated __sti() and __std() functions within the object files of the executable. Remember, it had to be portable, although that portability then was limited to machines running UNIX. Think for a moment how you might solve the problem. It's not a technically challenging issue, but at the time the successful distribution of cfront (and therefore of C++) depended on it.

Our solution was to use the **nm** command. (**nm** dumps the object file symbol table entries.) An executable was generated from the *.o* files. **nm** was then run on the resulting executable. Its output was piped into the munch program. (I think Rob Murray wrote **munch**, but nobody any longer claims to remember.) **munch** munched the symbol table names, looking for names that began with __sti or __std. (Yes, periodically to amuse ourselves we would begin a function with __sti such as __sti_ha_fooled_you). It then added the function names to a jump table of __sti() and __std() functions. Next, it wrote the tables into a small program text file. Then, odd as it may sound, the **CC** command was reinvoked to compile the file containing the generated tables. The entire executable was then relinked. _main() and exit() traversed the respective tables invoking each entry in turn.

This got the job done, but gosh, it sure felt like a long distance from computer science. With Release 1.0, a *patch* version for System V was implemented as a fast alternative to munch (I think Jerry Schwarz implemented it). **patch** presumed the executable was in System V COFF (Common Object File Format). It examined the executable and then found and chained together file specific __link nodes that contained a pointer to the __sti() and __std() functions. Next, it rooted the list to a global __head object defined within the new **patch** runtime library. The **patch** library included alternative implementations of _main() and exit() that traversed the linked list rooted by __head. (The typical porting pitfall was to compile cfront to generate **patch** output while linking in the **munch** library. I recall this bit Steve Johnson in his port of cfront to a Sun workstation after he left Bell Labs.) Eventually, alternative **patch** libraries for Sun, BSD, and ELF were donated by the user community and incorporated into the various cfront releases.

Once platform-specific C++ compilers began to appear, a hugely more efficient approach became possible by extending the link editor and object file formats to directly support static initialization and deallocation. For example, the System V Executable and Linking Format (ELF) was extended to provide .init and .fini sections that contain information on the objects requiring, respectively, static initialization and deallocation. Implementation-specific startup routines (usually named something like crt0.o) complete the platform-specific support for static initialization and deallocation.

Prior to Release 2.0, static initialization of nonclass objects was not supported—that is, the C language constraint was retained. So, for example, the following definitions were each flagged as invalid initializations:

```
extern int i;

// all require static initialization
// illegal in C and C++ prior to Release 2.0

int j = i;
int *pi = &v3d;
double sal = compute_sal( get_employee( i ) );
```

The addition of support for static initialization of nonclass objects in part was a side effect of supporting virtual base classes. How did virtual base classes become involved in the issue? The access of a virtual base class subobject within a derived class pointer or reference is a nonconstant expression requiring evaluation at runtime. For example, whereas the following addresses are known at compile time:

```
// constant expression initializations
Vertex3d *pv = new Pvertex;
Point3d *p3d = &v3d;
```

the location of the virtual base class Point subobject fluctuates with each subsequently derived class and therefore cannot be set during compilation. The initialization

```
// Point is a virtual base class of Point3d
// initialization of pt requires
// some form of runtime evaluation.
Point *pt = p3d;
```

requires the compiler to provide internal extensions to the support of class object static initialization to at least cover pointers and references of class objects; for example,

```
// Initial support of virtual base class conversion
// requires non-constant initialization support
Point *pt = p3d->vbcPoint;
```

There is not much distance to travel to provide the support necessary to cover all nonclass objects.

There are a number of drawbacks to using statically initialized objects. For example, if exception handling is supported, these objects cannot be placed within **try** blocks. This can be particularly unsatisfactory with statically invoked constructors because any throw will by necessity trigger the default terminate() function within the exception handling library. Another drawback is the complexity involved in controlling order dependency of objects that require static initialization across modules. (See [SCHWARZ89] for the first discussion of this problem and the introduction of what are now called Schwarz counters. For a comprehensive discussion of the issue, see [CARROLL95].) I recommend your not using global objects that require static initialization. Actually, I recommend your not using global objects at all (although this recommendation seems to meet with nearly universal dismissal, particularly from C programmers).

Local Static Objects

Say we have the following fragment code:

```
const Matrix&
identity() {
   static Matrix mat_identity;
   // ...
   return mat_identity;
}
```

What are the guaranteed semantics of the local static class object?

- mat_identity must have its constructor applied only once, although the function may be invoked multiple times.

- mat_identity must have its destructor applied only once, although again the function may be invoked multiple times.

One implementation strategy is to unconditionally construct the object at program startup. However, this results in the initialization of all local static class objects at program startup regardless of whether their associated functions are ever used. Rather, it's better to construct mat_identity only when identity() is first invoked (this is now required by Standard C++). How can we do that?

Here's how we did it in cfront. First, a temporary was introduced to guard mat_identity's initialization. On the first pass through identity(), the temporary evaluated as false. Then the constructor was invoked, and the temporary was set to true. This solved the construction problem. On the reverse end, the destructor needed to be conditionally applied to mat_identity, but only if mat_identity had been constructed. Determining whether it had was simple: If the guard was true, it had been constructed. The difficulty was that because cfront generated C code, mat_identity was still local to the function and I could not C-legally access it within the static deallocation function. "*Oh, bother,*" as Winnie the Pooh would say. The solution, oddly enough, was to do exactly what is anathema in a block-structured language: I took the local object's address! (Of course, since the object was static, its address in the downstream component would be transferred to the global program data segment.) In any case, here is cfront's output (slightly prettified):

```
// generated temporary static object guard
static struct Matrix *__0__F3 = 0 ;

// the C analog to a reference is a pointer
// identity()'s name is mangled based on signature

struct Matrix*
identity__Fv ()
{
   // the __1 reflects the lexical level
   // this permitted support for code such as
   //    int val;
   // int f() { int val;
   //              return val + ::val; }
   // where the last line becomes
   //    ....return __1val + val;

   static struct Matrix __1mat_identity ;
```

```
// if the guard is set, do nothing, else
// (a) invoke the constructor: __ct__6MatrixFv
// (b) set the guard to address the object
__0__F3
    ? 0
    : (__ct__1MatrixFv ( & __1mat_identity ),
      (__0__F3 = (&__1mat_identity)));
...
}
```

Finally, the destructor needed to be conditionally invoked within the static deallocation function associated with the text program file, in this case *stat_0.c*:

```
char __std__stat_0_c_j ()
{
    __0__F3
      ? __dt__6MatrixFv( __0__F3 , 2)
      : 0 ;
    ...
}
```

Bear in mind that the use of the pointer is peculiar to cfront; the conditional destruction, however, is required under all implementations. (As I write this, the Standards committee seems likely to change the semantics of destruction for local static class objects. The new rule requires that the static local class objects in the compilation unit be destroyed in reverse order of construction. Since these objects are constructed on demand (as each function is first entered), neither the set nor order of these constructed objects can be predicted during compilation. Support for this rule, then, is likely to require keeping a runtime list of the static class objects that are created.)

Arrays of Objects

Say we have the following array definition:

```
Point knots[ 10 ];
```

What needs to be done? If Point defines neither a constructor nor a destructor, then we need do no more than what is done for an array of built-in types, that is, allocate memory sufficient to store ten contiguous elements of type Point.

Point, however, does define a default constructor, so it must be applied to each of the elements in turn. In general, this is accomplished through one or more runtime library functions. In cfront, we used one instance of a function we named vec_new() to support creation and initialization of arrays of class objects. More recent implementations, including Borland, Microsoft, and Sun, provide two instances—one to handle classes without virtual base classes, one to handle classes containing virtual base classes, the latter usually named vec_vnew(). Its signature is generally the following, although there are variants across implementations:

```
void*
vec_new(
    void *array,        // address of start of array
    size_t elem_size,  // size of each class object
    int elem_count,    // number of elements in array
    void (*constructor)( void* ),
    void (*destructor)( void*, char )
)
```

where constructor and destructor are pointers to the default constructor and destructor, respectively, of the class. array holds either the address of the named array (knots, in the example) or 0. If 0, then the array is being dynamically allocated on the heap through the application of operator **new**. (Sun has separated the handling of named and dynamically allocated arrays of class objects into two separate library functions–_vector_new2 and _vector_con–each of which also has a virtual base class instance.)

The elem_size argument indicates the size of each element within the array. (I return to this in Section 6.2, where I discuss the operators **new** and **delete**.) Within vec_new(), the constructor is applied to the elem_count elements in turn. The destructor is necessary in implementations that support exception handling (it must be applied in the event the constructor being applied throws an exception). Here is a likely compiler invocation of vec_new() for our array of ten Point elements:

```
Point knots[ 10 ];
vec_new( &knots, sizeof( Point ), 10, &Point::Point, 0 );
```

If Point also defined a destructor, it would need to be applied to each of the elements in turn upon the termination of knots's lifetime. Not surprisingly, this is accomplished through an analogous vec_delete() (or

vec_vdelete() for classes with virtual base classes) runtime library functions. (Sun separates out handling the deallocation of named versus dynamically allocated arrays.) Its signature is generally the following:

```
void*
vec_delete(
    void *array,        // address of start of array
    size_t elem_size,  // size of each class object
    int elem_count,    // number of elements in array
    void (*destructor)( void*, char )
)
```

although some implementations add an additional argument carrying op-
tional values to conditionally direct the logic of vec_delete(). (The proliferation of separate specialized functions is the alternative to this
additional argument.) Within vec_delete(), the destructor is applied to
the elem_count elements in turn.

What if the programmer provides one or more explicit initial values for
an array of class objects, such as the following:

```
Point knots[ 10 ] = {
    Point(),
    Point( 1.0, 1.0, 0.5 ),
    -1.0
};
```

For those elements explicitly provided with an initial value, the use of
vec_new() is unnecessary. For the remaining uninitialized elements,
vec_new() is applied the same as for an array of class elements without an
explicit initialization list. The previous definition is likely to be translated as
follows:

```
Point knots[ 10 ];

// Pseudo C++ Code

// initialize the first 3 with explicit invocations
Point::Point( &knots[0]);
Point::Point( &knots[1], 1.0, 1.0, 0.5 );
Point::Point( &knots[2], -1.0, 0.0, 0.0 );

// initialize last 7 with vec_new ...
vec_new( &knots+3, sizeof( Point ), 7, &Point::Point, 0 );
```

Default Constructors and Arrays

At the programmer level, taking the address of a constructor is not permitted. Of course, this is exactly what the compiler does in its support of vec_new (). Invoking the constructor through a pointer, however, inhibits access of default argument values. This has always resulted in less than first-class handling of the initialization of an array of class objects.

For example, prior to cfront's Release 2.0, declaring an array of class objects meant the class had to declare either no constructors or a default constructor taking no arguments. A constructor taking one or more default arguments was not permitted. This was certainly nonintuitive and led to the following blunder. Here is the declaration for the complex library of Release 1.0. Do you see what's wrong with it?

```
class complex {
   complex(double=0.0, double=0.0);
   ...
};
```

Under the language rules then current, a user of the complex library as we released it could not declare an array of complex class objects. Obviously, we had ourselves tripped over a language pitfall. For Release 1.1, we fixed the class library. For Release 2.0, we fixed the language.

Again, consider for a moment how you might implement support for

```
complex::complex(double=0.0, double=0.0);
```

when the programmer writes

```
complex c_array[ 10 ];
```

and the compiler eventually needs to invoke

```
vec_new( &c_array, sizeof( complex ), 10,
         &complex::complex, 0 );
```

How are the default arguments made available to vec_new ()?

Obviously, there are several possible implementations. We elected within cfront to generate an internal stub constructor that takes no arguments. Within the body, the user-supplied constructor is invoked, with the default arguments made explicit. (Because the constructor's address is taken, it could not be made inline.)

```
// internally generated stub constructor
// to support array construction
complex::complex()
{
    complex( 0.0, 0.0 );
}
```

Internally, the compiler itself once again violates an explicit language rule: The class actually supports two constructors requiring no arguments. Of course, the stub instance is generated and used only if an array of class objects is actually created.

6.2   Operators new and delete

Although a use of operator **new** may seem to be a single operation, such as

```
int *pi = new int( 5 );
```

it is actually accomplished as two discrete steps:

1. The allocation of the requested memory through invocation of the appropriate operator **new** instance, passing it the size of the object:

   ```
   // invoke library instance of operator new
   int *pi = __new ( sizeof( int ));
   ```

2. The initialization of the allocated object:

   ```
   *pi = 5;
   ```

Further, the initialization is performed only if the allocation of the object by operator **new** succeeds:

```
// discrete steps of operator new
// given:   int *pi = new int( 5 );

// rewrite declaration
int *pi;

if ( pi = __new( sizeof( int )))
    *pi = 5;
```

Operator **delete** is handled similarly. When the programmer writes

```
delete pi;
```

the language requires that operator **delete** not be applied if pi should be set to 0. Thus the compiler must construct a guard around the call:

```
if ( pi != 0 )
    __delete( pi );
```

Note that pi is not automatically reset to 0 and a subsequent dereference, such as

```
// oops: ill-defined but not illegal
if ( pi && *pi == 5 ) ...
```

although ill-defined, may or may not evaluate as true. This is because an actual alteration or reuse of the storage that pi addresses may or may not have occurred.

The lifetime of the object addressed by pi ends with the application of **delete**. So any subsequent attempt to refer to that object through pi is no longer well defined and generally is considered bad programming. However, the use of pi as a pointer to an address in storage is still well defined, although of limited use; for example,

```
// ok: still addresses valid storage, even if
// the object stored there is no longer valid
if ( pi == sentinel ) ...
```

The distinction here is between the use of the pointer pi and the use of the object pi addressed and which has now had its lifetime ended. Although the object at that address is no longer valid, the address itself refers to valid program storage. pi, therefore, can continue to be used, but only in a limited way, much the same as if it were a void* pointer.

The allocation of a class object with an associated constructor is handled similarly. For example,

```
Point3d *origin = new Point3d;
```

is transformed into

```
Point3d *origin;
```

```
//Pseudo C++ code
if ( origin = __new( sizeof( Point3d )))
     origin = Point3d::Point3d( origin );
```

If exception handling is implemented, the transformation becomes somewhat more complicated:

```
// Pseudo 3.C++ code

if ( origin = __new( sizeof( Point3d ))) {
    try {
       origin = Point3d::Point3d( origin );
    }
    catch( ... ) {
       // invoke delete lib function to
       // free memory allocated by new ...
       __delete( origin );

       // propagate original exception upward
       throw;
    }
}
```

Here, if the constructor of the object allocated using operator **new** throws
an exception, the memory allocated is released. Then the exception is
rethrown.

The application of the destructor is similar. The expression

```
delete origin;
```

becomes

```
if ( origin != 0 ) {
    // Pseudo C++ code
    Point3d::~Point3d( origin );
    __delete( origin );
}
```

The various forms of the **delete** operator do not throw on exception.
Moreover, as a general rule of thumb, throwing an exception in a destructor
is ill-advised.

The general library implementation of operator **new** is relatively
straightforward, although there are two subtleties worth examining. (*Note:*
The following version does not account for exception handling.)

```
extern void*
operator new( size_t size )
{
    if ( size == 0 )
        size = 1;

    void *last_alloc;
    while ( !( last_alloc = malloc( size )))
    {
        if ( _new_handler )
            ( *_new_handler )();
        else return 0;
    }

    return last_alloc;
}
```

Although it is legal to write

```
new T[ 0 ];
```

the language requires that each invocation of operator **new** return a unique
pointer. The conventional way of solving this is to return a pointer to a default 1-byte memory chunk (this is why size is set to 1). A second interesting element of the implementation is the need to allow the user-supplied
_new_handler(), if present, to possibly free up memory. This is the reason for the loop each time _new_handler() is actually invoked.

Operator **new** in practice has always been implemented in terms of the
standard C malloc(), although there is no requirement to do so (and
therefore one should not presume it will always be done). Similarly, operator **delete** has, in practice, always been implemented in terms of the standard C free():

```
extern void
operator delete( void *ptr )
{
    if ( ptr )
        free( (char*) ptr );
}
```

The Semantics of new Arrays

When we write

```
int *p_array = new int[ 5 ];
```

`vec_new()` is not actually invoked, since its primary function is to apply the default constructor to each element in an array of class objects. Rather, the operator **new** instance is invoked:

```
int *p_array = (int*) __nw( 5 * sizeof( int ));
```

Similarly, if we write

```
// struct simple_aggr { float f1, f2; };
simple_aggr *p_aggr = new simple_aggr[ 5 ];
```

`vec_new()` again is not likely to be invoked. Why? `simple_aggr` does not define either a constructor or destructor, so the allocation and deletion of the array addressed by `p_aggr` involves only the obtaining and release of the actual storage. This is sufficiently managed by the simpler and more efficient operators **new** and **delete**.

If a class defines a default constructor, however, some version of `vec_new()` is invoked to allocate and construct the array of class objects. For example, the expression

```
Point3d *p_array = new Point3d[ 10 ];
```

is generally transformed into

```
Point3d *p_array;

p_array = vec_new( 0, sizeof( Point3d ), 10,
                   &Point3d::Point3d,
                   &Point3d::~Point3d );
```

Recall that the destructor is passed to `vec_new()` in case an exception is thrown during construction of the individual array elements. Only the already constructed elements need the destructor applied to them. Because the memory was allocated for the array within `vec_new()`, `vec_new()` is responsible for freeing it in the event of an exception being thrown.

Prior to Release 2.0, the programmer was responsible for providing the actual size of the array being deleted by an application of operator delete. Thus if we had earlier written

```
int array_size = 10;
Point3d *p_array = new Point3d[ array_size ];
```

we then would have had to write

```
delete [ array_size ] p_array;
```

and hope that in fact p_array had not had its original array deleted already and a new array assigned with a different number of elements. In Release 2.1, the language was modified. The user no longer has to specify the number of array elements to be deleted. Thus we could now write

```
delete [] p_array;
```

although for backward compatibility, both forms are usually still accepted. The first implementation, of course, was in cfront. Jonathan Shopiro did the actual library implementation. Support requires first the storage and then the retrieval of the element count associated with the pointer.

Concern over the impact of searching for the array dimension on the performance of the **delete** operator led to the following compromise. The compiler searches for a dimension size only if the bracket is present. Otherwise, it assumes a single object is being deleted. If the programmer fails to provide the necessary bracket, such as

```
delete p_array;   // oops
```

then only the first element of the array is destructed. The remaining elements are undestructed, although their associated memory is reclaimed. The less error-prone strategy of checking all delete operations for a possible array entry was rejected as being too costly.

An interesting difference between implementations is whether the element count, when explicitly supplied, should be used. In Jonathan's original version of the code, he gives precedence to the user's explicit value. Here is a pseudo-version of what he wrote, with commentary:

```
// first check to see if the last item allocated
// ( __cache_key ) is the item currently being deleted.
//
// if it is, no search need take place.
// if not, then look for the stored element count

int elem_count = __cache_key == pointer
        ? ((__cache_key = 0), __cache_count)
          : // fetch element count

// num_elem: element count passed to vec_new()
// for array allocated from heap, this is only set
// for the form: delete [10] ptr
// otherwise cfront passed it a -1 indicating `fetch'
```

```
if ( num_elem == -1 )
    // prefer explicit user size if choice!
    num_elem = ans;
```

Nearly all new C++ compilers choose not to consider the explicit user value, if present:

```
x.c", line 3: warning(467):
    delete array size expression ignored (anachronism)
    foo() { delete [ 12 ] pi; }
```

Why did Jonathan choose to give precedence to the user-specified value, while newer compilers do not? At the time of its introduction, no user code existed that did not explicitly provide the array size. Had cfront continued to a Release 4.0, we would have labeled the idiom an anachronism and likely have generated a similar warning.

How is this caching of the element count implemented? One obvious way is to allocate an additional word of memory with each chunk of memory returned by the vec_new() operator, tucking the element count in that word (generally, the value tucked away is called a *cookie*). However, Jonathan and the Sun implementation chose to keep an associative array of pointer values and the array size. (Sun also tucks away the address of the destructor—see [CLAM93a].)

The general concern with the cookie strategy was that if a bad pointer value should get passed to delete_vec(), the cookie fetched would of course be invalid. An invalid element count and bad beginning address would result in the destructor's being applied on an arbitrary memory area an arbitrary number of times. Under the associative array strategy, however, the likely result of a bad address's being passed is simply the failure to fetch an element count.

Within the original implementation, two primary functions were added to support the storage and retrieval of the element count cookie:

```
// array_key is the address of the new array
// mustn't either be 0 or already entered
// elem_count is the count; it may be 0

typedef void *PV;
extern int __insert_new_array(PV array_key, int elem_count);

// fetches (and removes) the array_key from table
// either returns the elem_count, or -1


extern int __remove_old_array(PV array_key);
```

The following is a prettified representation of the original cfront implementation of vec_new(), with commentary:

```
PV __vec_new(PV ptr_array, int elem_count,
             int size, PV construct )
{
// if ptr_array is 0, allocate array from heap
// if set, programmer wrote either
//      T array[ count ];
// or
//      new ( ptr_array ) T[ 10 ]

int alloc = 0; // did we allocate here within vec_new?
int array_sz = elem_count * size;

if ( alloc = ptr_array == 0)
      // global operator new ...
      ptr_array = PV( new char[ array_sz ] );

// under Exception Handling,
// would throw exception bad_alloc
if ( ptr_array == 0 )
   return 0;

// place (array, count) into the cache
int status = __insert_new_array( ptr_array, elem_count );
if (status == -1) {
   // under Exception Handling
   // would throw exception bad_alloc
   if ( alloc )
      delete ptr_array;
   return 0;
}

if (construct) {
   register char* elem = (char*) ptr_array;
   register char* lim = elem + array_sz;
   // PF is a typedef for a pointer to function
   register PF fp = PF(construct);
   while (elem < lim) {
      // invoke constructor through fp
      // on `this' element addressed by elem
      (*fp)( (void*)elem );

      // then advance to the next element
      elem += size;
   }
}
```

```
    return PV(ptr_array);
    }
```

vec_delete() works similarly, but its behavior is not always what the
C++ programmer either expects or requires. For example, given the following two class declarations:

```
class Point { public:
    Point();
    virtual ~Point();
    // ...
};

class Point3d : public Point { public:
    Point3d();
    ~Point3d();
    // ...
}
```

the allocation of an array of ten Point3d objects results in the expected invocation of both the Point and Point3d constructor ten times, once for each element of the array:

```
// Not at all a good idea
Point *ptr = new Point3d[ 10 ];
```

What happens, however, when we delete the array of ten Point3d elements addressed by ptr? Obviously, we need the virtual mechanism to
kick in to have the expected invocation of both the Point and Point3d destructor ten times, once for each element of the array:

```
// oops: not what we need!
// only Point::~Point invoked ...
delete [] ptr;
```

The destructor to be applied to the array, as we've seen, is passed to
vec_delete() based on the type of the pointer being deleted. In this case,
the Point destructor is passed. This is obviously not what we want. Moreover,
the size of each element is also passed; this is how vec_delete() iterates
across the array elements. In this case, the size of the Point class object, not of
the Point3d class object, is passed. Oops. The whole operation fails miserably.
Not only is the wrong destructor applied, but after the first element, it is applied to incorrect chunks of memory.

What should a programmer do? The best thing is to avoid addressing an array of derived class objects with a pointer to its base class if an object of the derived class is larger than that of the base. If you really must program this way, the solution is programmer-based rather than language-based:

```
for ( int ix = 0; ix < elem_count; ++ix )
{
    Point *p = &((Point3d*)ptr)[ ix ];
    delete p;
}
```

Essentially, the programmer must iterate through the array, applying the **delete** operator to each element. In this way, the invocation is virtual and both the Point3d and Point destructors are applied to each object.

The Semantics of Placement Operator new

A predefined overloaded instance of operator **new** is that of the placement operator **new**. It takes a second argument of type void*. The invocation looks as follows:

```
Point2w ptw = new ( arena ) Point2w;
```

where arena addresses a location in memory in which to place the new Point2w object. The implementation of this predefined placement operator new is almost embarrassingly trivial. It simply returns the address of the pointer passed to it:

```
void*
operator new( size_t, void* p )
{
    return p;
}
```

If all it does is return the address of its second argument, why use it at all? That is, why not simply write

```
Point2w ptw = ( Point2w* ) arena;
```

since in effect that's what actually happens? Well, actually it's only half of what happens, and it's the second half that the programmer cannot explicitly reproduce. Consider these questions:

1. What is the second half of the placement **new** operator expansion that makes it work (and that the explicit assignment of `arena` does not provide for)?

2. What is the actual type of the pointer represented by `arena` and what are the implications of that type?

The second half of the placement **new** operator expansion is the automatic application of the Point2w constructor applied to the area addressed by `arena`:

```
// Pseudo C++ code
Point2w ptw = ( Point2w* ) arena;
if ( ptw != 0 )
    ptw->Point2w::Point2w();
```

This is what makes the use of the placement operator **new** so powerful. The instance determines where the object is to be placed; the compilation system guarantees that the object's constructor is applied to it.

There is one slight misbehavior, however. Do you see what it is? For example, consider this program fragment:

```
// let arena be globally defined
void fooBar()
    {
    Point2w *p2w = new ( arena ) Point2w;
    // ... do it ...
    // ... now manipulate a new object ...
    p2w = new ( arena ) Point2w;
}
```

If the placement operator constructs the new object "on top of" an existing object and the existing object has an associated destructor, the destructor is not being invoked. One way to invoke the destructor is to apply operator **delete** to the pointer. But in this case, that's the absolutely wrong thing to do:

```
// not the right way to apply destructor here
delete p2w;
p2w = new ( arena ) Point2w;
```

The **delete** operator applies the destructor—this is what we want. But it also frees the memory addressed by p2w—this is definitely not what we want, since the next statement attempts to reuse it. Rather, we need to explicitly invoke the destructor and preserve the storage for reuse:

```
// the correct way of applying destructor
p2w->~Point2w;
p2w = new ( arena ) Point2w;
```

The only remaining problem is a design one: Does the first invocation of the placement operator in our example also construct the new object "on top of" an existing object, or is the arena addressed "raw"? That is, if we have

```
Point2w *p2w = new ( arena ) Point2w;
```

how can we know whether the area addressed by arena needs first to be destructed? There is no language-supported solution to this. A reasonable convention is to have the site applying **new** be responsible for also applying the destructor.

The second question concerns the actual type of the pointer represented by arena. The Standard says it must address either a class of the same type or raw storage sufficient to contain an object of that type. Note that a derived class is explicitly not supported. For a derived class or otherwise unrelated type, the behavior, while not illegal, is undefined.

Raw storage might be allocated as follows:

```
char *arena = new char[ sizeof( Point2w ) ];
```

An object of the same type looks as you might expect:

```
Point2w *arena = new Point2w;
```

In both cases, the storage for the new Point2w exactly overlays the storage location of arena, and the behavior is well defined. In general, however, the placement **new** operator does not support polymorphism. The pointer being passed to **new** is likely to address memory preallocated to a specific size. If the derived class is larger than its base class, such as in the following:

```
Point2w p2w = new ( arena ) Point3w;
```

application of the Point3w constructor is going to wreak havoc, as will most subsequent uses of p2w.

One of the more "dark corner-ish" questions that arose when the **new** placement operator was introduced in Release 2.0 was the following example brought up by Jonathan Shopiro:

placement operator was introduced in Release 2.0 was the following example brought up by Jonathan Shopiro:

```
struct Base { int j; virtual void f(); };
struct Derived : Base { void f(); };

void fooBar() {
    Base b;
    b.f(); // Base::f() invoked
    b.~Base();
    new ( &b ) Derived; // 1
    b.f(); // which f() invoked?
}
```

Since the two classes are the same size, the placement of the derived object within the area allocated for the base class is safe. Supporting it, however, would probably require giving up the general optimization of invoking statically all virtual functions calls through objects, such as b.f(). Consequently, this use of the placement **new** operator is also unsupported under the Standard (see Section 3.8 of the standard). The behavior of the program is undefined: We cannot say with certainty which instance of f() is invoked. (Most implementations, if they were to compile this, would probably invoke Base::f(), while most users would probably expect the invocation of Derived::f().)

6.3   Temporary Objects

If we have a function of the form

```
T operator+( const T&, const T& );
```

and two objects of class T—a and b—the expression

```
a + b;
```

may result in a temporary being generated to hold the returned object. Whether a temporary results depends in part on the aggressiveness of the compiler and in part on the program context in which the expression occurs. For example, consider the following program fragment:

```
T a, b;
T c = a + b;
```

temporary. However, the more probable transformation is to directly copy construct the result of that expression into c (see Section 2.3 for a discussion of the transformation of the addition operator), thus eliminating both the temporary and the associated calls of its constructor and destructor.

Moreover, depending on the definition of the operator+(), the named return value (NRV) optimization (again, see Section 2.3) is likely to be applied. This would result in the direct evaluation of the expression within c and the avoidance of both the call of the copy constructor and the call of the named object's destructor.

The resulting value of c is the same in all three cases. The difference is the cost of initialization. Is there any guarantee what a compiler will do? Strictly speaking, no. The Standard allows the implementation complete freedom regarding temporary generation:

> In some circumstances it might be necessary or convenient for the processor to generate a temporary object. Precisely when such temporaries are introduced is implementation-defined. (Section 12.2)

In theory, the Standard allows the implementation complete freedom. In practice, the competition of the marketplace virtually guarantees that any expression of the form

```
T c = a + b;
```

where the addition operator is defined as either

```
T operator+( const T&, const T& );
```

or

```
T T::operator+( const T& );
```

is implemented without the generation of a temporary.

Note, however, that the equivalent assignment statement

```
c = a + b;
```

cannot safely eliminate the temporary. Rather, this results in the following general sequence:

```
// Pseudo C++ code
// T temp = a + b;
T temp;
a.operator+( temp, b );        // 1
```

```
a.operator+( temp, b ); // 1

// c = temp
c.operator =( temp );   // 2
temp.T::~T();
```

In the line marked //1, the unconstructed temporary is passed to opera-
tor+(). This means that either the result of the expression is copy constructed into the temporary or the temporary is used in place of the NRV. In
the latter case, the constructor that would have been applied to the NRV is
applied to the temporary.

In either case, directly passing c, the target of the assignment, into the
operator function is problematic. Since the operator function does not invoke a destructor on its additional argument (it expects "raw" memory),
the destructor needs be invoked prior to the call. However, then the semantics of the transformation would be to replace assignment:

```
c = a + b; // c.operator=( a + b );
```

with its implicit invocation of the copy assignment operator, with a sequence of destruction and copy construction:

```
// Pseudo C++ code
c.T::~T();
c.T::T( a + b );
```

The copy constructor, destructor, and copy assignment operator can be
user-supplied functions, so there can be no guarantee that the two sequences result in the same semantics. Therefore the replacement of assignment with a sequence of destruction and copy construction is generally
unsafe and the temporary is generated. So an initialization of the form

```
T c = a + b;
```

is in practice always more efficiently translated than is an assignment of the
form

```
c = a + b;
```

A third form of the expression is without any target:

In this case, a temporary is necessarily generated to hold the expression. Although this may, in itself, seem bizarre, its occurrence in practice occurs rather commonly in subexpressions. For example, if we have

```
String s( "hello"), t( "world" ), u( "!" );
```

either

```
String v;
v = s + t + u;
```

or

```
printf( "%s\n", s + t );
```

results in a temporary being associated with the s + t subexpression.

This last expression raises the somewhat esoteric issue of what is the lifetime of a temporary; this deserves a closer look. Prior to Standard C++, the temporary's lifetime—that is, when its destructor is applied—was explicitly left unspecified; it was explicitly said to be implementation dependent. This meant that an expression such as the call to printf() could not be proved to be generally safe, since its correctness depended on when the temporary associated with s + t was destroyed.

(The presumption in this example of a String class is that the class defines a conversion operator of the form

```
String::operator const char*() { return _str; }
```

where _str is a private member addressing storage allocated during the construction of the String object and deallocated within its destructor.) Thus if the temporary is destroyed prior to invoking printf(), the address passed to it by the conversion operator is likely to be invalid. The actual results are implementation dependent based on how aggressive the underlying **delete** operator is in actually freeing the memory addressed. Some implementations, while marking the memory as free, do not actually alter it in any way. Until the memory is claimed by something else, it can be used as if it had not been deleted. While obviously not an exemplary approach to software engineering, this idiom of accessing memory after it has been freed is not uncommon. Many implementations of malloc(), in fact, provide a special invocation

```
malloc( 0 );
```

to guarantee just this behavior.

For example, here is one possible pre-Standard transformation of the expression that, although legal under the pre-Standard language definition, is likely to be disastrous:

```
// Pseudo C++ code: pre-Standard legal transformation
// temporary is destroyed too soon ...

String temp1 = operator+( s, t );
const char *temp2 = temp1.operator const char*();

// oops: legal but ill-advised (pre-Standard)
temp1.~String();

// undefined what temp2 is addressing at this point!
printf( "%s\n", temp2 );
```

An alternative (and, in this case, preferred) transformation is to apply the String destructor after the call to `printf()`. Under the Standard, this is the required transformation of this expression. The exact wording is as follows:

Temporary objects are destroyed as the last step in evaluating the full-expression that (lexically) contains the point where they were created. (Section 12.2)

What is a full-expression? Informally, it is the outermost containing expression. For example, consider the following:

```
// tertiary full expression with 5 sub-expressions
(( objA > 1024 ) && ( objB > 1024 ))
       ? objA + objB : foo( objA, objB );
```

There are five subexpressions contained within the one `?:` full-expression. This means that any temporaries generated within any of the subexpressions must not be destroyed until the entire tertiary expression has been evaluated.

This lifetime of temporaries rule becomes somewhat complex to support when the temporary is conditionally generated based on runtime semantics of the program. For example, what's hard about an expression such as

```
if ( s + t || u + v )
```

is that the u + v subexpression is only conditionally evaluated based on s + t evaluating as false. The temporary associated with the second subexpression must be destroyed, but, obviously, must not be unconditionally destroyed. That is, it is desirable to destroy the temporary only in those cases when it has been created!

Prior to the lifetime of temporaries rule, the standard implementation was to attach both the initialization *and* destruction of the temporary to the evaluation of the second subexpression. For example, with the following class declaration:

```
class X {
public:
    X();
    ~X();
    operator int();
    X foo();
private:
    int val;
};
```

and the following conditional test of two objects of class X:

```
main() {
    X xx;
    X yy;

    if ( xx.foo() || yy.foo() )
    ;

    return 0;
}
```

cfront generates the following program transformation of main() (the output has been slightly prettified and commented):

```
int main (void ){
    struct x __1xx ;
    struct x __1yy ;

    int __0_result;

    // name_mangled default constructor:
    // X::X( X *this )
    __ct__1xFv ( & __1xx ) ;
    __ct__1xFv ( & __1yy ) ;

    {
```

```
// generated temporaries ...
struct x __0__Q1 ;
struct x __0__Q2 ;
int __0__Q3 ;

/* each side becomes a comma expression of
 * the following sequence of steps:
 *
 *    tempQ1 = xx.foo();
 *    tempQ3 = tempQ1.operator int();
 *    tempQ1.X::~X();
 *    tempQ3;
 */

// __opi__1xFv ==> X::operator int()

if ((((
        __0__Q3 = __opi__1xFv(((
        __0__Q1 = foo__1xFv( &__1xx )), (&__0__Q1 )))),
        __dt__1xFv( &__0__Q1, 2) ), __0__Q3 )
    || (((
        __0__Q3 = __opi__1xFv(((
        __0__Q2 = foo__1xFv( & __1yy )), (&__0__Q2 )))),
        __dt__1xFv( & __0__Q2, 2) ), __0__Q3 ));

    {{
        __0_result = 0 ;
        __dt__1xFv ( & __1yy , 2) ;
        __dt__1xFv ( & __1xx , 2) ;
    }

        return __0_result ;
}}}
```

This strategy of placing the temporary's destructor in the evaluation of each subexpression circumvents the need to keep track of whether the second subexpression is actually evaluated. However, under the Standard's lifetime of temporaries rule, this implementation strategy is no longer permissible. The temporaries must not be destroyed until after evaluation of the full expression—that is, both sides—and so some form of conditional test must be inserted now to determine whether to destroy the temporary associated with the second subexpression.

There are two exceptions to the lifetime of temporaries rule. The first concerns an expression used to initialize an object; for example,

```
bool verbose;
...
String progNameVersion =
      !verbose
        ? 0
        : progName + progVersion;
```

where `progName` and `progVersion` are String objects. A temporary is created to hold the result of the addition operator

```
String operator+( const String&, const String& );
```

The temporary must be conditionally destructed based on the outcome of the test of verbose. Under the lifetime of temporaries rule, the temporary should be destroyed as soon as the full ?: expression is evaluated. However, if the initialization of `progNameVersion` requires invocation of a copy constructor

```
// Pseudo C++ Code
progNameVersion.String::String( temp );
```

then destruction of the temporary following evaluation of the ?: expression is certainly not what one wants. The Standard, therefore, requires

> ...the temporary that holds the result of the expression shall persist until the object's initialization is complete.

Even with all the firming up regarding the lifetime of temporaries that the Standard accomplished, it is still possible for programmers to have a temporary destroyed out from under them. The primary difference now is that the behavior is well defined. For example, here is an initialization that is guaranteed to fail under the new lifetime of temporaries rule:

```
// Oops: not a good idea
const char *progNameVersion =
   progName + progVersion;
```

where again `progName` and `progVersion` are String objects. The code generated for this looks something like:

```
// Pseudo C++ Code
String temp;
operator+( temp, progName, progVersion );
progNameVersion = temp.String::operator char*();
temp.String::~String();
```

`progNameVersion` now points into undefined heap memory.

The second exception to the lifetime of temporaries rule concerns when a temporary is bound to a reference. For example,

```
const String &space = " ";
```

generates code that looks something like

```
// Pseudo C++ Code
String temp;
temp.String::String( " " );
const String &space = temp;
```

Obviously, if the temporary were destroyed now, the reference would be slightly less than useless. So the rule is that a temporary bound to a reference

> persists for the lifetime of the reference initialized or until the end of the scope in which the temporary is created, whichever comes first.

A Temporary Myth

A general perception is that the generation of temporaries within current C++ implementations contributes to inefficiencies in program execution that make C++ a poor second choice over FORTRAN in scientific and engineering computing. Further, it is thought that this lack of efficiency offsets the greater abstracting facilities of C++ (see [BUDGE92], for example). (For arguments against this position, see [NACK94].) An interesting study in this regard is that of [BUDGE94] published in *The Journal of C Language Translation*.

In a comparison of FORTRAN-77 and C++, Kent Budge and his associates programmed a complex number test case in both languages. (complex is a built-in type in FORTRAN; in C++, it is a concrete class with two members, one real and one imaginary. Standard C++ has made the complex class part of the standard library.) The C++ program implemented inline arithmetic operators of the form

```
friend complex operator+( complex, complex );
```

(Note that passing class objects containing constructors and destructors by value rather than by reference, such as

```
friend complex
operator+( const complex&, const complex& );
```

is generally not good programming style in C++. Apart from the issue of copying by value possibly large class objects, the local instance of each formal argument has to be copy constructed and destructed and may result in the generation of a temporary. In this test case, the authors claim that converting the formal arguments to **const** references did not significantly increase performance. This is only because each function invocation is inlined.)

The test function looked like:

```
void func( complex *a, const complex *b,
           const complex *c, int N )
{
    for ( int i = 0; i < N; i++ )
        a[i] = b[i]+c[i] - b[i]*c[i];
}
```

where the addition, subtraction, multiplication, and assignment operators for the complex C++ class are inline instances. The C++ code generated five temporaries:

1. A temporary to hold the value of the subexpression `b[i]+c[i]`

2. A temporary to hold the value of the subexpression `b[i]*c[i]`

3. A temporary to hold the result of subtracting item 2 from item 1

4. Two temporaries, one each to hold the results of items 1 and 2 in order to carry out item 3

Time comparisons against the FORTRAN-77 code showed the FORTRAN code to be nearly twice as fast. Their first assumption was to blame the temporaries. To verify that, they hand-eliminated all temporaries in the intermediate cfront output. As expected, the performance increased two-fold and equaled that of FORTRAN-77.

Not stopping there, Budge and his associates experimented with a different approach. Rather than eliminating the temporaries, they "disaggregated" them. That is, they hand-coded the temporary aggregate class structure into pairs of temporary doubles. They discovered that disaggregation resulted in performance as efficient as that achieved by temporary elimination. They noted the following:

The translation systems we tested are evidently able to eliminate local variables of built-in type, but not local variables of class type. This is a limitation of C back-ends, not of the C++ front-end, and it

The translation systems we tested are evidently able to eliminate local variables of built-in type, but not local variables of class type. This is a limitation of C back-ends, not of the C++ front-end, and it appears to be pervasive, since it appears in both [sic] Sun CC, GNU g++, and HP CC. [BUDGE94]

The paper analyzes the generated assembly and shows that the cause of the performance degradation is the large number of program stack accesses to read and write the individual class members. By disaggregating the class and moving the individual members into registers, they were able to achieve nearly doubled performance. This led them to conclude the following:

Disaggregation of structs is achievable with modest effort, but has not generally been recognized as an important optimization prior to the introduction of C++ [BUDGE94].

In a sense, this study is simply a persuasive argument for good optimization. There already exist some optimizers, I'm told, that do put pieces of temporary classes into registers. As compiler implementations shift their focus from language feature support (with the completion of Standard C++) to quality of implementation issues, optimizations such as disaggregation should become commonplace.[1]

---

[1] SGI, for example, told me that they support disaggregation in their "Mongoose" compiler for their OS 6.2.

Chapter 7

On the Cusp of the Object Model

In this chapter, I discuss three prominent extensions to the language that affect the C++ Object Model: templates, exception handling (EH), and runtime type identification (RTTI). EH (and RTTI, which in a sense is a side effect of EH) is an exception to the other language features covered here in that I have never had the opportunity to actually implement it. My discussion, therefore, relies on [CHASE94], [LAJOIE94a], [LAJOIE94b], [LENKOV92], and [SUN94a].

7.1   Templates

C++ programming styles and idioms have been profoundly transformed since the introduction of templates (with cfront, Release 3.0, in 1991) and experience using them. Originally viewed as a support for container classes such as Lists and Arrays, templates are now the foundation for generic programming (the Standard Template Library). They also are used as idioms for attribute mix-in where, for example, memory allocation strategies ([BOOCH93]) or mutual exclusion mechanisms for synchronizing threads ([SCHMIDT94]) are parameterized. They further are used as a technique for template metaprograms, in which class expression templates are evaluated at compile time rather than runtime, thereby providing significant performance improvements ([VELD95]).

That said, however, it is also true that programming with templates is currently one of the most frustrating aspects of C++ programming. Error messages are often generated far from the actual site of the problem. Compilation times often rise exponentially, and one begins to positively dread changing a header file with multifile dependencies, particularly if one is in the midst of debugging. It also isn't uncommon to find unexpected ballooning of program size. Further, all these behaviors are generally beyond the comprehension of the average programmer who simply wants to get his or her work done and who, if these problems persist, may come to view the language more as an obstacle than as an aid. It is not uncommon to find a designated template expert among the members of a project who trouble-shoots and attempts to optimize the generation of templates.

This section focuses on the semantics of template support, a sort of when, why, and how of what is done with templates within a compilation system. There are three primary aspects of template support:

1. Processing of the template declarations—essentially, what happens when you declare a template class, template class member function, and so on.

2. Instantiation of the class object and inline nonmember and member template functions. These are instances required within each compilation unit.

3. Instantiation of the nonmember and member template functions and static template class members. These are instances required only once within an executable. This is where the problems with templates generally arise.

I use *instantiation* to mean the process of binding actual types and expressions to the associated formal parameters of the template. For example, with the template function

```
template <class Type>
Type
min( const Type &t1, const Type &t2 ) { ... }
```

and its use

```
min( 1.0, 2.0 );
```

the instantiation process binds Type to **double** and creates a program text instance of min() (suitably mangled to give it a unique name within the executable) in which t1 and t2 are of type **double**.

Template Instantiation

Consider the following template Point class:

```
template <class Type>
class Point
{
public:
    enum Status { unallocated, normalized };

    Point( Type x = 0.0, Type y = 0.0, Type z = 0.0 );
    ~Point();

    void* operator new( size_t );
    void  operator delete( void*, size_t );

    // ...
private:
    static Point< Type > *freeList;
    static int chunkSize;
    Type _x, _y, _z;
};
```

First, what happens when the compiler sees the template class declaration? In terms of the actual program, nothing. That is, the static data members are not available. Nor is the nested enum or its enumerators.

Although the actual type of the enum Status is invariant across all Point instantiations, as well as the value of its enumerators, each can be accessed only through a particular instance of the template Point class. Thus we can write

```
// ok:
Point< float >::Status s;
```

but not

```
// error:
Point::Status s;
```

although both types, abstractly, are the same. (And, optimally, we'd want only a single instance of any invariant nested type to be generated. Failing that, we might want to factor out the nested type to a nontemplate base class in order to prevent multiple copies.)

Similarly, the static data members freeList and chunkSize are not yet available to the program. We cannot write

```
// error:
Point::freeList;
```

but must specify the explicit template Point class instantiation with which the freeList member is associated:

```
// ok:
Point< float >::freeList;
```

This use of the static member causes an instance associated with the **float** instantiation of the Point class to be generated within the program. If we write

```
// ok: another instance
Point< double >::freeList;
```

a second freeList instance is generated, this one associated with the **double** instantiation of the Point class.

If we define a pointer to a particular instance, such as

```
Point< float > *ptr = 0;
```

again, nothing happens in the program. Why? Because a pointer to a class object is *not* itself a class object; the compiler does not need to know anything about the layout or members of the class. So instantiating a **float** instance of Point is unnecessary. Until the C++ Standard, however, the effect of declaring a pointer to a specific template class was left undefined; the compilation system might or might not instantiate the template (for example, cfront did, to the dismay of quite a few programmers). Under the Standard, the compilation system is explicitly prohibited from doing so.

The behavior in declaring a reference to a particular instance of a template, however, such as

```
const Point< float > &ref = 0;
```

does result in the instantiation of a **float** instance of Point. The actual semantics of this definition expand as follows:

```
// internal expansion
Point< float > temporary( float (0) );
const Point< float > &ref = temporary;
```

Why? Because a reference cannot be an alias to "no object." The 0 is treated as an integer value that must be converted into an object of the type

```
Point< float >
```

If there is no conversion possible, then the definition is in error and is flagged at compile time.

So the definition of a class object, either implicitly by the compiler, as with the generation of temporary, or explicitly by the programmer, as in the following:

```
const Point< float > origin;
```

results in the instantiation of the template class. This means the actual object layout of the **float** instantiation is generated. Looking back at the template declaration, we see that a Point has three nonstatic members, each of type Type. Type becomes bound to type **float**, so origin is allocated space sufficient to contain three **float** members.

However, the member functions—at least those that are not used—should not be instantiated. Standard C++ requires that member functions be instantiated only if they are used (current implementations do not strictly follow this requirement). There are two main reasons for the use-directed instantiation rule:

1. *Space and time efficiency.* If there are a hundred member functions associated with a class, but your program uses only two for one type and five for a second type, then instantiating the additional 193 can be a significant time and space hit.

2. *Unimplemented functionality.* Not all types with which a template is instantiated support all the operators (such as i/o and the relational operators) required by the complete set of member functions. By instantiating only those member functions actually used, a template is able to support types that otherwise would generate compile-time errors.

The definition of origin, for example, requires the invocation of the default Point constructor and destructor. Only these two functions must be instantiated. Similarly, when the programmer writes

```
Point< float > *p = new Point< float >;
```

only the **float** instance of the Point template itself, the class instance operator **new**, and the default constructor need to be instantiated. (It's interesting to note that although operator **new** is implicitly a static member of the class and so may not directly access any of its nonstatic members, it is still dependent on the actual template parameter type because its `size_t` first argument is passed the class size.)

When do these function instantiations take place? There are two current strategies:

- At compile time, in which case the functions are instantiated within the file in which `origin` and `p` are defined.

- At link time, in which case the compiler is reinvoked by some auxiliary tool. The template function instances may be placed within this file, some other file, or a separate repository.

Function instantiation is discussed in more detail in a subsection later in the chapter.

An interesting point raised in [CARGILL95] is whether, on an architecture in which types **int** and **long** are the same (or **double** and **long double**), the two type instantiations

```
Point < int > pi;
Point < long > pl;
```

should result in one or two instantiations. Currently, all implementations I am aware of generate two instantiations (with possibly two complete sets of member function instantiations). The Standard does not address this point.

Error Reporting within a Template

Consider the following template declaration:

```
1. template <class T>
2. class Mumble
3. {
4. public$:
5.    Mumble( T t = 1024 )
6.         : _t( t )
7.    {
8.       if ( tt != t )
9.          throw ex ex;
10.   }
11.   private:
12.      T tt;
13.   }
```

The declaration of the Mumble template class contains a collection of both blatant and potential errors:

1. Line 4: The use of the $ character is incorrect. This error is two-fold: (1) The $ is not a valid character for an identifier, and (2) only public, protected, and private labels are permitted in the body of a class declaration (the presence of the $ no longer identifies it as the keyword label **public**). (1) is a lexical error, while (2) is a syntactic/parsing error.

2. Line 5: The initialization of t to the integer constant 1024 may or may not be legal depending on the actual type of T. In general, this can be diagnosed only for each instantiation of the template.

3. Line 6: _t is not the member name; tt is. This kind of error is generally discovered within the type-checking phase during which each name is either bound to a definition or an error is generated.

4. Line 8: The not equal operator (!=) may or may not be defined depending on the actual type of T. As with item 2, this can be diagnosed only for each instantiation of the template.

5. Line 9: We accidentally typed ex twice. This is an error discovered during the parsing phase of the compilation (a legal "sentence" of the language cannot have one identifier following another).

6. Line 13: We forgot to terminate the class declaration with a semicolon. Again, this is an error discovered during the parsing phase of the compilation.

In a nontemplate class declaration, these six blatant and potential errors are resolved by the compiler at the point at which the declaration is seen. This is not the case with templates, however. For one thing, all type-dependent checking involving the template parameters must be deferred until an actual instantiation occurs. That is, the potential errors on lines 5 and 8 (items 2 and 4, above) of the example are checked and reported for each instantiation and are resolved on a type-by-type basis. Thus for

```
Mumble< int > mi;
```

both lines are correct. For

```
Mumble< int* > pmi;
```

line 8 is correct, but line 5 is a type error—you cannot assign a pointer an integer constant (other than 0). With the declaration

```
class SmallInt
{
public:
   SmallInt( int );
   // ...
};
```

within which the not-equal operator is not defined, the instance

```
Mumble< SmallInt > smi;
```

generates an error for line 8, while line 5 is correct. Of course,

```
Mumble< SmallInt* > psmi;
```

once again reverses that: Line 8 is again correct, but line 5 is again in error.

What, then, are the errors that are flagged when handling the template declaration? In part this depends on the processing strategy for the template. In the original cfront implementation, the template is fully parsed but not type-checked. Type-checking is applied only to each particular instantiation. So under a parsing strategy, all the lexing and parsing errors are flagged during the handling of the template declaration.

The lexical analyzer would catch the illegal character on line 4. The parser itself would likely flag the

```
public$: // caught
```

as an illegal label within the class declaration. The parser would not flag the reference to an unnamed member:

```
_t( t )  // not caught
```

It would catch the presence of ex twice in the throw expression of line 9 and the missing semicolon on line 13.

In a popular alternative implementation strategy (for example, see [BALL92a]), the template declaration is collected as a sequence of lexical tokens. The parsing is delayed until an actual instantiation. When an actual instantiation is seen, the set of tokens is pushed through the parser and then type-checking is invoked, and so on. What errors does a lexical tokenizing of the template declaration flag? Very few, in fact; only the illegal character used in line 4. The rest of the template declaration breaks up into a legal collection of tokens.

In current implementation, that is, a template declaration has only limited error checking applied to it prior to an instantiation of an actual set of parameters. Non–syntax-related errors within a template that a user might consider blatantly obvious are likely to compile without complaint and be flagged as an error only after a particular instance is defined. This is more an issue of current practices than an aspect of the template facility itself. The handling of template functions underscores this the most dramatically.

Nonmember and member template functions are also not fully type-checked until instantiated. In current implementations, this leads to error-free compilations of some rather blatantly incorrect template declarations. For example, given the following template declaration of Foo:

```
template < class type >
class Foo {
public:
    Foo();
    type val();
    void val( type v );
private:
    type _val;
};
```

cfront, the Sun compiler, and Borland all compile this *without complaint*:

```
// current implementations do not flag this definition
// syntactically legal; semantically in error:
// (a) bogus_member not a member function of class
// (b) dbx not a data member of class

template < class type >
double Foo< type >::bogus_member() { return this->dbx; }
```

Again, this is an implementation decision. There is nothing inherent in the template facility that disallows more rigorous error checking of the non–type-dependent portions of a template declaration. Certainly, errors like these could be discovered and flagged. Currently, however, it is simply not done.

Name Resolution within a Template

There is a distinction between the program site at which a template is defined (called in the Standard the *scope of the template definition*) and the program site at which a template is actually instantiated (called the *scope of the template instantiation*). An example of the first is

```
// scope of the template definition

extern double foo ( double );

template < class type >
class ScopeRules
{
public:
    void invariant() {
        _member = foo( _val );
    }

    type type_dependent() {
        return foo( _member );
    }
    // ...
private:
    int  _val;
    type _member;
};
```

and an example of the second is

```
//scope of the template instantiation

extern int foo( int );
// ...
ScopeRules< int > sr0;
```

There are two invocations of foo() within the ScopeRules template class. Within the scope of the template definition, only one declaration of foo() is in scope. Within the scope of the template instantiation, however, two declarations are in scope. If we have an invocation such as

```
// scope of the template instantiation
sr0.invariant();
```

the question is, which instance of foo() is invoked for the call:

```
// which instance of foo()?
_member = foo( _val );
```

The two instances in scope at this point in the program are

```
// scope of the template declaration
extern double foo ( double );

// scope of the template instantiation
extern int foo( int );
```

and the type of _val is **int**. So which do you think is chosen? (*Hint:* The only way to answer this correctly—apart from guessing—is to know the answer.) Obviously, the instance chosen is the nonintuitive one:

```
// scope of the template declaration
extern double foo ( double );
```

The program site of the resolution of a nonmember name within a template is determined by whether the use of the name is dependent on the parameter types used to instantiate the template. If the use is not dependent, then the scope of the template declaration determines the resolution of the name. If the use is dependent, then the scope of the template instantiation determines the resolution of the name. In this first example, then, the resolution of foo () is *not* dependent on the type parameter used to instantiate ScopeRules:

```
// the resolution of foo() is not
// dependent on the template argument
_member = foo( _val );
```

This is because _val is an invariant template class member of type **int**; that is, the actual type used to instantiate the template has no effect on the type of _val. Moreover, function resolution is determined by the signature of the function only and not its return type. Thus the type of _member does not influence the choice of which foo () to invoke, and the invocation of foo () is not dependent on the template argument. The invocation must be resolved from the scope of the template declaration. Within that scope is only the one candidate instance of foo () from which to choose. (Note that this behavior cannot be reproduced with a simple macro expansion, such as a use of **#define** macros of the preprocessor.)

Let's look at a type-dependent usage:

```
sr0.type_dependent();
```

Which foo () does its call resolve to?

```
return foo( _member );
```

This instance clearly is dependent on the template argument that determines the actual type of _member. So this instance of foo() must be resolved from the scope of the template instantiation, which in this case includes both declarations of foo(). Since _member is of type **int** in this instance, it's the integer instance of foo() that is invoked. Were ScopeRules instantiated with an argument of type **double**, then the double instance would be invoked. Were it instantiated with an **unsigned int** or **long,** the invocation would be ambiguous. Finally, were it instantiated with a class type for which a conversion existed for neither instance, the invocation would be flagged as an error. Regardless of the outcome of the invocation, the candidate declarations reflect the scope of the template instantiation site and not of the template declaration.

This means an implementation must keep two scope contexts:

1. The scope of the template declaration, which is fixed to the generic template class representation

2. The scope of the template instantiation, which is fixed to the representation of the particular instance

The compiler's resolution algorithm must determine which is the appropriate scope within which to search for the name.

Member Function Instantiation

The most difficult aspect of template support is template function instantiation. Current implementations provide two instantiation strategies: a compile-time strategy in which the code source must be available within the program text file and a link-time strategy in which some meta-compilation tool directs the compiler instantiation.

There are three main questions an implementation has to answer:

1. How does the implementation find the function definition?

   One solution is to require that the template program text file be included the same as if it were a header file. The Borland compiler, for example, follows this strategy. Or we could require a file-naming convention. For example, we could require that the template program text for a declaration found in a file *Point.h* be placed in a file *Point.C* or *Point.cpp,* and so on. cfront follows this strategy. The Edison Design Group compiler supports both.

2. How does the implementation instantiate only those member functions that are actually used by the application?

One solution is simply to ignore this requirement and instead generate all the member functions of an instantiated class. The Borland compiler, for example, follows this strategy, while supporting **#pragma**s to suppress or instantiate specific instances. An alternative strategy is to simulate linkage of the application to see which instances are actually required and generate only those. cfront follows this strategy. The Edison Design Group compiler supports both.

3. How does the implementation prevent the instantiation of member definitions within multiple *.o* files?

   One solution is to generate multiple copies and then provide support from the linker to ignore all but one instance. Another solution is the use-directed instantiation strategy of simulating the link phase to determine which instances are required.

The current weakness of both compile-time and link-time instantiation strategies is a sometimes significant increase in compile time while the template instances are being generated. Obviously, there is going to be a first-time instantiation requirement for the template functions. Implementations break down, however, when those functions are reinstantiated unnecessarily or when the overhead for determining whether the functions need to be reinstantiated takes too long.

The original intention of C++ template support envisioned a use-directed automatic instantiation mechanism that required neither user intervention nor multiple instantiations of the same file. This has proved considerably more difficult to achieve than anyone at the time imagined (see [STROUP94]). **ptlink**, the original instantiation tool accompanying Release 3.0, provided a use-driven automatic instantiation mechanism but was far too complex for even sophisticated users to understand and was unacceptably slow for large applications.

The Edison Design Group has developed a "second-generation" directed-instantiation mechanism that comes closest (of those I am aware of) to the original intention of the template facility. Briefly, it works as follows:

1. The initial compilation of a program's source files does not result in any template instantiations. However, information about instances that could have been instantiated is generated within the object file.

2. When the object files are linked together, a *prelinker* program is executed. It examines the object files looking for references to and corresponding definitions of template instances.

3. For each reference to a template instance for which there is no definition, the prelinker identifies a file in which it could have been instantiated (using the information generated in step 1). In this way, it assigns the necessary program instantiations to particular files. These are registered in a prelinker- generated *.ii* file stored in an *ii_file* directory.

4. The prelinker reexecutes the compiler to recompile each file for which the *.ii* files have changed. This is repeated until a transitive closure of all necessary instantiations is achieved.

5. The object files are linked together into an executable.

The primary cost of this directed-instantiation scheme is the set-up time of the *.ii* files the first time the program is compiled. A secondary cost is the need to run the prelinker for every compile afterwards in order to ensure a definition exists for all referenced templates. After the initial set-up and successful first link, recompilation consists of the following:

1. For each program text file being recompiled, the compiler checks the associated *.ii* file.

2. If the associated *.ii* file lists a set of templates to be instantiated, those templates (and only those templates) are instantiated in the course of compiling the program text file.

3. The prelinker must be run to ensure all referenced templates have been defined.

The presence of some form of automated template mechanism is, in my opinion, a necessary component of a programmer-friendly C++ compilation system, although admittedly no current system is problem-free. Still, as a developer, I would not use or recommend a system without such a mechanism.

Unfortunately, no mechanism is without its bugs.[1] The Edison Design Group's compiler uses an algorithm introduced in cfront, Release 2.0 [KOENIG90a], to automatically generate (in most cases) a single instance of a virtual table for each class within a program. For example, given the following class declaration:

```
class PrimitiveObject : public Geometry
{
public:
    virtual ~PrimitiveObject();
    virtual void draw();

    ...
};
```

---

[1] Since fixed, of course, the discussion remains instructive, however.

that is included in 15 or 45 program text files, how can the compiler ensure that only one virtual table instance is generated (generating 15 or 45 is easy!)?

Andy Koenig came up with the following observation: The address of every virtual function is placed within the virtual tables of the classes for which it is active.[2] By having the function's address taken, the definition of the virtual function must be present somewhere within the program; otherwise, the program will not link. Moreover, only one instance of the function can be present or the program will not link. So, place the virtual table in the file within which is defined the first non-inline, nonpure virtual function defined by the class. In our example, the compiler generates the virtual table within the file within which the virtual destructor is stored.

Unfortunately, this single definition observation does not necessarily hold true under templates. Not only may multiple definitions be generated under the "compile everything in the module" model of template support, but link editors now permit multiple definitions, choosing one and ignoring the rest.

Okay, very interesting, but what does this have to do with the Edison Design Group's automatic instantiation mechanism? Consider the following library function:

```
void foo( const Point< float > *ptr )
{
    ptr->virtual_func();
}
```

The virtual function call is translated into something like:

```
// Pseudo C++ code
// ptr->virtual_func();
( *ptr->__vtbl__Point< float >[ 2 ] )( ptr );
```

thus resulting in an instantiation of the **float** instance of the Point class and that of `virtual_func()`. Because the address of each virtual function is placed within the table, if the virtual table is generated each virtual function must also be instantiated. This is why the Standard has the following, otherwise puzzling clause in Section 14.3.2:

> If a virtual function is instantiated, its point of instantiation is immediately following the point of instantiation for its class.

However, if the compiler follows cfront's virtual table implementation scheme, the table will not be generated until a definition of the virtual

---

[2] This has been relaxed by the standard.

destructor for the **float** instance of Point is instantiated. Except, at this point, there is no explicit use of the virtual destructor to warrant its instantiation.

The Edison Design Group's automatic template mechanism does not realize the implicit use its own compiler makes of the first non-inline, non-pure virtual function and so does not mark it for instantiation within a *.ii* file. As a result, the linker comes back complaining of the absence of the

```
__vtbl__Point< float >
```

symbol and refuses to create an executable. Oh, bother! Automatic instantiation breaks down in this case, and the programmer must explicitly force the destructor to be instantiated. Currently, this is supported under this compilation system with the use of **#pragma** directives. The Standard, however, has extended template support to allow the programmer to explicitly request the instantiation within a file of an entire class template:

```
template class Point3d< float >;
```

an individual member function of a template class:

```
template float Point3d<float>::X() const;
```

and an individual template function:

```
template Point3d<float> operator+(
    const Point3d<float>&, const Point3d<float>& );
```

In practice, template instantiation seems to resist full automation.[3] Even when everything works right, the resulting set of object files may still prove too costly to recompile regularly if the application is large enough. Manual preinstantiation within a separate object module is tedious but often is the only effective solution.

7.2   Exception Handling

The primary implementation task in supporting exception handling (EH) is to discover the appropriate **catch** clause to handle the thrown exception. This requires an implementation to somehow keep track of the active area of each function on the program stack (including keeping track of the local class objects active at that point in the function). Also, the implementation must provide some method of querying the exception object as to its actual

---

[3] The standards committee (July 1996) voted on modifications to provide for a simpler and more efficient template instantiation model.

type (this leads directly to some form of runtime type identification (RTTI)). Finally, there needs to be some mechanism for the management of the object thrown—its creation, storage, possible destruction (if it has an associated destructor), clean up, and general access. (There also may be multiple objects active at one time.) In general, the EH mechanism requires a tightly coupled handshake between compiler-generated data structures and a runtime exception library. The implementation tradeoff is between program size versus the runtime speed of the program when no exception is being handled:

- To maintain execution speed, the compiler can build up the supporting data structures during compilation. This adds to the size of the program, but means the compiler can largely ignore these structures until an exception is thrown.

- To maintain program size, the compiler can build up the supporting data structures "on the fly" as each function is executed. This affects the speed of the program but means the compiler needs to build (and then can discard) the data structures only as they are needed.

According to [CHASE94], the Modula-3 Report has actually "institutionalized" a preference for maintaining execution speed at the expense of program size by recommending "that 10,000 instructions may be spent in the exceptional case to save one instruction in the normal case." That tradeoff is not universal, however. At a recent conference in Tel Aviv, I was speaking with Shay Bushinsky, one of the developers of "Junior," a chess program that tied for third place with IBM's "Deep Blue" in the winter 1994 world computer chess championship. Surprisingly, the program runs on a Pentium-based personal computer (Deep Blue uses 256 processors). He told me that when they recompiled it under the version of the Borland compiler that incorporated EH, it no longer fit in available memory even though nothing in the program changed. As a result, they had to fall back to an earlier version of the compiler. For "Junior," a bigger but noninvasive runtime program is not an option. (Nor, on the other hand, would the runtime impact of building up the data structures on the fly likely be acceptable. Support for EH brings with it additional overhead whether or not an exception is thrown.)

It is also worth noting (in passing) that EH literally killed off cfront. It is simply not possible to provide an acceptably robust EH mechanism without the support of the code generator (and linker). The UNIX Software Laboratory (USL) sat on the C-generating implementation of EH delivered by Hewlett-Packard for over a year (see [LENKOV92] for a discussion of their portable implementation and its performance). USL finally threw up its collective hands and canceled plans for a Release 4.0 and for any further development of cfront.

A Quick Review of Exception Handling

Exception handling under C++ consists of the following three main syntactic components:

1. *A **throw** clause.* A **throw** clause raises an exception at some point within the program. The exception thrown can be of a built-in or user-defined type.

2. *One or more **catch** clauses.* Each **catch** clause is the exception handler. It indicates a type of exception the clause is prepared to handle and gives the actual handler code enclosed in braces.

3. *A **try** block.* A **try** block surrounds a sequence of statements for which an associated set of **catch** clauses is active.

When an exception is thrown, control passes up the function call sequence until either an appropriate **catch** clause is matched or main() is reached without a handler's being found, at which point the default handler, terminate(), is invoked. As control passes up the call sequence, each function in turn is popped from the program stack (this process is called *unwinding the stack*). Prior to the popping of each function, the destructors of the function's local class objects are invoked.

What is slightly nonintuitive about EH is the impact it has on functions that seemingly have nothing to do with exceptions. For example, consider the following:

```
1. Point*
2. mumble()
3. {
4.     Point *pt1, *pt2;
5.     pt1 = foo();
6.     if ( !pt1 )
7.         return 0;
8.
9.     Point p;
10.
11.    pt2 = foo();
12.    if ( !pt2 )
13.        return pt1;
```

```
14.
15.     ...
16.     }
```

If an exception is thrown within the first call of foo () (line 5), then the function can simply be popped from the program stack. The statement is not within a **try** block, so there is no need to attempt to match up with a **catch** clause; nor are there any local class objects requiring destruction. If an exception is thrown within the second call of foo () (line 11), however, then the EH mechanism must invoke the destructor for p before unwinding the function from the program stack.

Under EH, that is, lines 4–8 and lines 9–16 are viewed as semantically distinct regions of the function with differing runtime semantics should an exception be thrown. Moreover, EH support requires additional bookkeeping. An implementation could either associate the two regions with separate lists of local objects to be destroyed (these would be set up at compile time) or share a single list that is added to and shrunk dynamically at runtime.

On the programmer level, EH also alters the semantics of functions that manage resources. The following function includes, for example, both a locking and unlocking of a shared memory region and is no longer guaranteed to run correctly under EH even though it seemingly has nothing to do with exceptions:

```
void
mumble( void *arena )
{
    Point *p = new Point;
    smLock( arena ); // function call

    // problem if an exception is thrown here
    // ...

    smUnLock( arena ); // function call
    delete p;
}
```

In this case, the EH facility views the entire function as a single region requiring no processing other than unwinding the function from the program stack. Semantically, however, we need to both unlock shared memory and delete p prior to the function being popped. The most straightforward (if not the most effective) method of making the function "exception proof" is to insert a default **catch** clause, as follows:

```
void
mumble( void *arena )
{
    Point *p;
    p = new Point;
    try {
        smLock( arena );
        // ...
    }
    catch ( ... ) {
        smUnLock( arena );
        delete p;
        throw;
    }

    smUnLock( arena );
    delete p;
}
```

The function now has two regions:

1. The region outside the **try** block for which there is nothing for the EH mechanism to do except pop the program stack

2. The region within the **try** block (and its associated default **catch** clause)

Notice that the invocation of operator **new** is not within the **try** block. Is this an error on my part? If either operator **new** or the Point constructor invoked after the allocation of memory should throw an exception, neither the unlocking of memory nor the deletion of p following the **catch** clause is invoked. Is this the correct semantics?

Yes, it is. If operator **new** throws an exception, memory from the heap would not have been allocated and the Point constructor would not have been invoked. So, there would be no reason to invoke operator **delete**. If, however, the exception were thrown within the Point constructor following allocation from the heap, any constructed composite or subobject within Point (that is, a member class or base class object) would automatically be destructed and then the heap memory freed. In either case, there is no need to invoke operator **delete**. (I revisit this at the end of this section.)

Similarly, if an exception were thrown during the processing of operator **new**, the shared memory segment addressed by arena would never have become locked; therefore, there would be no need to unlock it.

The recommended idiom for handling these sorts of resource management is to encapsulate the resource acquisition within a class object, the destructor of which frees the resource (this style becomes cumbersome, however, when resources need to be acquired, released, then reacquired and released a second or subsequent times):

```
void
mumble( void *arena )
{
    auto_ptr <Point> ph ( new Point );
    SMLock sm( arena );

    // no problem now if an exception is thrown here
    // ...

    // no need to explicitly unlock & delete
    // local destructors invoked here
    // sm.SMLock::~SMLock();
    // ph.auto_ptr <Point>::~auto_ptr <Point> ()
}
```

The function now has three regions with regard to EH:

1. One in which the standard `auto_ptr` is defined

2. One in which the SMLock is defined

3. One that follows the two definitions and spans the entire function

If an exception is thrown within the `auto_ptr` constructor, there are no active local objects for the EH mechanism to destroy. If, however, an exception is thrown within the SMLock constructor, the `auto_ptr` object must be destroyed prior to the unwinding of the program stack. Within the third region, of course, both local objects must be destroyed.

EH support complicates the constructors of classes with member class and base class subobjects with constructors. A class that is partially constructed must apply the destructors for only these subobjects and/or member objects that have been constructed. For example, if a class X has member objects A, B, and C, each with a constructor/destructor pair, then if A's constructor throws an exception, neither A, B, nor C needs its destructor invoked. If B's constructor throws an exception, A's destructor needs to be invoked, but not C's. Providing for all these contingencies is the compiler's responsibility.

Similarly, if the programmer writes

```
// class Point3d : public Point2d { ... };
Point3d *cvs = new Point3d[ 512 ];
```

this is what happens:

1. Memory is allocated for the 512 Point3d objects from the heap.

2. If (1) succeeds, the Point2d constructor then Point3d constructor is applied on each element in turn.

What if the Point3d constructor for element 27 throws an exception? For element 27, only the Point2d destructor needs to be applied. For the first 26 constructed elements, both the Point3d and Point2d destructors need to be applied. Then the memory allocated must be freed.

Exception Handling Support

When an exception is thrown, the compilation system must do the following:

1. Examine the function in which the throw occurred.

2. Determine if the throw occurred in a **try** block.

3. If so, then the compilation system must compare the type of the exception against the type of each **catch** clause.

4. If the types match, control must pass to the body of the **catch** clause.

5. If either it is not within a **try** block or none of the **catch** clauses match, then the system must (a) destruct any active local objects, (b) unwind the current function from the stack, and (c) go to the next active function on the stack and repeat items 2–5.

Determine if the Throw Occurred within a try Block

A function, recall, can be thought of as a set of regions:

- A region outside a **try** block with no active local objects

- A region outside a **try** block but with one or more active local objects requiring destruction

- A region within an active **try** block

The compiler needs to mark off these regions and make these markings available to the runtime EH system. A predominant strategy for doing this is the construction of program counter-range tables.

Recall that the program counter holds the address of the next program instruction to be executed. To mark off a region of the function within an active **try** block, the beginning and ending program counter value (or the beginning program counter value and its range value) can be stored in a table.

When a throw occurs, the current program counter value is matched against the associated range table to determine whether the region active at the time is within a **try** block. If it is, the associated **catch** clauses need to be examined (we look at this in the next subsection). If the exception is not handled (or if it is rethrown), the current function is popped from the program stack and the value of the program counter is restored to the value of the call site and the cycle begins again.

Compare the Type of the Exception against the Type of Each Catch Clause

For each throw expression, the compiler must create a type descriptor encoding the type of the exception. If the type is a derived type, the encoding must include information on all of its base class types. (It's not enough to simply encode the public base class types because the exception could be caught by a member function; within the scope of a member function, conversion between a derived and nonpublic base class is permitted.)

The type descriptor is necessary because the actual exception is handled at runtime when the object itself otherwise has no type information associated with it. RTTI is a necessary side effect of support for EH. (I look further at RTTI in Section 7.3.)

The compiler must also generate a type descriptor for each **catch** clause. The runtime exception handler compares the type descriptor of the object thrown with that of each **catch** clause's type descriptor until either a match is found or the stack has been unwound and terminate() invoked.

An exception table is generated for each function. It describes the regions associated with the function, the location of any necessary cleanup code (invocation of local class object destructors), and the location of **catch** clauses if a region is within an active **try** block.

What Happens When an Actual Object Is Thrown during Program Execution?

When an exception is thrown, the exception object is created and placed generally on some form of exception data stack. Propagated from the throw site to each **catch** clause are the address of the exception object, the type descriptor (or the address of a function that returns the type descriptor object associated with the exception type), and possibly the address of the destructor for the exception object, if one if defined.

Consider a **catch** clause of the form

```
catch( exPoint p )
{
    // do something
    throw;
}
```

and an exception object of type exVertex derived from exPoint. The two types match and the **catch** clause block becomes active. What happens with p?

- p is initialized by value with the exception object the same as if it were a formal argument of a function. This means a copy constructor and destructor, if defined or synthesized by the compiler, are applied to the local copy.

- Because p is an object and not a reference, the non-exPoint portion of the exception object is sliced off when the values are copied. In addition, if virtual functions are provided for the exception hierarchy, the vptr of p is set to exPoint's virtual table; the exception object's vptr is not copied.

What happens when the exception is rethrown? Is p now the object propagated or the exception object originally generated at the throw site? p is a local object destroyed at the close of the **catch** clause. Throwing p would require the generation of another temporary. It also would mean losing the exVertex portion of the original exception. The original exception object is rethrown; any modifications to p are discarded.

A **catch** clause of the form

```
catch( exPoint &rp )
{
    // do something
    throw;
}
```

refers to the actual exception object. Any virtual invocations resolve to the instances active for exVertex, the actual type of the exception object. Any changes made to the object are propagated to the next **catch** clause.

Finally, here is an interesting puzzle. If we have the following throw expression:

```
exVertex errVer;

// ...
mumble()
{
    // ...
    if ( mumble_cond ) {
        errVer.fileName( "mumble()" );
        throw errVer;
    }
    // ...
}
```

Is the actual exception `errVer` propagated or is a copy of `errVer` constructed on the exception stack and propagated? A copy is constructed; the global `errVer` is not propagated. This means that any changes made to the exception object within a **catch** clause are local to the copy and are not reflected within `errVer`. The actual exception object is destroyed only after the evaluation of a **catch** clause that does not rethrow the exception.

In a review of C++ compilers for the PC (see [HORST95]), Cay Horstmann measured the performance and size overhead introduced by EH. In one case, Cay compiled and ran a test case that created and destroyed a large number of local objects that have associated constructors and destructors. No actual exceptions occurred, and the difference in the two programs was the presence of a single `catch(...)` within `main()`. Here is a summary of his measurements for the Microsoft, Borland, and Symantec compilers. First, the difference in program size as a result of the presence of the **catch** clause:

Table 7.1 Object Size with and without Exception Handling

	w/o EH	w/EH	%
Borland	86,822	89,510	3%
Microsoft	60,146	67,071	13%
Symantec	69,786	74,826	8%

Second, the difference in execution speed as a result of the presence of the **catch** clause:

Table 7.2 Execution Speed with and without Exception Handling

	w/o EH	*w/EH*	%
Borland	78 sec	83 sec	6%
Microsoft	83 sec	87 sec	5%
Symantec	94 sec	96 sec	4%

EH implementations within C++ compilers vary the most when compared with support of other language features. In part this is because of its runtime nature and reliance on the underlying hardware and the different priorities of the UNIX and PC platforms in terms of execution speed and program size.

7.3   Runtime Type Identification

In cfront, a portion of the internal type hierarchy to represent programs looks as follows:

```
// the root class of the program hierarchy
class node { ... };

// root of the `type' subtree: basic types,
//    `derived' types: pointers, arrays,
//     functions, classes, enums ...
class type : public node { ... };

// the class representation
class classdef : public type { ... };

// two representations for functions
class fct : public type { ... };
class gen : public type { ... };
```

where gen is short for generic and represents an overloaded function.

Thus whenever one had a variable or member of type type* and knew it represented a function, one still had to determine whether its specific derived type was a fct or gen. Except in one particular instance. (Or at least one particular instance for one particular span of time.) The only category of function (apart from the destructor) prior to Release 2.0 that could not be overloaded was that of the conversion operator, such as

```
class String {
public:
   operator char*();
   // ...
};
```

Prior to the introduction of **const** member functions in Release 2.0, conversion operators could not be overloaded because they do not take arguments. This changed with the introduction of const member functions. Declarations such as the following were now possible:

```
class String {
public:
   // ok with Release 2.0
   operator char*();
   operator char*() const;
   // ...
};
```

That is, prior to the internal version of Release 2.0 supporting **const** member functions, it was always safe (and faster) to short-circuit access of the derived object by an explicit cast, such as the following:

```
typedef type *ptype;
typedef fct *pfct;

simplify_conv_op( ptype pt )
{
   // ok: conversion operators can only be fcts
   pfct pf = pfct( pt );
   // ...
}
```

This code is then tested and correct prior to the introduction of **const** member functions. Notice that there is even a programmer comment documenting the safety of the cast. Subsequent to the introduction of **const** member functions, both the comment and code are no longer correct. This code fails miserably with the revised String class declaration, since the **char*** conversion operator is now stored internally as a gen and not a fct.

A cast of the form

```
pfct pf = pfct( pt );
```

is called a *downcast* because it effectively casts a base class down its inheritance hierarchy, thus forcing it into one of its more specialized derived classes. Downcasts are potentially dangerous because they circumvent the type system and if incorrectly applied may misinterpret (if it's a read operation) or corrupt program memory (if it's a write operation). In our example, a pointer to a gen object is incorrectly cast to a pointer to a fct object, pf. All subsequent use of pf in our program is incorrect, except for a test of whether it is 0 or for a comparison against another pointer.

Introducing a Type-Safe Downcast

One criticism of C++ had been its lack of support for a type-safe downcast mechanism—one that performs the downcast only if the actual type being cast is appropriate (see [BUDD91] for this and other sober criticisms of C++). A type-safe downcast requires a runtime query of the pointer as to the actual type of the object it addresses. Thus support for a type-safe downcast mechanism brings with it both space and execution time overhead:

- It requires additional space to store type information, usually a pointer to some type information node.

- It requires additional time to determine the runtime type, since, as the name makes explicit, the determination can be done only at runtime.

What would such a mechanism do to the size, the performance, and the link compatibility of such common C constructs as the following?

```
char *winnie_tbl[] = { "rumbly in my tummy", "oh, bother" };
```

Obviously, there would be a considerable space and efficiency penalty placed on programs that made no use of the facility.

The conflict, then, is between two sets of users:

1. Programmers who use polymorphism heavily and who therefore have a legitimate need for a type-safe downcast mechanism

2. Programmers who use the built-in data types and nonpolymorphic facilities and who therefore have a legitimate need not to be penalized with the overhead of a mechanism that does not come into play in their code

The solution is to provide for the legitimate needs of both parties, although perhaps at the expense of a "pure" design elegance. Do you see how that might be done?

The C++ RTTI mechanism provides a type-safe downcast facility but only for those types exhibiting polymorphism (those that make use of inheritance and dynamic binding). How does one recognize this? How can a compiler look at a class definition and determine whether this class represents an independent ADT or an inheritable subtype supporting polymorphism? One strategy, of course, is to introduce a new keyword. This has the advantage of clearly identifying types that support the new feature and the disadvantage of having to retrofit the keyword into older programs.

An alternative strategy is to distinguish between class declarations by the presence of one or more declared or inherited virtual functions. This has the advantage of transparently transforming existing programs that are recompiled. It has the disadvantage of possibly forcing the introduction of an otherwise unnecessary virtual function into the base class of an inheritance hierarchy. No doubt you can think of a number of additional strategies. This latter strategy, however, is the one supported by the RTTI mechanism. Within C++, a polymorphic class is one that contains either an inherited or declared virtual function.

From an implementation viewpoint, this strategy has the additional advantage of significantly minimizing overhead. All class objects of polymorphic classes already maintain a pointer to the virtual function table (the vptr). By our placing the address of the class-specific RTTI object within the virtual table (usually in the first slot), the additional overhead is reduced to one pointer per class (plus the type information object itself) rather than one pointer per class object. In addition, the pointer need be set only once. Also, it can be set statically by the compiler, rather than during runtime within the class construction as is done with the vptr.

A Type-Safe Dynamic Cast

The **dynamic_cast** operator determines at runtime the actual type being addressed. If the downcast is safe (that is, if the base type pointer actually addresses an object of the derived class), the operator returns the appropriately cast pointer. If the downcast is not safe, the operator returns 0. For example, the following is how we might rewrite our original cfront downcast. (Of course, now that the actual type of pt can be either a fct or a gen, the preferred programming method is a virtual function. In this way, the actual type of the argument is encapsulated. The program is both clearer and more easily extended to handle additional types.)

```
typedef type *ptype;
typedef fct *pfct;
```

```
simplify_conv_op( ptype pt )
{
   if ( pfct pf = dynamic_cast< pfct >( pt )) {
      // ... process pf
   }
   else { ... }
}
```

What is the actual cost of the **dynamic_cast** operation? A type descriptor of pfct is generated by the compiler. The type descriptor for the class object addressed by pt must be retrieved at runtime; its retrieval goes through the vptr. Here is a likely transformation:

```
// access of type descriptor for pt
((type_info*) (pt->vptr[ 0 ]))->_type_descriptor;
```

type_info is the name of the class defined by the Standard to hold the required runtime type information. The first slot of the virtual table contains the address of the type_info object associated with the class type addressed by pt (see Section 1.1, Figure 1.3). The two type descriptors are passed to a runtime library routine that compares them and returns a match or no-match result. Obviously, this is considerably more expensive than a static cast, but considerably less so than an incorrect downcast such as our downcasting a type to a fct when it really addresses a gen.

Originally, the proposed support for a runtime cast did not introduce any new keywords or additional syntax. The cast

```
// original proposed syntax for run-time cast
pfct pf = pfct( pt );
```

was either static or dynamic depending on whether pt addressed a polymorphic class object. The gang of us at Bell Laboratories (back then, anyway) thought this was wonderful, but the Standards committee thought otherwise. Their criticism, as I understand it, was that an expensive runtime operation looks exactly the same as a simple static cast. That is, there is no way to know, when looking at the cast, whether pt addresses a polymorphic object and therefore whether the cast is performed at compile time or runtime. This is true, of course. However, the same can be said about a virtual function call. Perhaps the committee should also have introduced a new syntax and keyword to distinguish

```
pt->foobar();
```

as a statically resolved function call from its invocation through the virtual mechanism.

References Are Not Pointers

The **dynamic_cast** of a class pointer type provides a true/false pair of alternative pathways during program execution:

- A return of an actual address means the dynamic type of the object is confirmed and type-dependent actions may proceed.

- A return of 0, the universal address of no object, means alternative logic can be applied to an object of uncertain dynamic type.

The **dynamic_cast** operator can also be applied to a reference. The result of a non–type-safe cast, however, cannot be the same as for a pointer. Why? A reference cannot refer to "no object" the way a pointer does by having its value be set to 0. Initializing a reference with 0 causes a temporary of the referenced type to be generated. This temporary is initialized with 0. The reference is then initialized to alias the temporary. Thus the **dynamic_cast** operator, when applied to a reference, cannot provide an equivalent true/false pair of alternative pathways as it does with a pointer. Rather, the following occurs:

- If the reference is actually referring to the appropriate derived class or an object of a class subsequently derived from that class, the downcast is performed and the program may proceed.

- If the reference is not actually a kind of the derived class, then because returning 0 is not viable, a **bad_cast** exception is thrown.

Here is our `simplify_conv_op()` function reimplemented with a reference argument:

```
simplify_conv_op( const type &rt )
{
    try {
      fct &rf = dynamic_cast< fct& >( rt );
      // ...
    }
    catch( bad_cast ) {
      // ... mumble ...
    }
}
```

where the action to perform ideally indicates some sort of exceptional failure rather than simply a flow-of-control transfer.

Typeid Operator

It is possible to achieve the same runtime "alternative pathway" behavior with a reference by using the **typeid** operator:

```
simplify_conv_op( const type &rt )
{
    if ( typeid( rt ) == typeid( fct ))
    {
        fct &rf = static_cast< fct& >( rt );
        // ...
    }
    else { ... }
}
```

although clearly at this point, the better implementation strategy is to introduce a virtual function common to both the gen and fct classes.

The **typeid** operator returns a **const** reference of type type_info. In the previous test, the equality operator is an overloaded instance:

```
bool
type_info::
operator==( const type_info& ) const;
```

and returns **true** if the two type_info objects are the same.

What does the type_info object consist of? The Standard (Section 18.5.1) defines the type_info class as follows:

```
class type_info {
public:
    virtual ~type_info();
    bool operator==( const type_info& ) const;
    bool operator!=( const type_info& ) const;
    bool before( const type_info& ) const;
    const char* name() const;
private:
    // prevent memberwise init and copy
    type_info( const type_info& );
    type_info& operator=( const type_info& );

    // data members
};
```

The minimum information an implementation needs to provide is the actual name of the class, some ordering algorithm between type_info objects (this is the purpose of the before() member function), and some form of type descriptor representing both the explicit class type and any subtypes of the class. In the original paper describing the EH mechanism (see [KOENIG90b]), a suggested type descriptor implementation is that of an encoded string. (For alternative strategies, see [SUN94a] and [LENKOV92].)

While RTTI as provided by the type_info class is necessary for EH support, in practice it is insufficient to fully support EH. Additional derived type_info classes providing detailed information on pointers, functions, classes, and so on are provided under an EH mechanism. MetaWare, for example, defines the following additional classes:

```
class Pointer_type_info: public type_info { ... };
class Member_pointer_info: public type_info { ... };
class Modified_type_info: public type_info { ... };
class Array_type_info: public type_info { ... };
class Func_type_info: public type_info { ... };
class Class_type_info: public type_info { ... };
```

and permits users to access them. Unfortunately, neither the naming conventions nor the extent of these derived classes is standardized, and they vary widely across implementations.

Although I have said that RTTI is available only for polymorphic classes, in practice, type_info objects are also generated for both built-in and nonpolymorphic user-defined types. This is necessary for EH support. For example, consider

```
int ex_errno;
...
throw ex_errno;
```

where a type_info object supporting the int type is generated. Support for this spills over into user programs:

```
int *ptr;
...
if ( typeid( ptr ) == typeid( int* ))
   ...
```

Use of typeid(expression) within a program, such as

```
int ival;
...
typeid( ival ) ... ;
```

or of `typeid( type )`, such as

```
typeid( double ) ... ;
```

returns a `const type_info&`. The difference between the use of **typeid** on a nonpolymorphic expression or type is that the type_info object is retrieved statically rather than at runtime. The general implementation strategy is to generate the type_info object on demand rather than at program outset.

7.4   Efficient, but Inflexible?

The traditional C++ Object Model provides efficient runtime support of the object paradigm. This efficiency, together with its compatibility with C, are primary elements of the widespread popularity of C++. There are, however, certain domain areas—such as dynamically shared libraries, shared memory, and distributed objects—in which this object model has proved somewhat inflexible.

Dynamic Shared Libraries

Ideally, a new release of a dynamically linked shared library should just "drop in." That is, the next time an application is run, it transparently picks up the new library version. The library release is noninvasive in that the application does not need to be rebuilt. However, this noninvasive drop-in model breaks under the C++ Object Model if the data layout of a class object changes in the new library version. This is because the size of the class and the offset location of each of its direct and inherited members is fixed at compile time (except for virtually inherited members). This results in efficient but inflexible binaries; a change in the object layout requires recompilation. Both [GOLD94] and [PALAY92] describe interesting efforts in pushing the C++ Object Model to provide increased drop-in support. Of course, the tradeoff is a loss of runtime speed and size efficiency.

Shared Memory

When a shared library is dynamically loaded, its placement in memory is handled by a runtime linker and generally is of no concern to the executing process. This is not true, however, under the C++ Object Model when a class object supported by a dynamically shared library and containing virtual functions is placed in shared memory. The problem is not with the process that is placing the object in shared memory but with a second or any subsequent process wanting to attach to and invoke a virtual function through the shared object. Unless the dynamic shared library is loaded at exactly the same memory location as the process that loaded the shared object, the virtual function invocation fails badly. The likely result is either a segment fault or bus error. The problem is caused by the hardcoding within the virtual table of each virtual function. The current solution is program-based. It is the programmer who must guarantee placement of the shared libraries across processes at the same locations. (On the SGI, the user can specify the exact placement of each shared library in what is called a *so_location* file.) A compilation system-based solution that preserves the efficiency of the virtual table implementation model is required. Whether that will be forthcoming is another issue.

The Common Object Request Broker Architecture (CORBA), the Component (or Common) Object Model (COM), and the System Object Model (SOM) are (roughly) attempts to define distributed/binary object models that are language independent. (See [MOWBRAY95] for a detailed discussion of CORBA, plus secondary discussions of SOM and COM. For C++-oriented discussions, see [HAM95] (SOM), [BOX95] (COM), and [VINOS93] and [VINOS94] (CORBA).) These efforts may in the future push the C++ Object Model toward greater flexibility (through additional levels of indirection) at the expense of runtime speed and size efficiency.

As the demands of our computing environment evolve (consider Web programming and the use of Java language applets), the traditional C++ Object Model, with its emphasis on efficiency and compatibility with C, may prove an increasing constraint on the Model's use. At this moment, however, the Object Model has accounted for the nearly universal applicability of C++ in fields as diverse as operating systems and device drivers to particle physics and the genome project as well as my own current field of 3D computer graphics and animation.

Index

Abstract Base Class, *see* Base Class
Abstract Data Type, 2, 19, 21, 165–168
   see also Class, Object-Based
Access Level, *see also* Layout of Data,
     Nonstatic Data Members
  no space penalty, 5
  order of multiple access levels undefined,
    17, 76
  program to determine layout, 77
Address Points, 138
ADT, *see* Abstract Data Type
Advice
  auto_ptr for local resource management,
    259
  avoid arrays and ploymorphisms, 223
  avoid copy assignment operator in vir-
    tual base class, 189
  avoid global objects, especially class ob-
    jects, 209
  avoid non-static data in virtual base class,
    139
  avoid pure virtual destructors, 161
  avoid unnecessary object creation, 205
  define copy constructor if return many
    objects by value, 60
  don't depend on copy constructor side-
    effects, 59
  initialize class members with other class
    members inside constructor, 65
  initialization is more efficient than assign-
    ment of class objects, 229
  use composition to combine C, C++, 18
Algol, 134
Aliasing, pointer problem, 44
Alignment, 23, 60
Anna, 19
Arguments to Functions, *see* Function
    Arguments
Arrays
  class objects, 211–215
  construction, 212–214
  delete, 220
  dimension size and **delete**, 220–222

new allocation, 218–224
one element, 16–17
polymorphism, ill-behaved, 223–224
program transformation, 213
auto_ptr, 259

Ball, Michael, xii, 135, 137
Base Class, *see also* Class, Inheritance,
    Virtual Inheritance, Virtual Base Class
  abstract base class, 159–162
  default derived class constructor, 37
  integrity of base class, 85–87
  layout, within derived class, 17, 26,
    83–105
  ordering of base classes under multiple
    inheritance, 95
  pointer, vs. derived, 26
  problem of second base class under mul-
    tiple inheritance, 92–94
  vptr placement, 89–91
Binding
  data member 73–74
  member rewriting rule, 74
  type within member argument list, 74–75
Bitwise Copy Semantics, 185
  exhibited by class, 42–45
  four cases not exhibited by class, 45–50
Blake, William, viii
Borland, 52, 175, 212, 247, 255, 263–264
BSS, 164
Budge, Kent 235–237
Buroff, Steve, 15
Bushinsky, Shay, 255

C++ Object Model, *see also* Class,
    Inheritance, Object-Oriented
    Programming
  benefits and drawbacks, 9
  data members, 72,
  evolution, 71
  explanation of, vii, 8–12
  inheritance, 9–10, 83–105
  multiple inheritance, 91–95

program transformation, 11–12
virtual inheritance, 95–101
C++ vs. C, combining, 90
composition, 17–18
inheritance, 17–18
C++ vs. C, compatibility, 12
C++ vs. C, data representation, 5
C++ vs. C, pitfall, 16–17
C++ vs. C, tentative definition, 164, 206
Cargill, Tom, 122, 244
Cast, 25
catch Clause, 256, 260–261, 262
Cfront, traditional implementation
array and default constructor, 214
array element size, 222
class vs. **struct**, 14–16
conditional test inside constructor, 179
const member function, 265
conversion operator, 265
copy assignment operator, 175
death under exception handling, 255
inline member functions, 152–153
local static class objects, 210–211
multiple inheritance layout, 95
named return value optimization, 57
new and **delete** of class objects, 142
pointer to member functions, 147
static initialization, 206–207
static member access with side-effect, 79
static member function, 123
templates, 246, 247
temporary generation, 232–233
thunks, 134
virtual base class, 97
virtual functions, 133
virtual table generation, 252–253
vptr placement, 89
class vs. **struct**, 12–18
Class, *see also* Base Class, Constructor,
Destructor, Inheritance, Layout of
Data, Multiple Inheritance, Virtual
Inheritance
empty class, 69
memory requirements to represent object,
23, 70
object construction and copy, 163–172
polymorphic class, 267
COM, 273
Conversion
base and derived class, 91
difficulty under multiple inheritance, 92
downcast, 93
virtual base class, 97

Conversion Operator, 18
difficulty of use, 31
Constructor, 8 *see also* Copy Constructor,
Default Constructor, Member
Initialization List
augmentation, 88, 169, 173, 176–179, 182
computational constructor, 54–55
inline vs. initialization list, 166–167,
192–193
inserting, 203
local static objects, 210
ordering under inheritance, 172–173
protected, 160
split function optimization, 179, 184
synthesized by compiler, 32–50
unnecessary call, 142
Coplien, Jim, 206
Copy Assignment Operator, 8, 184–190
bitwise copy semantics, 185
ill-behaved under virtual inheritance,
187–189
trivial vs. non-trivial, 186
Copy Constructor
advice: don't depend on side-effects, 59
bitwise copy semantics, 43–45
compiler suppresses invocation, 49
memberwise initialization, 41–43
pointer aliasing problem, 44
program transformations:
argument initialization, 51–52
explicit initialization, 50–51
return value initialization, 53–59, 171
synthesized by compiler, 43–50
trivial vs. non-trivial, 43, 60–61
virtual base class, 47–49
virtual function, 46–47
whether to provide an instance, 59–61
CORBA, 8, 273

Danny, 19
Data Abstraction, 1
Data Encapsulation
layout costs, 5–6
performance, 101–106
Data Members, *see also* Layout of Data,
Static Data Members, Nonstatic Data
Members
binding, 72–74
layout, 75–77, 83–105
Daughter, *see* Anna
Default Constructor
augmentation, 35
base class subobjects

Default Constructor (*continued*)
  common misunderstandings, 40
  implementation vs. program need, 33, 35
  inline instance, 34
  member class subobjects, 34–36
  synthesized by compiler, 32–40
  transformation, 36
  trivial vs. non-trivial, 33
  virtual base class, 38–39
  virtual functions, 37–38
delete, 215–227, *see also* **vec_delete**
  array, 220
  array dimension size, 220–222
  free ( ), **218**
  implementation, 218
  placement delete, 225
Demangling, *see* Name Demangling
Derivation, *see* Inheritance
Derived Class, *see* Inheritance, Multiple
    Inheritance, Virtual Inheritance
Destructor, 8, 196–199
  augmentation, 88, 175, 198
  delete, 197
  insertion within program, 203–205
  local static object, 211
  order of execution, 198
  order of local static objects, 211
  pure virtual declaration, 160–161
  split function optimization, 198
  synthesis, 196–198
  trivial vs non-trivial, 196
  virtual, 168–169
Disneyland, 19
downcast, 93, 265–267
dynamic_cast, 22, 126, 267–269
  original proposal, 268
  with reference, 269
Dynamic Libraries, 272

Edison Design Group, xii, 250–254
Efficiency, *see* Performance
Encapsulation, *see* Data Encapsulation
Exception Handing, 254–264
  auto_ptr, 259
  delete, 258, 260
  determine occurrence of **throw**, 260–261
  determine type of **throw** object, 261
  function regions, 257–258
  impact on C++ programs, 256–257
  new, 258, 260
  performance and size, 263–264
  resource management, 257–259
  thrown object behavior, 261–263
  type descriptor, 126, 261
explicit, 32

Fake Static, 206
Faulkner, William, 14
Flynn, Erroll, 16
FORTRAN-77, performance comparison
    with C++, 235–237
Foundation Project, v, 179
free ( ), underlying **delete**, 218
Function Arguments,
  class objects, transformation, 51–53
  and inline functions, 154–155
  type binding within class, non-intuitive,
    74–75

g++, 65, 237
Global Object Initialization, *see* Static
    Initialization

Horstmann, Cay, 263
HP, 237, 255

IBM, 138
Inheritance, *see also* Single, Multiple, Virtual
    Inheritance, Nonstatic Data
    Members, Layout of Data
  integrity of base class, 85–87
  layout of members, 17, 83–105
  object construction and copy, 172–176
  ordering of constructors, 172–173
  performance, data member access, 105
  pitfall, 85
  polymorphism and object construction,
    168–172
  support within C++ Object Model,
    9–10
  virtual functions, 128–139
Initialization, *see also* Static Initialization,
    Constructors
  arrays of class objects, 211–213
  local static class objects, 210–211
  temporary lifetime, 234
Initialization List, 166–167, 192–193
  arrays of class objects, 213
Inline Function, 5, 151–157
  complexity measure, 152
  formal arguments, 154–155
  implementation dependent, 152
  local variables, 155–156
  must_inline, 152
  temporary generation, 155–157

Java, 273
Johnson, Steve, 207

Knuth, 134
Koenig, Andy, xii, 206, 253

Lajoie, Josée, xiii, 59
Layout of Data, 75–77
  across access levels, 17, 76–77
  base and derived Members, 17
  class object, 26
  multiple inheritance, 91–95
  pointer, 26
  reference, 26
  single inheritance, concrete, 83–87
  single inheritance, polymorphic, 88–91
  virtual base class, 71
  virtual inheritance, 95–101
  virtual table, 129, 136, 139
  virtual table pointer, 89–91
  within an access level, 17, 76
Local Static Class Object, 209–211
  construction, 210
  order of destruction, 211

malloc(), 218, 230
Mangling, *see* Name Mangling
Member Functions, 5, 113–157
  see also Nonstatic Member Functions,
    Static Member Functions, Virtual
    Functions
  binding, data members, 72–74
  binding, within argument list, 74–75
  member rewriting rule, 74
Memberwise Initialization, 40–43
Member Initialization List, 62–67
  avoid inefficiencies, 62–63
  invoking member function within, 66
  member function and base class, 66
  order of actual initialization, 64–65
  order dependency pitfall, 64
  program transformations, 63
memcpy(), 60–61
  danger of use within constructor, 61
  program transformation, 61
memset(), 61
Metaware, 95, 98, 271
Microsoft, 18, 90, 98, 138, 148, 149, 212,
  263–264
Mixing Programming Paradigms, 20
Moo, Barbara, xii
Multiple Entry Points, 138
Multiple Inheritance, 9–10
  conversion overhead, 92–94
  layout of nonstatic data members, 91–95
  pointer to data member, 108–109
  pointer to member functions, 147–149
  problem of second base class, 92–94,
    131–138
  virtual functions, 131–138
Murray, Rob, v, 14, 179, 207

new, 215–227, *see also* **vec_delete**
  arrays, 212, 218–224
  exception handling, 256, 260
  implementation, 218
  malloc(), 218
  placement new, 224–227
  plain ol' data, 215, 219
Name Demangling, 119–120
Name Mangling, 79, 117–120
Named Return Value Optimization
  criticisms with, 57–58
  explanation of, 55–59
  performance, 57, 228
  program transformation, 56, 116, 171,
  requires copy constructor, 57, 60
Nonstatic Data Member, 8, 72, 80–82
  see also Data Member, Layout of Data,
    Pointer to Class Member
  access, 81
  access, performance, 101–106
  address, bound member vs formal,
    107–108
  base class integrity, 85–87
  layout under inheritance, 10, 83–105
Nonstatic Member Functions, 114–117
NRV, *see* Named Return Value
  Optimization

Object, *see* Class
Object-Based Programming
  vs. object-oriented, 18–29
Object Construction, *see* Construction,
  Initialization
Object Model *see* C++ Object Model
  simple, 6–7
  table-driven, 7–8
Object-Oriented Programming, *see also*
  Polymorphism
  objects do not support OO programming,
    28
  paradigm, 22
  requires Indirection, 20
  slicing of derived object, 29
  vs. Object-Based, 18–29
Ontogeny, 182
Optimizer, 103, 104, 106, 110
O'Riordan, Martin, 90, 122
Overloaded Function, 12

Performance, under increasing abstraction
  data member access, 101–106
  effects of optimizer, 103, 104, 106, 110
  member functions, 139–144
  named return value optimization, 57
  object construction and copy, 190–196

Performance, under increasing abstraction
(*continued*)
  pointer to data members, 109–112
  pointer to member functions, 149–151
Phylogeny, 182
Pitfall
  data layout under inheritance, 85–87
  depending on Copy Constructor invoca-
    tion, 59
  member initialization list, 64
  using objects with polymorphism, 20
Placement Delete, 225
Placement New, 224–227
  and polymorphism, ill-behaved, 226–227
Plain Ol' Data, 163, 164
POD, *see* Plain Ol' Data
Pointers
  aliasing problem and copy constructor, 44
  base vs. derived class pointer, 26
  memory requirements, 23
  type and representation, 24–25, 26
  use with object-oriented programming,
    21
Pointer to Class Member, 7
  address of data member, 81
  pointer to data members, 106–109
  pointer to data members, performance,
    109–112
  pointer to member functions, 144–151
  pointer to member functions, perfor-
    mance, 149–151
Polymorphic Class, 267
Polymorphism, *see also* Object-Oriented
    Programming
  active vs. passive, 126
  delays resource commitment, 29
  effects of introducing, 89
  forms of polymorphism within C++,
    21–22
  natural vs. unnatural, 91–92
  non-public class hierarchy, 21–22
  object construction and copy, 168–172
  overheads with support, 88
  requires indirection (pointer or refer-
    ence), 21, 28
  slicing of derived object, 29
  void*, 21
Procedural Programming, 14, 18
Program Transformations
  array of class objects, 213
  assignment of class objects, 228–229
  conditional expression, 201–203
  copy constructor
    argument initialization, 51–52, 169
    explicit initialization, 50–51

    return value initialization, 53–59, 171
      with use of memcpy, 61
  default constructor with multiple class
    subobjects, 36
  delete invocation, 217
  dynamic_cast invocation, 268
  inline function, 156
  member initialization list, 63
  multiple inheritance, conversion, 94
  named return value optimization, 56, 171
  new invocation, 215, 217, 219
  nonstatic member function, 115–117
  pointer to member function, 147–148
  static initialization, 210–211
  static member function, 121–124
  temporary generation, 231
    and false/true conditional expres-
      sion, 232–233
    and object initialization, 234–235
  types of program transformation, vi
  under C++ object model, 11–12
  virtual base class member access, 97
  virtual function invocation, 38, 120
  virtual inheritance, 177–178
  virtual table pointer initialization,
    182–183
Pure Virtual Function, *see* Virtual Function

References
  bound to temporary, 235
  distinguished from pointer, 269
  memory requirements, 23
  use with **dynamic_cast**, 269
  use with object-oriented programming,
    21
Reference-Based Programming, *see* Object-
    Oriented Programming
Return Value
  class object, *see* Copy Constructor
  optimization, *see* Named Return Value
    Optimization
RTTI, *see* Runtime Type Identification
Runtime Type Identification, 8, 126, 264–272

Schwarz, 31, 207
Schwarz Counter, 32, 209
Schwarz Error, 32
SGI, xii, 273
Shakespeare, William, 14
Shared Memory & C++ Object Model,
    272–273
Shopiro, Jonathan, xiii, 54, 122, 220–221,
    226
Single Inheritance, *see* Inheritance
Slicing of Derived Object, 29, 47

Snow White and Some Dwarves, 36
so_locations, 273
SOM, 8, 273
Son, *see* Danny
Split Functions, as optimization, 137, 179, 184, 188, 197
Stack Unwinding, 256
Static Data Members, 8, 72, 78–80
  see also Data Members
  access via side-effect, 79
  address of, 79
Static Initialization, ix-x, 205–209
  class objects, 206–207
  drawbacks, 209
  interaction with exception handling, 209
  non-class objects, 208
  order dependency across modules, 209
Static Local Object, *see* Local Static Object
Static Member Functions, 114, 121–124
  see also Member Functions
  access via side-effect, 79
  address of, 124
  motivation for introduction, 122
  program transformation, 121
Stroustrup, Bjarne, xii
struct vs. **class**, 12–18
Subobject, 10
Sun, 135, 137, 207, 212, 221, 237, 247
Symantec, 263–264

Templates, 15, 239–254
  difficulties with usage, 239
  error reporting, 244–247
  impact on C++ programming, 239
  instantiation, 240–244
  member function instantiation, 250–254
  scope and name resolution, 247–250
  use-directed instantiation, 243, 251–253
Temporaries, 227–237
  conditional expression, 231–233
  disaggregation, 236–237
  expressions, 202
  full-expression, 231
  implementation-dependent, 227–228
  initialization vs. assignment, 228–229
  inline functions, 155–157
  lifetime, 230–235
  object initialization, 234
  performance impact, 235–237
  reference, 235
Tentative Definition, 164, 206
this Pointer,
  absence of within static member function, 122

adjustment under multiple inheritance, 131–134
adjustment under virtual inheritance, 139
nonstatic member function insertion, 115–116
throw clause, 256, 260–261
Thunk, 134, 148, see also Vcall Thunk
Timings, *see* Performance
Transformation, *see* Program Transformation
try Block, 260–261
typeid, 22, 270–272
type_info, 9, 268, 270
Type-safe linkage, 119

Usenix C++ Implementor's Workshop, 122
USL, 255

Value-Based Programming, *see* Object-Based
Vcall Thunk, 148, *see also* Thunk
vec_delete, 213, 221
vec_new, 212–213, 219, 222
Vinoski, Steve, viii
Virtual Base Class, *see also* Virtual Inheritance
  access, data members, 81
  copy constructor, 47–49
  default constructor of derived class, 38–39
  layout, 71
  optimization of empty instance, 70
  presence disables bitwise copy, 39, 48
  requires run-time access, 39
Virtual Base Class Table, 98
Virtual Function, 8, 17, 38, 46, 124–139
  see also Object-Oriented Programming, Polymorphism
  address points, 138
  bad design choice, 161–162
  const virtual function, 162
  copy constructor, 46–47
  default constructor, 37–38
  first reaction to, 114
  implementation model, 38, 46
  inheritance, 129–131
  multiple entry points, 138
  multiple inheritance, 131–138
  performance, 141
  pointer to member function, 145–147
  pointer vs. object invocation, 27
  program transformation, 38, 120–121
  pure virtual destructor, 161
  pure virtual function, 160–161
  suppressing virtual mechanism, 29
  this pointer adjustment, 133–138

Virtual Function, (*continued*)
    thunk, 134
    virtual inheritance, 138–139
Virtual Inheritance, 9–10, 95–101, *see also*
        Virtual Base Class
    conversion, 97
    copy assignment operator, 187–189
    destructor, 198
    implementation challenge, 96
    implementation, pointer vs. offset, 98–101
    initialization by most derived class,
        177–178
    invariant region, 96
    layout strategy, 97
    object construction and copy, 176–179
    shared/fluctuating region, 96
    split function optimization, 179

    static initialization, 208–209
    virtual functions, 138–139
Virtual Table (vtbl), 8, 38, 46, 88, 127–131
    interaction with templates, 252–253
    under multiple inheritance, 135–136
    under virtual inheritance, 139
Virtual Table Pointer (vptr), 8, 27, 88, 127–131
    copy assignment operator, 27
    initialization within constructor, 38, 47,
        88, 169, 179–184
    overhead and split function optimization,
        142–144
    placement within class object, 76, 89–91
    presence disables bitwise copy, 47
    reset within destructor, 198
    under multiple inheritance, 135–136
    under virtual inheritance, 139

BN BD 5